Füll 50

JOHN MULHOLLAND'S
BOOK OF MAGIC

JOHN MULHOLLAND'S
BOOK OF **MAGIC**

CHARLES SCRIBNER'S SONS · New York

PREFACE

FROM the beginning of civilization, magic has delighted people of all ages and every nationality. Magic is superb entertainment for it combines the challenge of a puzzle, the thrill of a detective story, the amusement of a comedy, and the charming fantasy of a fairy tale. Magic is universally enjoyed for, seemingly, it is the accomplishment of what everyone knows cannot be done. Being able to witness the unreal is great fun. Magic, too, is enjoyable for the performer. A magician always finds pleasure in seeing the good time people have at his entertainments and he finds their regard gratifying.

Realizing that magic deals only with what to other people is impossible, modern magicians have to keep ahead of scientists who daily open doors through which just yesterday only magicians could enter. It is true that it still is possible to show a number of the feats of magic Reginald Scot described in a book published in 1584. This is because some things, even now, can be realized only by magic, but science keeps going ahead. Magicians are not troubled by the great advances their adversaries, the scientists, make, for watching the incredible has never-ending appeal and magicians rely on imagination forever being able to keep fancy ahead of fact.

There are many misconceptions about the art of entertaining by mystifying, and confusion begins in the very terms generally employed. Conjuring and magic, the words most commonly used for a performance of trickery, also refer to the work of devils and evil spirits. Wizardry, a word less frequently found, has the same double connotation. Legerdemain, prestidigitation, sleight of hand, though having but a single meaning, infer, by their roots, the erroneous idea that a show of mysteries depends upon the quick and dexterous hands of the performer. Actual sleight of hand does require mastering unusual digital techniques and developing muscles of the hand rarely needed in any other work. While there are feats of magic which only can be accomplished by dexterity of hand even those are not

PREFACE

based upon speed. Learning real sleight of hand may be compared, at least in training of the hands, to learning to play the piano. To become adept each requires about the same number of years. I have spent as long as five years practicing a routine of sleights before I felt ready for public performance. Learning non-sleight of hand is similar to learning to play a tom-tom. True one must practice that drum in order to strike the head in the proper spot and to hit the drum with the correct rhythm but the task is not difficult and takes little time to master. As the reader will find there is a vast amount of excellent magic which does not depend upon specially trained muscles. However, even such magic is termed sleight of hand by the public. Whereas, at times, it is a bother to a performer that the terms for his art are so misleading, it also is a boon to him that people are confused by words even before the show starts and real confusion begins.

The purpose of this book is to teach effective modern magic which can be learned without difficulty. All the magic has been selected because of having won public approval and yet none requires the use of sleight of hand. Some of the tricks described can be shown in minutes after reading the text. These depend solely upon knowing the secrets, and using just enough memory to recall the order of the details of performance. Other tricks taught in these pages can be learned in an hour, or at most a few hours, of rehearsal. Several of the tricks require the use of equipment, and for these full instructions are given so that the reader can make everything needed. Among the tricks will be found magic suitable for any occasion and any audience.

Many of the tricks in this book I have devised. Others, it is gratefully acknowledged, are, at least in part, based on ideas of other magicians. All the magic is described as I do it in my shows. My audiences have enjoyed witnessing these feats of magic and I have had fun doing them. May you and your audiences also find pleasure in their performance.

J.M.

CONTENTS

CONTENTS

CONTENTS

CONTENTS

Useful information for a magician; such as how to practice;
what magic to show when, where and for whom; how to avoid
errors and control stage fright; and further notes on properties,
patter and people

JOHN MULHOLLAND'S

BOOK OF MAGIC

One. MAGIC AND THE MAGICIAN

LEARNING magic is very much like learning a second language. It is quite easy for anyone to memorize a few simple words, or even a short sentence or two, of a foreign tongue. It is a very difficult and lengthy task to learn to know another language really well and, unless one has a linguistic aptitude it is probably impossible. The same thing holds true in magic. It is quite easy to learn to perform certain tricks well, but many years of diligent effort are required to become a master of the craft. The study of magic has this advantage—the world looks upon a man as a magician if he can perform even a half-dozen tricks in an interesting manner. A magician's reputation rests upon how mystifying and entertaining he can make the feats he performs rather than in how large his repertoire.

Understanding what magic is, and what manner of man is the performer, make it a great deal easier to become a magician. If you will study the next few pages carefully you will save yourself effort in acquiring your magic— as well as saving face in public by having your tricks work.

Magic is the pretended performance of those things which cannot be done. The success of a magician's simulation of doing the impossible depends upon misleading the minds of his audiences. This, in the main, is done by adding, to a performance, details of which the spectators are unaware, and of leaving out others which they believe you have not left out. In short a performance of magic is largely a demonstration of the universal reliability of certain facts of psychology.

Because magic depends largely upon psychology and in order to make use of that subject, the first thing to remember is to be natural or be yourself.

MAGIC AND THE MAGICIAN

That really is rather hard to do for, in magic, there seems to be an all compelling urge to adopt gestures, mannerisms, and even a tone of voice which are unnatural. The personality you now have will be of great aid to you and it is impossible to put too much stress on the advisability of continuing to be you. There is a real likelihood of a person with an assumed manner being thought a show-off, and a magician is an entertainer—not a smart-aleck. Of course it is entirely possible to assume another personality when performing magic, but it doubles the task of learning to appear in public. You have spent a number of years becoming the person you are now and are infinitely, and unquestionably, more pleasant to be with than anyone else you soon could learn to be. Learning to do things which you never have done before is enough of a chore without bothering to learn to be some other person doing things he never has done. So it not only is better, but very much easier, to remain as you are.

Speaking of a magician's being an entertainer, in my definition "magic is the art of creating illusion agreeably." Magic, to be entertaining, must give the effect of being the accomplishment of the impossible by a pleasant person. The means used to perform the wonders has to be held a complete mystery. If you are caught in a trick you are not a magician. If you are not caught, but later disclose how you have fooled your audience, you probably will be thought rude even though you have been asked for an explanation. The reason the secrets must be kept is that magic is entertaining only for so long as it is mystifying and when the secrets are told the pleasure is taken away. Then, too, a detailed explanation never can be grasped at once; and a simplified one makes the trick sound so easy that only one of feeble mind could have been fooled by it: In either case you probably will not be believed. There are no exceptions; in magic it is advisable never to mention the methods employed. If you are asked to explain a trick you have just done, the best answer, perhaps, is, "I have promised never to tell." So as to say this truthfully it might be a good idea to make that promise to me now.

A magician not only should be agreeable but even a trifle over-agreeable, for the audience knows that what just has been seen cannot have been true and, on that account, may feel a little antagonistic towards the performer. By over-agreeable I mean always act as if you considered the audience as doing you a favor in watching instead of your doing the favor by performing. It always has been my conviction that the audience has honored the performer by coming to see his show and that he should return the honor by agreeably doing his best. Naturally, I am referring to those planned shows which people know are to occur.

Extemporaneous magic brings out another point in being agreeable. It is wise never to offer to show a trick unless you have been requested to do so provided, of course, you are known to the group to be a magician. If your magic previously has been liked you undoubtedly will be asked to perform. If your talent for the mysterious is not known it is permissible to bring forth your trick, if you do it casually and at a moment when entertainment seems indicated. In telling a humorous story one doesn't begin with, "I want to tell a screamingly funny story I just heard." If the tale isn't apropos, and doesn't grow out of the conversation, it might better be left untold and, anyway, that is a most unamusing way to begin. So in magic the person who starts by saying, "I want to show you a trick" gives the effect of thinking more of his own pleasure than that of his friends. If the time seems ripe for a trick, perhaps a trick with a coin, you can begin, when a lull comes in the conversation, by saying, "It seems odd, to me, the metals the government puts into the coins these days." That sounds as though it might be interesting, were it continued, and you have everyone's attention. If immediately, and with no preliminary fuss, a trick with a coin is done the show is started. That is, further tricks may be shown if that one seemed to have been enjoyed—if not that is where the performance stops. Again tricks are like stories and should be given only for so long as the audience is amused and wants more. Both should be stopped before the audience has had enough. My suggestion, undoubtedly needless to mention, is not always to begin with a trick with a coin but rather to say something to attract attention to whatever object is to be used. It is better never to give the idea how, or even that, the object is to be used and definitely nothing should be said about a trick being about to occur.

Not only is it inadvisable to mention that you are about to show a trick with such and such an object, because it is the least interesting way of beginning, but it is easier to get away with the trick by not telling beforehand what you are about to do. "Forewarned is forearmed" also applies to an audience, so never tell in advance what you intend doing.

Magic is devised to fool the minds of the spectators rather than their eyes. The hand is not quicker than the eye, but the eyes see a great many things of which the mind takes no notice. Those details which pass unnoticed are the extra ones which make the trick possible. It would be easier to demonstrate this point were we to meet personally, for a description of a trick is rather unsatisfactory. Magic really exists only during its performance. But I shall attempt to show you, without doing a trick, how details which the eyes can see pass unnoticed by the mind. To begin I want you to pronounce and think about these words:

AIVA NID NACS

Nothing but odd sounding, meaningless, hog-latin as it is. But that is merely because of the details being confusing. When the spaces are taken out and the letters are read backwards we have the word—Scandinavia. Your eye could see that but the mind did not record it. Another example:

Now will you please read this sentence carefully

How many times did the letter E appear in the previous sentence? You had to go back and count and then you may have missed one of the seven on the first try. And did you happen to notice that there was no period at the end of the sentence? Why should you know how many times one letter of the alphabet is used in a sentence, or that a period is missing? And why should you know how to spell Scandinavia backwards and divided? There is no reason at all, and I am merely attempting to show you that those things which we have no reason to notice remain "unseen." The reverse is also true, and we "see" a thing where we believe it to be.

Because audiences fail to notice certain things which are plainly visible, and accept as seen certain things which are not there, a magician is able to perform a vast array of mysteries. It is usually thought that a magician depends upon quickness to keep audiences from seeing through his tricks but that is not true. The fact is that a normal eye can see a motion at least 200 times faster than the most highly trained finger can move. The magician depends upon the faultiness of human observation. However, he must not call attention to the presence or absence of the object by movement or gesture. Movement of any kind attracts attention and a rapid action is very apparent. Therefore in performing a trick always move at your normal rate of speed. However, try to make one movement follow another smoothly and evenly.

The effectiveness of a magician's performance depends, to a considerable extent, upon natural, smooth, and even action. In order to make one's actions smooth it is most necessary to study and memorize each movement made. This not only aids the performance of the trick but enhances the show. Making everything he does seem as if it were the natural thing to do, the magician can lull the suspicions of the audience to a very great degree. In order to make every gesture seem natural the magician in his preparatory practice must study the details of what he does so that he can perform his actions without hesitation. That again makes for smoothness and rhythm.

The most helpful aid in the actual doing of the tricks is a confident manner. Please do not misunderstand me to have said a cocky manner. A confident manner cannot merely be assumed. It can come only from inner assurance that one really knows what he is doing. When the details of performance are studied to the end that you know exactly what happens next and, without hesitation, or embarrassment, can do that next step, and the one after that, a confident manner comes automatically.

A magician should know all the details of every trick he publicly performs as well as he knows his name, or where he lives. He should not have to stop to consider, or worry to remember. This does not mean endless repetition in practice but rather a careful and studied analysis when he is learning what to do. No trick in this book is hard although a few depend upon an unusual, and seemingly unnatural, manner of making some action. When the reason is understood for doing what is required in a new manner it becomes easy to do after a few repetitions. All other details in actions are what one would do normally. But as each action, normal and unusual, is necessary for the success of the trick all have to be memorized and in order. If you do know each step so that the trick will run off smoothly you need have no worry about a confident manner.

The confident manner, the easy natural actions, and particularly what the magician says as he performs all tend to help make the spectators ignore many things which they actually can see, or about which they might feel suspicious. This accompanying talk, technically called patter, should be merely stories about the tricks. Patter should be as interesting as possible and as sensible. Remember that the idea of claiming to do the impossible is not altogether sensible and the patter should not add, too much, to the burden on the credulity of the audience. The patter may be far-fetched but must sound reasonable. As an example, it is permissible to claim that the magic word "Ipswobego" will cause an object to disappear but in the next trick, where something quite different occurs, it is well to devise another magic word. The audience will accept, while realizing it is silly, that a magic word caused something to happen. They will not accept, because it becomes too absurdly silly, that the same word will cause something else to happen. However, it ceases to be silly if, in the manner of saying the word, the magician acts as if he were using the word for a blind to conceal his "real" dark secret. In short, much depends upon the type of person the magician may be. If you are naturally serious, continue so and make your patter such that you would accept it were you the spectator. If you are naturally jovial your patter may be lighter and more far-fetched. You must tailor your patter to fit your personality. If you are not an easy talker cut your patter down. Patter makes it easier for the audience to understand the object of your trick; patter makes the trick more entertaining; patter makes it easier to do the trick. Even a simple statement of what you are going to do aids in these several ways.

In a number of places in this book will be found suggestions for the patter for a trick. This has been done because, in each instance, the effectiveness of the trick depends to a large extent upon the plot of the story. The reader may prefer stories of his own and if that is the case he should use them. However, he must make certain that his stories encompass the various points in which the suggested patter aids the performance. He also must have stories which fit his personality so that he can tell them well.

Patter, for a magician, may be summed up as the conversational accompaniment of his actions. Of course, the magician, in his patter, always assumes that he can perform the impossible and it is, therefore, untrue. Even though it is quite permissible, for an entertainer in action, to embroider, fringe, accordion pleat, and otherwise ornament the truth, it is not easy to extemporize for few people are natural, or convincing, prevaricators. However, patter is very easy if the magician knows exactly what he intends to say and says it as he usually speaks. In planning patter, it is well to remember that, the less the magician says the easier it is to think out and to remember.

One last word about patter—always speak as if you were talking to the person farthest away. If you begin speaking directly to him you will find that you naturally will use sufficient volume to be heard. Listen to how loudly you are speaking and then keep your voice that loud. It is downright rude to speak so that you are not heard, as, of course, everyone knows, but many performers forget this fact and fail to speak up.

Another method used in mystification depends upon the audience's not knowing that prior preparation has been made by the magician. As an example, people familiar with cards know that an ordinary deck consists of 52 cards. If before the magic even has been suggested the magician secretly has removed four cards from the deck it never will be suspected. It is not suspected because the audience, not knowing what the trick is to be, has no reason to think that what looks like a deck of cards is not really a full deck. Not one person in a million can tell, merely by looking, whether the deck contains 48 or 52 cards. Prior preparation frequently is used in magic and many, newly in the ranks of mystifiers, are apt to be self-conscious in bringing forth anything prepared. A self-conscious magician generates suspicion towards both his paraphernalia and himself. Just remember that what looks all right to the audience must be all right. The spectators can see only what they observe and they observe only what they know about. As they do not know about any previous preparation there has been no such preparation as far as they are concerned. If you will accept this as fact—and it is a fact—you never will be self-conscious.

The magician should remember that the methods he uses are absolutely immaterial to his audiences whose only interest in his magic is that it be entertaining and mystifying. Only results count and the how does not matter. Many people think they would enjoy discovering the secret of the magician, but actually are really pleased only when he astonishes them. When a person first takes up the performance of magic he is apt to believe his audience will be suspicious of those secret parts of the performance necessary to have the feats work, and he will worry about his audience's acceptance of what he says, and what he does, as well as what he uses. Provided he really knows what he is doing and saying, and does and says what is needed in an easy and assured way, these worries are needless as has been noted. However, what he uses does excite suspicion when it seems to be something created solely for the performance of trickery. Apparatus magic can, at times, make difficulties for the magician. That is because in our world today mechanics and electronics play so huge a part that when people see an object they never have seen before, they jump to the conclusion that it is just one more result of science. No one today can be astonished by the abilities of any mechanism and a magician therefore must make his audience accept that what they see is contrary to science rather than caused by it. Knowing the public's attitude a magician is wise to use only apparatus designed to minimize suspicion.

MAGIC AND THE MAGICIAN

Perhaps it would be well to explain what a magician means by "apparatus." A deck of cards, a coin, a handkerchief, and all the other articles a magician might use in his mysteries are not apparatus when they are exactly as they should be. Usually such items are described as "properties," or "props." However, if what seems to the audience to be a deck of cards actually is a box, or what looks like a coin actually is printed paper, or what apparently is a handkerchief really is a bag, then these things fall into the category of apparatus. Incidentally magicians use the word "fake" for any piece of apparatus, made to aid their trickery, which simulates a common object. A fake need not be small and, as examples, magicians have used chairs and tables which, while normal in appearance, are constructed to do, or aid in doing, things no furniture designer ever envisioned. Because no one is suspicious about what appears to be a familiar common object, the best apparatus for magic is something which is accepted as being an article with which everyone is familiar. Such articles may be most tricky in fact, but because they appear to be ordinary are accepted as being as innocent as they appear. To the public, as well as to Gertrude Stein, "a rose is a rose is a rose" and the magician, without worry, may depend upon that fact. Once a person decides that an object is what it appears to be he is apt to think no more about it.

Another type of apparatus which does not excite suspicion is the object which the audience immediately thinks it recognizes when it is named. For example, the magician introduces a small stand (which later in the book the reader will discover is required for the magic) by saying: "This little show window display rack will be very useful in keeping the tags in the plain sight of everyone." The stand does look very much like some of the racks on which shopkeepers display their wares and the audience will accept it as such. The rack mentioned, while made for the trick, happens to be innocent of trickery but it is well always when using any piece of equipment at all unusual to make the audience accept it as the commonest of objects. What people believe they recognize as a common object they always will accept.

Also acceptable is the apparatus which can be described as if it were commonplace somewhere in the world. It is most interesting how people will accept the odd shaped cup as being just a cup when the performer calls attention to "this Indonesian cup." He then must follow by giving a reason for using a cup from these far off islands. The usual reason offered is the magician's desire to be "authentic," as: "I shall perform this feat exactly the way the Javanese magician used to do it." What could be more reasonable, or natural, than using an Indonesian cup when doing Indonesian magic? Audiences are very inclined to follow such reasoning without question. But here a bit of warning—the magician's story must be authentic. Do not decorate your cup with Chinese characters and call it Indonesian, for someone in the audience is apt to be aware of the incongruity. Never make the audience suspicious by making a statement which they can know to be false. Such as, "when I was in Indonesia," when many of those in your audience are well aware that you have never been to that country. It is just as easy to say, "This is magic I learned from a colleague who was taught the feat in Indonesia." One statement may be no more true than the other, but one is not accepted by the audience and the other is accepted without question.

The magician's task is much harder when he attempts to use apparatus solely designed for a trick and which does not look like anything the spectator ever has seen, or can be made to think he has seen, or might see, somewhere in the world. The reader need not worry in regard to this point, for no such apparatus will be found in these pages.

One last piece of general advice. The task of learning magic is greatly reduced if in reading about a trick the description of the effect is reread at least once to insure knowing exactly what is supposed to happen. When the effect to be created is fully understood it becomes far easier to follow the explanation of the method used, the construction of any needed equipment, and to remember the instructions for performance.

Magic, you see, is merely a matter of knowledge, preparation, and memory put together with practice. The magician, a man like yourself, is one who is agreeable, natural, and assured.

And now for the tricks.

Two. SUNDRY MYSTERIES

THE tricks in this chapter are excellent in themselves, but their particular value lies in the fact that the magician always is ready to do them. Each one can be performed extemporaneously and with borrowed objects—that is, the magician is prepared to do the tricks any time, after he has studied and practiced them in private. The tricks do not have to be shown impromptu but even as part of a show, it is well occasionally to use the other person's cards, or coins, or rings. Being able to perform magic any time, anywhere proves a man to be a magician rather than merely the possessor of a few tricks, and, besides, it is a source of great personal satisfaction.

THE FREELY SELECTED CARD

MOST of the designs adorning the backs of the cards of the modern bridge size (or narrow) playing cards are not reversible. This also is true with the patterns on many standard size decks. In other words, the picture, or design, on the back of each card can be either right side up or upside down. Magicians call cards with such backs "a one-way deck." A deck with the backs so designed that the pattern is the same whichever end is uppermost is called a "reversible deck."

I

If, in a one-way deck, all the cards are arranged with the back design right side up, it is simple to discover a particular card which has been turned upside down. For instance, a spectator selects one card from a pack having all the back designs facing in one direction. While the spectator looks at his card, the magician turns the deck end for end. Once the spectator returns his card to the deck the magician can locate the card easily for the back design of the chosen card is opposite to that of all the other cards. While it might appear obvious what he is doing were the magician merely to look at the backs as he runs through the cards, it becomes unnoticeable when the magician distracts the minds of all the spectators by giving them another idea to consider.

The theme of the magician's patter is that the eyes of anyone looking at the cards in the deck will change expression instantly upon seeing the card of which he is thinking. "Remember, no matter how hard you may fight against it, your eyes will tell your secret." The magician holds the pack at arm's length and high enough so that, when he looks into the eyes of the spectator, he still can see the cards. The cards are pushed from the top of the deck, slowly from one hand to the other. When the card with the upside down back appears, the magician waits until it has been placed at the front of those in the other hand. Then he announces: "Your eyes flickered. This (holding that hand high) must be your card."

In order neither to be awkward nor to turn the deck and then find the spectator, with a case of fidgets, has turned his card about too, the magician, after the card has been selected, squares the deck and holds the cards with both hands, one end is grasped in each hand (see illustration). When the spectator is ready to put the card back in the deck, the magician, in a most natural way, can offer either end of the deck for the card's insertion depending upon which hand he releases.

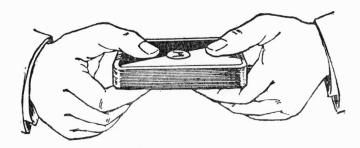

Once the card is back in the deck, the magician may shuffle the deck both fairly and thoroughly, provided he takes care no other cards become reversed during the shuffle.

II

This method of locating a freely selected card may be used with other conclusions. In one of them the magician begins counting the cards aloud after he has finished shuffling the deck. He explains that he wants to divide the deck exactly in half, which is quite as distracting a suggestion as watching the eyes. Provided he comes across the reversed card in the upper half of the deck, the magician merely divides the deck after counting twenty-six and lays both halves, face down, upon the table. He does not hesitate, nor otherwise change his speed and manner, when he sees the reversed card, but he does remember its numerical location.

With the two halves of the deck on the table, the magician asks a spectator to point to one pile. If the half-deck containing the selected card is indicated, the magician expresses thanks, turns the cards face up, and requests the spectator to lay his hand flat on the pile. If the other pile is indicated, the magician, as in the opposite instance, first thanks the spectator and then says, "Very well, that is the pile I shall use." The other deck, as previously described, is turned face up and the spectator puts his hand on the pile. Because the magician does not tell beforehand why he wants one deck chosen, the spectator's choice is meaningless though he is not aware of the fact. He remembers that he was given a choice and the trick becomes more impressive.

Before describing the climax, it should be noted that when the selected card is not in the first half of the deck, the magician puts those cards on the table exactly as he does when the card is in that half. However he does not also put down the second half. Holding those cards he says, "I must be certain this is a complete deck and there also are twenty-six cards here." He counts those cards aloud, too, and again beginning with one and counting to twenty-six. He, of course, notices and remembers the number of the position of the chosen card as this is the real reason for counting the cards.

With a spectator holding his hand on the pile having the selected card, the magician begins the trick. He announces to the audience that he is going to cut the pack he is holding, to reveal cards one after another. He holds the cards, and so opens them that the audience cannot see the cards at which he looks. The best way to do this is to hold the cards flat in one hand and with the other lift the nearest edge of the cards as though the pack were a book on its side with the binding towards the audience.

As the magician successively opens the half-deck, he says aloud, though in a flat voice, as if talking to himself: "A four, a Jack (Jack counts eleven), four and eleven are fifteen, and a two, two and fifteen make seventeen." Turning towards the spectator holding the other cards, and in a more animated manner, the magician goes on talking, "The number is seventeen. The cards always know. The selected card is the seventeenth card under your hand." The spectator counts the cards and finds that the magician is correct.

The reason for having the cards face up in the pile given to the spectator is that he would be quite apt to notice, were he given a chance to look at the backs, that the selected card is upside down.

Of course, the numbers given in the suggested patter were merely by way of example. First, the magician must know the numerical location of the card. He got the position, when he counted aloud in dividing the deck, from the top down, but the number he must know, when he turns the cards over, is from the face down. All that he need do to get this number is to subtract the number he memorized, as he counted, from twenty-seven. He subtracts from twenty-seven, though there are but twenty-six cards in the pile, because he wants to know the number of the chosen card rather than to know how many cards are above that card, and subtracting from twenty-seven will give that number.

When he knows the location of the selected card, the magician mentally, and quickly, thinks of several figures, which when added total the location number. He then cuts the cards and pretends to discover cards with those numbers. He can announce before cutting that he is going to cut the pack three times, if he makes use of the dodge of calling the King a zero. It is simple to think of three figures which when added total any number above five. Pretending to find one or more Kings, and calling each a zero, then makes it possible to get three figures with no higher a total than two.

One is never used for that card would be in view when the half-deck was turned face up. In the unusual circumstance that the selected card is twenty-sixth when the deck first is counted, take two cards from the top and put them on the bottom of that half before turning over the cards. No point is made of this and it seems to the audience merely that the deck is being squared.

III

Another method of disclosing the selected card in a magical manner relies on the same one-way back secret. As in the preceding tricks, one card is selected, returned to the reverse deck and the cards shuffled.

The magician then announces that he is going to divide the deck into three piles. As if it were the logical way to make the division, he begins sliding cards from one hand into another. He holds the cards so that he can see the backs, but at the same time does not permit the audience to see the faces of the cards nor yet to have a good view of the backs. He slides the cards into the other hand as if he were counting them, but he does not count aloud. He does not count silently either but, by his actions, he gives the audience something to think about, which is quite apart from his secret. Some of the cards he slides on to the faces of those in the other hand and some to the back, or top. This method of putting cards from one hand to the other, if noticed at all, will not look odd for many people count cards that way when it does not matter whether they are kept in order.

The reason for putting the cards into the other hand, first one way and then the other, is that the magician wants the selected card on the bottom of one of the three piles and, at the same time, wants the piles to be approximately the same size. When the card comes in view, the magician puts it on the face of the pile in his other hand. It does not matter in which third of the deck the card appears provided only that the magician gets it on the bottom of one of the three piles. The piles should be put on the table in a straight row and the one with the selected card must be the middle pile. Depending on which part of the deck the chosen card is found regulates the order in which the piles are placed on the table. When the card is found in the first third, the pile is put down with the other piles on either side thus: 2 - 1 - 3. When the card comes in the second third, the piles are placed in the normal order: 1 - 2 - 3. When in the last third, the piles go down: 1 - 3 - 2. In short, the magician contrives, in laying down the three piles of cards, to have the important heap in the middle.

The magician thereupon asks one of the spectators to place his right hand on one of the piles. The spectator should be one who is in a position to reach any pile with equal ease. No suggestion is made to the spectator that he is making a choice. He merely is given an instruction: "Please put your right hand on one of those piles." Somewhat better than three-quarters of the time the hand will go on the center pack. Whether or not this happens, the magician says, "Thank you, and please hold your hand there." Were the center heap the one on which the spectator laid his hand, the magician immediately picks up the other two piles, puts them together and sets them on the table to one side. He then asks for the name of the selected card and when it is given says, "I want you to lift your hand a few inches off the cards and strike them—not hard but something more than a tap. Fine! Now turn over the heap and you will find your selected card."

Were the spectator not to put his right hand on the center heap, he, after being thanked and told to keep the right hand in position, is instructed to place his left hand on one of the other piles. Again the chances are in favor of the magician for the spectator is apt to select the other outside pile. In such case, the magician again expresses his thanks and requests the spectator to pick up the two heaps he holds and to lay them aside. The magician does the trick with the center heap as in the first instance.

In the rare event that the spectator places one hand on an outer pile and the other on the center, the magician still is pleased and grateful. The magician first lays aside the third heap and then asks the spectator to raise one hand. If the hand is taken from the other outside heap it, too, is laid aside and the trick goes on as before. If he lifts his hand from the center heap, he is told not to lift it too high and then given instruction to strike the cards as in each previous instance. The fact that the spectator is left holding the other pack is ignored by the magician and means nothing to the spectator.

Seemingly permitting a member of the audience to make a selection from two or more objects and yet control that selection is a device magicians call "the conjurer's choice." There are various ways of using the conjurer's choice though the two already given are the most convincing. The fact that the magician thanks the spectator for his choice, besides being courteous, adds to the spectator's belief, odd though it may seem, that he really has made a selection.

If the magician does not have an opportunity secretly to arrange the cards so that the back designs all face in one direction, he cannot make use of a one-way deck. Sometimes he has an opportunity to prepare before the spectators see the cards. At other times he may get a chance to leave the room and take the cards with him. It can be done, however, right in front of everyone by "playing a game of solitaire." He calls no attention to his game and if he should be questioned he answers that it is a new game and that he doubts if he can explain the rules. He holds the deck in one hand, backs up, in the manner used in playing solitaire. One card at a time is taken from the pack, turned face up, and put on the table. The cards are laid in six piles. Prior to the description of the supposed game, it should be noted what really happens. Before the magician takes each card from the deck, he notices whether the design is right or wrong way up and lays the card accordingly on a pile at the right or at the left. When all the cards are on the table, the three piles of cards at the magician's left are ones with their backs all in one direction and those in the three piles to his right have the backs reversed. When all the cards are on the table, the piles are picked up, using both hands at once. By putting the outside piles on the next ones and each double heap on a center pile, the magician gathers the two halves of the deck. Each half is given a quarter turn, in an opposite direction to bring the ends together and the back design pointing the same way, and the halves are put together.

In playing the game, the cards should be put on the table as rapidly as possible, laying the cards first on one pile and then another. The same, or a higher or lower value card, seems naturally to go on a card already showing. Like suits reasonably can be put together. In other words with a little thought the cards may be put in piles so that it looks to anyone watching as if a system were followed. If no one is looking the cards may be put down in any old manner as long as the back design still is kept in mind. What misleads everyone completely is using six piles to divide the cards in half.

This "solitaire" method of putting a deck in order may be used in arranging cards for another excellent trick which does not depend on cards with one-way backs. The object is to sort the cards according to the color of the suits and have half the deck "red" and the other half "black." This time in playing the game, the cards are put on the table "back up" though still in six heaps. The magician holds the deck so that he can see the faces of the cards and again lays them on the table as if he were following a system. When all the cards are on the table the magician puts one pile on top of another until the deck is completed—half red, half black.

To start the trick, the magician holds the deck, back up, in one hand and begins slowly to push cards from the top of the deck into the other hand as he offers a choice of one card to a spectator. The first card having been taken from the deck, the magician, continuing to push cards from the deck into the other hand, turns to another spectator for the selection of a second card. There is no difficulty in contriving to have the first card taken from the top half of the deck and the second card from the lower half when only those halves respectively are offered for the selections. If the magician shows no interest in which card is chosen, a person naturally will select a card easy to get. The magician should not have trouble in making it easy to take a card from but one half of the deck at a time, nor in appearing unconcerned in the choice of cards.

After the spectators have looked at their cards, the magician offers the pack so that the cards may be replaced. He holds the cards as he did when the selections were made and runs them from one hand to the other. The only difference is that he offers the pack to the second spectator first. Therefore, the card from the lower half of the deck goes into the top half and the one from the upper half goes among the bottom cards.

When the magician looks at the faces of the cards, he finds one red card among the black and one black card among the red. He pulls these out of the pack and inquires of the spectators the names of the two chosen cards. Upon being answered, he shows he holds the selected cards.

Incidentally, the trick may be made more effective if the magician cuts the pack several times after the cards have been replaced. Even after the pack has been cut again and again the correct cards are the only red card among the black cards, and the only black card among the red.

In order to keep the secret quite out of the minds of the audience, the magician asks each person who chose a card to think strongly of the card and look into his eyes. He tells them: "Remember the eyes are a mirror of the mind." Of course, that is a mis-quotation but no magician ever would let such an atom-sized detail mar his regard for good patter for a good trick.

RINGS AND STRINGS

THE magician ties two pieces of heavy string around a borrowed pencil, or fountain pen. He puts several borrowed finger rings on the strings and ties them fast to the pencil. To hold the knots in place all four ends of the strings are threaded through another borrowed ring. Finally both strings are tied together at one end and given to one spectator, and the other ends, after being knotted, are handed to a second spectator. The strings not only are tied on the pencil and threaded through the rings and further tied, but spectators hold the ends of the strings so that the knots cannot be undone. The magician takes all the borrowed objects in his hands and with a slight pull magically frees them from the strings. The rings and pencil are unharmed and the strings, free of knots, still are held by the spectators. Because strings, rings and pencil are borrowed and are seen to be tied together so securely, the magician's ability to separate them is most astonishing.

The basis for the mystery is hundreds of years old and was described in all of the oldest books on magic in one, or another, manner of presentation. The trick was a favorite with the medieval magicians of England and the Continental countries, as well as the Oriental magicians from China to Egypt. The form of the trick given here has, to use the showman's phrase, "several extra added attractions" and likely will mystify even those who know one of the older presentations.

Each of the strings should be two to three feet long and the strings are hung over the pencil and tied together. Tying this knot is the first important step in the trick. The two strands of one string (held as one) are tied in a simple single knot to the two strands of the second string. (See illustration.) By strand is meant that part of the string which hangs on one side of the pencil. The audience will not notice the difference, but anyone tying the strings naturally would knot those strands hanging on one side of the pencil with the strands of the other side and such a knot would make the trick impossible. The magician must be certain he uses the right strands to make the knot. Once the strings are knotted properly—which puts the knot exactly in the center of the strings—the magician gives the ends of the strings to two spectators. Each person seems to be holding one end of each string while actually, though the magician makes no remark on the subject, each spectator holds both ends of one string.

The magician borrows four finger rings. Provided the magician gets an even number of rings it is immaterial how many he borrows. The magician takes two rings, assuming he borrowed four, and asks one spectator to thread those rings on the strings he holds. The second spectator follows suit with the remaining rings. The magician then ties the rings fast to the pencil. This knot is the second important step in the trick. The magician asks each spectator to give him one string and he ties a simple single knot and hands the strings back to the spectators to be held. Making the knot, which seems to complicate matters, actually permits the magician to exchange one strand

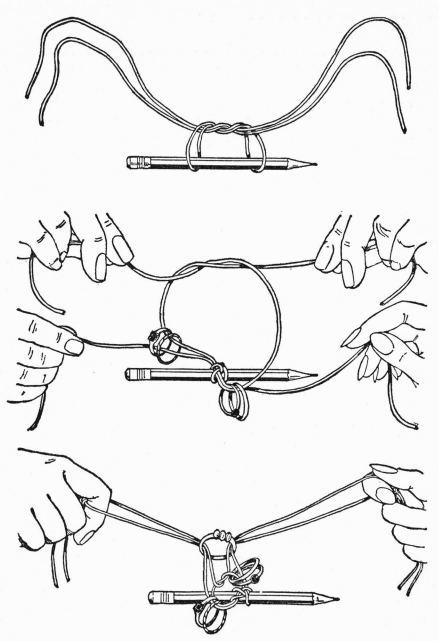

of string each spectator holds. Each spectator, at this point, will be holding one end of each string. Using only one strand of string to make the knot, beside being essential for the trick, actually appears to make the knots more involved.

SUNDRY MYSTERIES

The magician borrows another ring and the strings, first of one spectator and then the other, are threaded through the ring. The magician tells the audience that this last ring is used to hold the knots in place. Actually it has no connection with the working of the trick but its use makes the trick seem more astounding.

Finally the magician ties together the two strings of one spectator and, going to the other spectator, ties his two strings together.

While these various steps seem involved to the audience, each is very easily and quickly done. The lovely part of the trick, once the last knots are tied, is that merely sliding the pencil out of the knots automatically will release the pencil and rings, as well as free the strings of knots. The trick depends entirely upon the way the strings are tied.

If, in taking all the rings in one hand, the magician holds that hand over the knots so that they are hidden from the sight of the audience, he can pull the pencil free with the other hand without anyone's seeing what happened. Once the pencil is free of the strings, the hands should be held together to make it appear as if both rings and pencil came off simultaneously. The rings will come off of the strings as soon as the pencil is pulled free, but not until then, and it is a better trick when everything seems to happen at one time.

If the spectators are asked to pull on the strings at the time the release is made, the rings will come free more rapidly and the knots will disappear instantly. When the ends of the strings held by each spectator are tied together, for the announced reason of thereby making it impossible to untie the other knots, it is suggested that each spectator hold his strings by putting a finger through the loop which the knot makes. This will give each person a better grip and keep either one from spoiling the trick by losing his hold on the strings.

The effect is enhanced if the magician, carefully following the prescribed order and manner of making knots, acts as if he were devising, as he went along, the most secure way of tying the objects together. The trick also becomes more effective when, after the last knot is made, the magician reviews what he has done.

"For double strength, I have used two strings. Your pencil (turning to the lender) was tied tightly and securely to the strings. Several rings were strung on the string and they were tied fast to the pencil. Another ring holds those knots in place. Finally the ends of the strings were tied and these gentlemen have consented to hold them firmly. There are only two possible ways of freeing the rings, provided neither gentleman releases the ends he holds: one way is to cut the strings; and the other to use magic. I shall use magic. Watch! The rings and pencil are undamaged and the strings intact."

MAGIC SPELLING

I

THE magician takes a borrowed deck and shuffles it several times. Putting the deck on the table he asks some person to cut the cards. The magician immediately takes one pile of cards and lays it across the other, and moves away from the table. He tells the spectator who cut the cards to look at the card at the place where the pack was cut (the top card of the lower heap) and to put it back in the pack and thoroughly shuffle the deck. The spectator also is instructed to remember the name of his card and to be certain that the magician is given no chance to see which it is.

After that has been done, the magician takes the deck, looking at the faces, and runs through the cards. He seems quite disappointed as he finishes and, turning to the person who had selected the card says, "I can't seem to find your card by looking, but I am certain we can find it by magic." As he makes that statement, the magician squares the deck and puts it back on the table with the backs up. The person is asked to tell which card he had selected.

When the name of the card is given, the magician instructs the spectator to spell it out in full; that is, the value, "of," and the suit. For each letter one card is to be taken from the top of the pack and tossed on the table. After the card has been taken off the deck for the last letter, the magician instructs the spectator to turn the next card over for that will be the chosen card. Of course, the magician is right.

There are two parts to the explanation. First, the magician must know which card has been selected and, second, he must get it in position in the deck for the spelling out of the name of the card.

The second part is very simple. All that the magician needs to do is to spell out, for example, t-e-n-o-f-c-l-u-b-s, as he looks through the faces of the cards from the bottom of the deck to the top. He begins with the card after the "ten of clubs" (assuming that was the card) and pushes over one card for each letter spelled. When he has reached the end of his mental spelling, he nonchalantly cuts the deck at that point. In the case that the chosen card happens to be near the top of the deck, and the top is reached before completing the spelling, the magician, again beginning at the bottom of the pack, continues spelling and moves these bottom cards to the top upon reaching the last letter. In other words, although the audience never realizes the fact, for no one knows that the magician is aware which card was chosen, the magician puts the pack in order for the trick right in front of everyone.

This is an excellent trick to perform if some time, by chance, a glimpse of a card is caught by the magician. Of course, that cannot be depended upon to occur, but it happens quite frequently enough for the magician to be on the watch. When it does and advantage is taken by the magician, the audience is convinced it has seen a miracle.

The first part of this trick, that of knowing which card has been selected, is also very easy. It is necessary for the magician only to know which card is on top of the deck. The deck may be shuffled without removing the top card from its position and without any difficulty provided it is kept in mind which card is the top card. Shuffling not only keeps everyone from imagining that the magician would know the location of any given card, but also it gives the magician a chance to discover, as he picks up the deck, which card is on top of the deck.

The magician puts the deck on the table and asks that it be cut. The instant the deck is divided into two piles, the magician picks up what had been the lower half and puts it diagonally across the top half in the form of an X. Of course, the top card, the one known to the magician, is the top card of the lower heap and that is the one at which the spectator is told to look. However, everyone thinks, if a moment's pause is given between cutting the deck and having the spectator look at the card, that the card was taken where the pack was cut. The moment's pause comes when the magician moves away from the table after laying half the pack criss-cross on the other

half. Were it not for the psychological effect upon the audience, the result would be the same if the spectator were asked to take the top card of the deck before the deck was cut. With the added confusion of cutting the deck, the audience never imagines that the magician could know which card has been chosen.

II

Another effective spelling trick with cards is one done entirely by the magician. He runs through a deck of cards, face up, and takes out all the cards of one suit. Making these into a packet of cards, held face down, he begins to spell the values of the cards. As each letter is said the magician takes the top card off the packet and puts it on the bottom. The next card, after completing the spelling, is put on the table face up. In each instance the card put on the table is the one which has just been spelled. The magician continues spelling and putting cards on the table until all thirteen cards are out.

In other words the magician begins with the ace and spelling A-C-E takes three cards, one at a time as he spells from the top and puts them on the bottom of the packet. The next card is put face up on the table and is the ace. Next T-W-O is spelled and the two put on the table. This spelling continues right through the Queen. The last card proves to be the King.

All that is necessary is to know the order in which the cards have to be put to perform the spelling. Before the show all the cards of one suit (Hearts is suggested) are taken from the pack and put in the following order:

5-9-10-King-Jack-2-4-6-Queen-Ace-7-8-3

After the thirteen cards have been arranged, they are pushed back in the deck. The five goes near the top, the nine a few cards below, and so on. The pack is replaced in the box and the trick is prepared.

In performing the trick the deck is run through face up so that naturally the first card of the suit found will be the last card of the list. That is correct and the order will be reversed as the cards are taken from the pack and laid face up in a pile on the table. The original list was made backwards to take care of this reversal.

III

Some people prefer another form of the same trick. In this form all the court cards are taken from the deck and "Jack, Queen, King" are the words spelled. The card following the spelling of each word is put on the table as in the previous trick. The cards not only come out as spelled but the three cards of each suit come together. The order is:

JS-QC-JH-KD-JD-QH-QD-JC-KC-KS-KH-QS

In this trick as in the previous one, the first card in the list is put near the top of the pack, the next a few cards below, and so on. When the cards are taken from the pack, they are taken first from the bottom and the order is reversed as the packet is made.

CARD AUTOMATION

PARTICULARLY striking are those feats in which the magician does not seem to do anything and yet is successful in his magic. There are not many such effects and most are quite difficult to perform. This feat is very good, because it is easy to do, can be done with anyone's pack of cards, and because the spectators are quite willing to accept the performer's explanation to account for its performance. As this explanation is light years away from the true explanation the audience is particularly mystified.

The magician introduces this trick by making a statement for which there is a considerable basis of fact even though it has no connection with the trick. He explains that teachers, lawyers, detectives, and others who have long experience in listening to people account for their actions develop a technique by which they know when a person is trying to withhold information. Some emphasize, or slur, the critical part of their talk, while others speed up their words or become very deliberate with their speech. There are people who will speak normally but will show some physical mannerism, such as stroking the chin, at the moment of reaching the subject they wish to withhold. The magician goes on to claim that he has been making a study of how people talk and what people do as they talk and has reached the point where almost invariably he can discover when a person wants to withhold information. He offers to demonstrate this ability and suggests using his host's deck of cards for the experiment.

A volunteer, who feels that he has full control of his voice and actions, is invited to take part in the test. The magician intructs him to take the deck of cards and to deal the cards on to the table so as to make four piles.

One at a time he is to deal all the cards in the deck exactly as if he were dealing four bridge hands—except that he is to keep the cards in piles rather than scattering them on the table. When the last card is dealt the magician turns his back to the audience.

The volunteer then is asked to take one card from somewhere around the center of one of the four piles. He is told to look at the card, to remember which it is and to show it to some of the other spectators. With the magician continuing to keep his back toward the audience, the volunteer is instructed to put his card on any one of the piles. He also is told to put the four piles one on top of another in any sequence he wishes. Finally he is requested to square the deck.

At this point the magician turns so that he again is facing the spectators. He suggests to the volunteer that the deck be cut and that the cut be completed. The volunteer is told that he may cut the deck again if he wishes. After that cut is completed he is given permission to cut the deck even a third time.

The spectators are reminded that the volunteer selected one card but that even he does not know where in the deck that card may be found. Of course, as his back was turned, the magician could not possibly know either the location of the card or which card had been chosen. The volunteer is told that if he will read off the names of the cards as he goes through the deck, one card at a time, he will give away the card he is thinking of by either his voice or his manner. He is told to name the cards from the top down. Many people will find it easier to place the cards on the table as they are named and it may be wise to suggest doing this to make certain that each card is named and that none is skipped. Suddenly, as he recites the names of the cards, the volunteer is stopped and the magician correctly repeats the name of the chosen card. The audience is convinced that the magician has done nothing except, while his back was turned, to ask that one card be chosen from the deck and yet he is able to know which card that was. The trick is very impressive since the magician does only what he appears to do during the trick.

The feat is possible because of what the magician does before the trick is begun and about which the audience knows nothing. This secret act consists of putting four cards of like value on the top of the pack and four cards of another value at the bottom. It is immaterial which four cards are used in either instance, but, as example, say the four threes are on top

of the deck and the four aces are on the bottom of the deck. The act of dealing the cards into four piles automatically will put an ace on the top and
a three on the bottom of each pile. No matter which pile the chosen card
is placed upon, or in which order the four piles are picked up, or how many
times the deck is cut, the thought-of card will lie between a three and an
ace. The other threes and aces will not be separated by another card. Cutting the deck, by the way, does not mix the cards although it appears to
do so. The reason this is a fact is explained in Chapter 5, in "To Know
Which Card Has Been Selected."

As soon as the spectator names an ace the magician listens carefully to
the name of the next card. If it is not a three he will know it to be the chosen
card and stops the volunteer the moment he names the ace. There are two
possible chances in cutting the pack that the cards may be left in a position
where the magician might be confused were he not aware of those possibilities. By chance the cards may be cut so as to leave an ace on top of the
deck. Unless the volunteer so holds the deck that the magician sees the
bottom card, the magician cannot know if the card on the bottom is the
chosen card or a three, so he lets the volunteer continue giving the names
of the cards. If the chosen card does not show up following another of the
aces (and there are 3 chances out of 4 that it will) the magician stops the
volunteer just before he names the last card. The magician then tells the
volunteer that it did him no good to be tricky and to put the chosen card
at the bottom of the deck. In this instance the magician does not name the
card (for he hasn't heard which it is) but merely announces it to be the
selected card.

The other arrangement, chance may bring in cutting the pack, is that the
top card is the chosen card. That would mean that the second card was an
ace and the bottom card a three. If the second card is an ace, and the top
card not a three, the top card has to be the chosen card. Quite a little fun
can be generated by making the volunteer name the top two or three cards
a second time. This not only permits the magician to make certain that he
has gotten the name of the chosen card but will amuse the audience by the
way the volunteer will try to control his voice.

There will be occasions when it almost is impossible for the magician
secretly to arrange the cards so that four cards of one value are on top of the
pack and four cards of another value on the bottom. In such an instance he
can prepare for this feat by showing another card trick. In starting this trick

he explains to his audience that he has been reading of some of the fancy handling of cards which is done by professional gamblers. He goes on to say that he has not yet learned to handle the entire deck but that he can do some things with just a few cards. Picking up the deck and holding the cards with their faces towards him he says, "I'll use just four threes and the four aces," as he takes those cards from the pack. Remember the magician may use any two sets of four cards of equal value and will find it more simple to take cards as they come in the pack rather than having to bother searching for particular cards. However, to make the explanation less involved I shall continue as if the cards used were the threes and aces.

Once the magician has taken the eight cards from the deck he holds those cards in a fan in his left hand as a card player holds a hand of cards. The magician turns the fan of cards so that the spectators can see the four aces at the left of the fan and the four threes at the right. Turning the fan back so that the faces of the cards are away from the audience, the magician announces that he will arrange the cards so that the aces and threes alternate and seemingly proceeds to do so. However, there is a slight difference between his statement and the way the cards actually are arranged. In his final fan the cards are arranged—3, ace, 3, ace, ace, 3, 3, ace. It will be noticed that the fifth and sixth cards are in reverse order. As, one at a time, the aces are put between the threes the magician repeats, "three, ace, three, ace, three, ace, three, ace." As it cannot be seen that the third ace is put behind the three rather than in front of it the magician's statement is accepted. When the cards have been arranged the magician holds the eight cards face down in the way he would hold the deck were he dealing.

The magician now announces that he will take, one at a time, three cards from the top of the pile and place them on the bottom. The fourth card he will place on the table; and that he will continue to follow the same routine until he has four cards on the table and four in his left hand. While doing this counting he will separate the four cards of one value from the four of the other value. As the magician finishes his announcement he asks everyone to try to catch him making any false move. Then slowly, carefully, fairly he does exactly what he said he would do. As there is no false move none can be seen.

When he has finished counting the cards the magician will have the four threes in his hand and the four aces will be on the table. Were anyone else to try to do the same thing he would not have the same result because he would start, as the magician claimed he started, with the aces and threes alternating. However, the magician probably will not be challenged and he has shown the audience a mildly amusing feat. The important thing he has done, right in front of the eyes of the spectators, is to locate eight cards needed to perform a really impressive feat of magic. In putting those cards back "in" the deck he places the deck upon the four aces on the table and puts the four threes on top of the deck. In order that no one remembers later that this is what was done the magician cuts the deck several times and apparently mixes the cards well. There is a very simple means of doing this cutting so that the cards are just as he wants them when he finishes. Holding the deck in the left hand, face down, with the edges of the cards between his fingers on one side and his thumb on the other, the magician with the fingers of the right hand draws about a quarter of the cards off the bottom of the deck. These cards he puts on top of the deck. But, and this is the important point, in placing the cards on the top of the deck he puts them about a half of an inch forward. That is, when the cards are on top of the deck, the end of the deck towards the performer protrudes about a half of an inch beneath these cards. As soon as the cards are placed on top of the deck the fingers of the left hand grip these cards as well as the deck. The magician pulls from the bottom of the deck another dozen, or so, cards. These he places on top of those previously shifted from bottom to top. At this point he has reversed the position of about half of the deck from bottom to top and the cards which have been moved are, to him, noticeably separated from the rest of the deck. Again the magician takes about a quarter of the cards from the bottom of the deck and moves them to the top. Then finally, he grasps the protruding bottom cards and puts them on top of the deck. To the spectators the magician has mixed the cards by cutting the deck four times. Actually the cards are in exactly the same order as they were prior to his act of cutting the cards. Cutting the cards in this manner appears to be thoroughly mixing the cards and is accepted as doing so. This multiple cut is mastered in a few minutes with a deck of cards and is useful in making more convincing "mixing the cards," not only in the trick described but in several other tricks to be found in these pages. The cut is easy to learn to do because it is the normal way of cutting the cards while the deck is held in the hand, with the single difference that the cards when placed on top of the deck are made to protrude a fraction of an inch. And this difference makes no difficulty in handling the deck. The only practice needed is training the memory so that there is no hesitation in placing the cards on the deck correctly.

COINS, PAPER NAPKINS AND OLIVES

ACCORDING to Webster's Dictionary, sleight-of-hand is the term used for "a trick or tricks requiring skillful manual manipulation." When manual skill is not required for a trick, it is not sleight-of-hand. The term is very loosely used because the public does not, or at least should not, know the means used by the magician to accomplish his feats. A number of my professional colleagues are such brilliant masters of sleight-of-hand that it never occurs to anyone attending their performances that their mysteries could be accomplished by manual dexterity. On the other hand, I have heard spectators praise a magician's sleight-of-hand when none was used. This is by way of introducing several exceptionally effective tricks which are apt to be accredited to sleight-of-hand, but which do not need "skillful manual manipulation." The performer need only have enough dexterity with the fingers of the right hand to pick up a coin from the table and then to drop the coin. With his left hand, he must have enough control to open and close the fingers and to turn the wrist. Putting those simple movements together, while assuredly not sleight-of-hand, will produce startling feats of magic.

By the way, throughout this book in the instructions for the ways objects should be handled, it is assumed that the reader is right handed. If that is not the case, it may be necessary, in some instances, for him to transpose "right" and "left" in his reading.

It might be well, at this point, also to note that in this book the names used for each of the five fingers are those in general use in the United States. The "first finger" is that one next to the thumb and which some people designate as the index finger. The "second finger," the longest one in the hand, is next to the first finger and commonly referred to as the "middle finger." The "third finger" is between the second and fourth fingers and sometimes called the "ring finger." The "fourth" or smallest finger, variably called the "little finger" or "the pinky," is the last of the four fingers. The thumb is always called "the thumb" and is not given a number. By the "middle fingers" are meant the second and third fingers. The reader need not fear that he will be asked to do anything with any finger he cannot do, and this note is only to make certain that he and I have the same understanding of terms.

This sequence of natural moves will be found useful in causing an astounding array of small objects to disappear, but the better to learn them, a coin, no smaller than a quarter dollar, should be used. This is what the audience sees. A coin is picked up from a table with the fingers of the right hand, and put in the left hand which immediately is closed. The right hand is waved over the closed left hand, a magic word is spoken, or any other bit of by-play is used, and the left hand is opened to disclose the disappearance of the coin. Both hands are seen to be empty.

The trick will be described first in the situation where the magician is seated at a table, and first should be practiced that way. It is assumed that those to whom the trick is to be shown also are seated about the table, but not too close to the magician until he has developed confidence in the trick and his ability to perform it properly.

Everything the magician does is so markedly the natural thing to do that his task is not at all hard. In the beginning, the coin is placed on the table for that is the natural way to show the coin. Because the coin is to be put in the hand, it is natural to pick it up. It is also natural to slide the coin towards oneself in picking it up. And there is where the secret part of the trick comes in, for the hand continues its movement towards the body until it is past the edge of the table and the coin is dropped into the lap. Acting in manner and position of the fingers as though the coin were still held, "it" is put into the left hand and that hand is closed tightly. Nothing remains except to order the coin to disappear and to show the hands empty. There are the bare bones of the moves made by the magician. The moves are very easy to do, but they must be understood in detail and properly synchronized.

The best way to find what is supposed to be done is to take a coin from the table and actually put it in the hand. In doing this, it will be found that the hands move together and each hand does its share of the work. Copying these moves, when only pretending to put the coin in the left hand, will make the simulation more natural.

This is a detailed explanation of what each hand does. The right hand takes a coin from the pocket and drops it on the table. The coin should be dropped from the height of three or four inches. Dropping the coin seems to be the most convincing way to prove the existence of the coin and to show the absence of trickery. The coin should be dropped so that it falls about

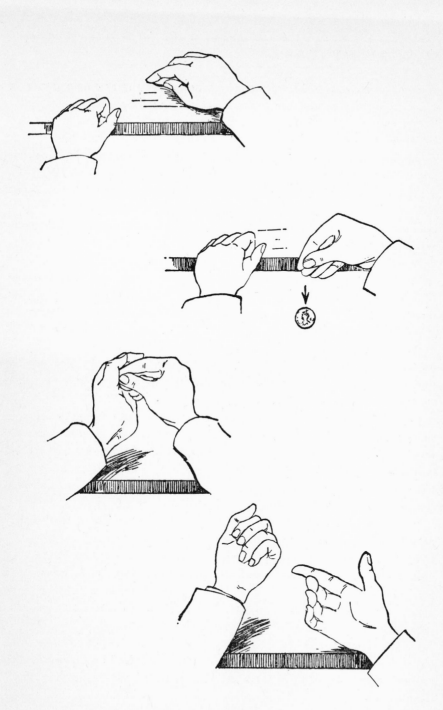

eight inches from the edge of the table and directly in front of the magician. The instant the coin is on the table, the magician makes a remark about the design such as, "A quarter with George Washington's portrait." This factual statement, while calling everyone's attention to the coin, does not explain what is about to happen and does give everyone something else to think about. When he speaks of the coin, the magician rests each hand on the edge of the table. The natural way to have the hands is palm down and fingers curled under and as far apart as the width of his shoulders.

The magician picks up the coin with the fingers of the right hand. It will be found that the fingers will cover the coin so that it is hidden from the sight of the audience. The motion of the right arm carries the right hand along the surface of the table towards the magician and an inch or two beyond the edge. This is when the coin is dropped. Then the right arm is lifted and the hand goes back over the table. The left hand begins moving before the coin is dropped. It is held in exactly the same position as when resting on the table. Actually it is a left arm movement.

The right and left hands should meet at a point about a foot from the edge of the table and several inches above its surface. In order to time this correctly, the left hand does not move as rapidly as does the right. Though the hands move at different rates of speed neither hand makes either a quick or jerky action.

When the right and left hand meet, both are palm side down. The wrist of each is turned to bring the fingers of the right hand to the palm of the left. The curled fingers of the left hand will mask from the sight of the spectators that no coin is put into the hand. The left fingers close about the fingers of the right hand and the right hand is withdrawn. At this point, the left hand is closed, as if holding the coin, and the back of the hand is towards the table. The magician points at his left hand with his right as he says, "I put the quarter into my hand." The reason for pointing is to give the audience a chance to see that the right hand is empty. This emptiness must be made plain without either speaking about the matter or being too obvious in showing the hand.

The magician gives the order for the disappearance of the coin and slowly, very slowly, opens his left hand. After everyone sees that the coin is gone, the magician slowly shows the back and palm of both hands with the fingers spread apart.

Unless the magician can be certain to remember to keep his knees together, not only to catch the coin, but to hold it until retrieved, he had better have a napkin or his handkerchief spread across his lap.

There is apt to be a mental hazard that makes these moves seem awkward the first few times they are tried, so the sequence and timing of the moves need to be practiced until the performer feels not only natural but confident. There is nothing odd or unusual about the moves and the only reason they may seem awkward is because of the claim to put a coin in the hand when that is not done. As there is no reason for the audience to suspect the deception the magician's qualms are needless.

Now for a few tricks which may be performed with the aid of these moves.

I

The magician causes a coin to disappear and later finds it under a salt shaker, an ash tray, or some other object on the table. This requires two coins of the same general appearance. One coin the magician secretly puts under an object on the table before he takes the other coin from his pocket. The second coin is introduced, caused to vanish, and—by disclosing the hiding place of the first coin—made to reappear.

The easiest way to hide the first coin under some object is to lift the object with the left hand and transfer it to the right hand and place it on the coin held secretly in that hand. The coin is held secretly in the right hand by putting it on the two middle fingers, where they join the palm, and closing the hand until the coin is gripped. As soon as the object is over the hand, the fingers are opened. It will be found easy to put an ash tray, saucer, or similarly sized object on the table with the coin underneath, by laying the hand on the table and, by turning the wrist, dropping the coin and dropping the dish over it. This requires a covering on the table to mask the sound of the falling coin.

It also is easy, once the object is over the coin in the right hand, to slide the fingers of the left hand under both object and coin and pick them up together. Thus held they may be put down together, and if done slowly and carefully, without making any noise with the coin. It is better to use this method with small coins.

The coin, instead of being found under something, may be found in a sugar bowl or in someone's pocket. In either case, it is necessary merely to drop the coin in place some time before the occurrence of the trick. When close to a person no difficulty will be found in dropping a coin into an out-side coat pocket. Care should be taken to notice whether the pocket looks as if it were filled, for dropping a coin on an eye-glass case or similarly hard object, is likely to be noisy.

Finally it should be noted that it is not essential that the coin be made to reappear, for the disappearance alone is a good trick.

II

Precisely the same moves are used in a totally different type of mystery. The magician tears a paper napkin into a dozen pieces and, with a wave of the hand, restores it to its original, though somewhat more mussed, condition.

Before he tears the first napkin, the magician secretly has annexed a second napkin which, to use the words of an early writer on magic, "is so like unto the first as not to be told apart." This napkin is squeezed into a compact ball and put, by the magician, on his lap.

Both hands are used to tear up the first napkin. This is done slowly and with care taken to show the hands otherwise to be empty. The emptiness of the hands is not remarked upon, but must be made obvious. The magician may talk about the grain of the paper and how much more readily he can tear it across one way than across the other, or he may content himself by counting aloud into how many pieces he has torn the napkin.

When the napkin is mutilated sufficiently, the magician puts the pieces together and squeezes them into a ball like the ball he has made of the whole napkin in his lap. Once the ball is made, it is dropped on the table—as was done with the coin—and the right hand presses the ball on the table as if to insure that it is as compact as possible. While this is being done, the left hand retrieves the whole-napkin-ball from his lap.

Exactly the same motions are done with the napkin on the table and the right hand as were done with the coin. The left hand, too, is moved in just the same way. The only difference being that a substitution of napkins is made because the whole napkin is in the left hand. The torn pieces are gotten rid of as was the coin and the audience believe the ball, when it is shown, in the left hand to be the ball of torn pieces and when it is shown to be a complete napkin their astonishment is great.

After having gotten confidence and smoothness in presenting this torn napkin trick, any size napkin may be used, but until that point is reached, it is better only to do the trick with one of small size.

III

The motions used to cause a coin to disappear are equally good to substitute one paper napkin for another. The moves used to exchange the napkins are equally good when used to exchange objects of different type.

For instance an olive can be transformed into a lump of sugar, a piece of paper can be changed into a potato chip, a blank domino can be turned into a double six.

Each of the above tricks is very effective and amusing when shown at a table. This however should be borne in mind—only one trick using this method should be shown on a single occasion in order that the secret be not discovered. And one further suggestion, always remember to pocket whatever has been discarded in the lap before arising from the table.

It is quite possible to utilize the same moves when standing. The difference being that, as he has no lap when standing, the magician does not use his lap to discard the objects.

To vanish a coin he uses a plate and a cloth. The cloth, which may be a table cover or merely a folded handkerchief, is under the plate and is used to eliminate noise. The coin is dropped on the plate for the announced purpose of testing the trueness of the sound. When it is picked up, the coin is dropped behind the plate exactly as it was dropped in the lap.

A book of fair thickness lying flat on the table will be found to be an excellent screen behind which to hide the torn paper napkin. The whole napkin, at the start of the trick reposes in the magician's left coat pocket. He gets it from his pocket at the same point in the trick in which he gets the one in his lap. No one will notice the motion, in either instance, if the magician will go after the napkin calmly, slowly, and in an indifferent manner.

The number of objects which may be exchanged or caused to disappear by this method is almost limitless. The magician's imagination and the material at hand are the main restrictions. Size also must be taken into account, but once the magician has practiced until he is both confident and comfortable in doing the trick, he will find it possible to handle objects even larger than his hand.

SUNDRY MYSTERIES

One time when I was at a dinner with Frank Buck, the writer, motion picture director and authority on wild animals, he took from his pocket a Cassowary egg. The contents of the egg nearly fill a quart bottle, which gives a rough idea of its size. One of the other guests suggested that the egg should be given to me for it very likely was one object I never had used in magic. True the egg was twice the size of my hand, but it disappeared quite as readily and as easily as would a quarter, or an olive. Not only did the egg disappear but it did so to the expressed amazement of my friends.

Three. TRICKY TRICKS

It is an advantage to any magician to be able to perform a number of completely extemporaneous feats which stress laughs and surprise rather than mystery. This Chapter is composed of such feats. The majority of the effects are presented as challenges but actually are intriguing and amusing hoaxes. All the effects are equally effective when shown to men at a bar, to young people at a soda fountain, or any other place where the magician feels a surprise and a laugh would make the party more enjoyable.

CAMEL AND THE NEEDLE'S EYE

I

St. Mark's statement to the effect that it is easier for a camel to go through a needle's eye than for a rich man to enter Heaven indicates that the good Saint felt he was comparing impossibilities. The spectators will be certain of the impossibility of dropping a quarter through a dime-size hole in a piece of paper. Though Heaven may lack rich men, a quarter will drop through a hole in a piece of paper no larger than the diameter of a dime—provided one knows how to do it.

Preparation for performing the feat of dropping a large coin through a small hole is accomplished at the time the hole is made in the paper. Provided the paper is not stiff, any kind of paper may be used such as newspaper, writing paper, or thin wrapping paper. The paper is folded in half and then into quarters so that at the center of the paper two folds cross. A dime is placed on the folded paper so that the point of the folded center is right in the middle of the dime. Holding the coin and paper together tightly, the paper is torn along the edge of the dime. When still folded the paper torn off is shaped like a quarter of a pie. When opened, this piece is circular and the size of a dime. Likewise, the hole in the remaining paper is, when the paper is unfolded, precisely dime-size. Folding the paper and tearing it by using the dime as guide is the easiest as well as the quickest way of making such a size hole in a piece of paper. Not only is this the quickest way of making a hole in paper of the desired size, but it gives an obvious excuse for folding the paper. And the folds are required for the performance of the feat.

After the hole has been torn, the paper is unfolded and laid flat on a table and a quarter is put on the paper near the hole so that a comparison of sizes can be made. The spectators are asked what they think the possibilities are of dropping the quarter through the small hole in the paper without altering either coin or paper. After everyone agrees that the idea is completely impractical, the performer shows that it can be done.

The performer begins his demonstration by raising both the top and bottom of the paper from the table. The coin will slide into the crease previously made in the paper. The performer then moves his hands on the paper so that

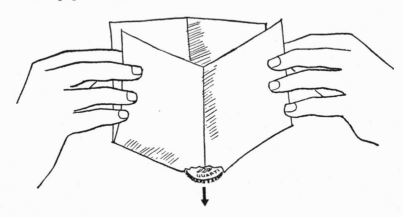

one is at either end of the folded paper and holding together the double thickness of paper. He then raises his hands and brings them together. This will make the paper bend along the other fold and bring the quarter, on edge, to the hole. In holding a folded paper in this way the diameter of the hole widens enough for the coin to drop through the hole. A trial will verify the truth of this odd fact of the hole's becoming bigger without tearing the paper.

II

This demonstration may well be followed by another depending upon a play on words. It should be remembered that the performer always used the word "drop" in speaking of the quarter "dropping" through the hole in the paper only the size of a dime. This time he uses the word "push." He makes another hole in the paper only half the size of a ten cent piece. He reminds the spectators that they just have seen how the quarter went through the hole exactly the size of a dime. Then he asks them, "Do you believe that I can push that same quarter through this hole which is only half the size of the first?" The spectators will agree the feat is impossible because they witnessed how only barely did the quarter go through the larger hole. They all are conditioned to the idea of the coin's going through the hole in the paper and will not notice that the performer used the word "push." As soon as all agree that it can't be done, the performer takes a pencil, sticks it through the hole and, putting the end of the pencil against the coin, "pushes it through the hole."

III

Not only have the spectators been "sold" but they now will suspect the words the performer uses. In this third demonstration, they will analyze everything he says expecting tricky wording. However, he fools them again by doing exactly what he states he can do. He tells the spectators, "I can cut this paper so that it will have a hole large enough for me to walk through." He then asks, "Would you like to see me do it?" The paper the performer holds should be about the size of ordinary business stationery—8½″ x 11″— and again any paper may be used. Incidentally, a piece of letter-size paper can be cut quickly so that the circumference of the hole will measure more than 12′ which will be found large enough to walk through when it is held open. Paper cut to this size will have strength enough to hold together as it is held. The same size paper can be cut so that the hole will have a 36′ circumference but then will be too delicate to permit the feat to be done.

It will have been noticed that the performer promised "to cut the paper so it will have a hole large enough to walk through." Due to paper's having "grain," it will tear straight lengthwise but is almost impossible to tear straight crosswise. Therefore, it is necessary to use scissors to cut the paper for this feat. Unless the performer carries a small pair of scissors with him, and many men do, the feat only can be done where scissors are available.

Prior to cutting the paper, which is assumed to be 8½" x 11", fold it in half lengthwise. Then starting at the fold, and ½" from one end of the paper, the double paper is cut with the scissors to within ¾" of the sides of the paper. The cut runs ½" from the end of the paper. Always cutting from the folded edge parallel cuts are made 1" apart the length of the paper. Each of these cuts, like the first one, stops when it is ¾" from the edges of the paper. The paper then is turned around and starting after the first cut (1¼" from the

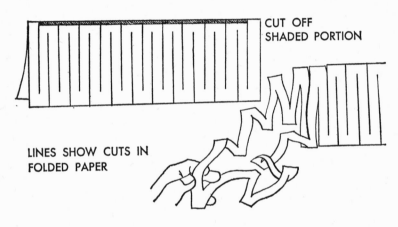

CUT OFF
SHADED PORTION

LINES SHOW CUTS IN
FOLDED PAPER

end of the paper), cuts are made from the edges of the paper towards the center fold. These cuts go half way between the other cuts and parallel to them, ending before the last cut. These cuts stop when each is ¾" from the center fold. When these cuts are made, the paper again is turned around. The fold of the paper is cut away, beginning after the first cut and continuing up to the last cut, leaving only a fold at each end of the paper uncut. The cutting then is completed. The paper, much like a folding screen, will open to make a huge loop of paper. Because paper tears easily, the loop must be handled with care but it will be found quite big enough to step through. I know I find no difficulty and I am 6'3" tall and weigh over 190 pounds. If the reader is very much larger, he may find it advantageous to start with a bigger piece of paper.

Anyone will swear this feat cannot be done—that is anyone not in possession of two little details. He who has these details finds it all so easy.

The performer balances a strip of paper on the mouth of an empty bottle. The paper strip, about 1″ wide and 1′ long, may be torn from newspaper, writing paper, or any flexible paper. The bottle may have contained beer, ginger ale, or any other beverage which comes in a small mouthed bottle. On top of the paper strip and directly centered on the mouth of the bottle, the performer places a stack of coins. A silver quarter is at the bottom of the pile. On top of the quarter is a nickle, above that coin is a penny and the top coin is a ten cent piece. All that is needed is 41¢, a bottle and a strip of paper.

The challenge is to remove the paper strip from between the stack of coins and the bottle and without touching either the coins or the bottle, or permitting either of them to be touched by anyone or anything. After due consideration, the majority of people will give up. The small minority who attempt to remove the paper fail in their efforts.

The performer, when it comes time to show how it can be done, first tears off one end of the paper strip. He does this by grasping the paper between thumb and first finger, as near to the bottle as is possible without touching it. With care the strip can be torn within an inch of the bottle. The first finger of the left hand is put under and across the strip of paper, in preparing to tear it, and the thumb presses the paper against the finger. The right hand pulls the strip down so that it is torn along the left finger. This is a very simple thing to do but the action must not be hurried. Trying to tear the

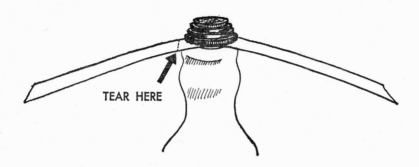

TEAR HERE

paper quickly is apt to pull the paper which will cause the stack of coins to topple off the bottle.

After one end of the paper strip has been torn off, the performer moistens the tip of the second finger of his right hand. Then, with considerable force, he strikes the remaining long end of the paper strip with the moistened finger. He strikes down on the paper. The paper will slide out from between the bottle and the stack of coins. Moistening the finger makes it grip the paper. Inertia will hold the coins in place.

Those who happen to remember what they were told in their physics classes about inertia will be confounded by the fact that the strip extends on both sides of the bottle. No such person ever conceived of the idea of removing the extra paper in my experience and until it is removed the feat cannot be done.

While using a stack of coins makes the feat seem more difficult, it actually, because of the added weight, makes it easier. Using the particular coins suggested, because of the variation in size, also makes the trick easier while making it appear to be harder to do.

FALLING DOWN

ANOTHER challenge having to do with a piece of paper and a coin is so easy for the performer and so impossible for the spectator. It is impossible for the spectator largely because his thinking has been lead in the wrong channels by the suggestions of the performer.

The performer, prior to making his challenge, reminds his listeners that while a pound of feathers is exactly the same weight as a pound of lead, were both feathers and lead dropped simultaneously from the top of the Washington Monument, the lead would be first to reach the ground. That, of course, is because the much larger package of feathers would have its fall delayed by air resistance. A rocket is designed to minimize the force of air and a parachute is designed to make use of the same force. The performer's purpose in reminding the spectators of these facts is to get them thinking in the terms of air resistance and weight and bulk and so lead them away from the true solution to his challenge.

The performer shows a coin and also a piece of paper slightly smaller in size than the coin. He challenges anyone to drop both the coin and the piece of paper at the same time and cause the paper to drop with the same rapidity as does the coin. While most people will immediately say it can't be done, a very few will try to do it. When they, too, are convinced that the feat is impossible, the performer shows them how it can be done.

Remember that the piece of paper is just a little smaller than is the coin, for this is essential. The performer holds the coin by the edges and flat. His hand is above the coin with his fingers pointing towards the floor. The instant he releases his fingers, the coin will fall and be flat in its descent. Prior to releasing the coin, the performer places the piece of paper on the flat top surface of the coin. The paper is placed carefully on the coin so that it does not stick over the edge of the coin at any point. Dropping the coin and paper together in this way both will drop at the same speed. This, obviously, is because the coin as it falls keeps the air from getting under the paper to delay its fall.

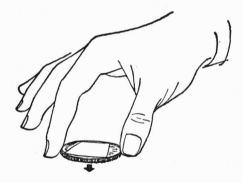

THE SUBMARINE COIN

HERE is another feat offered as a challenge to the spectators. After everyone gives up the performer demonstrates how easily it can be accomplished.

At the beginning the performer shows a plate having a dime resting on it. Covering the coin is an inverted tumbler and the glass is filled with water. The challenge is to pick up the silver ten cent piece without wetting the fingers. Some may, by holding the glass and plate tightly together, invert the glass so that it is rightside up but they find that is of little help as the coin drops from the plate to the bottom of the glass where it still is covered by water. At this point, almost invariably the task is relinquished. Even those very few who go to the next step of pouring the water into something else and without letting the coin slide out of the glass are left with a very moist coin which they don't know how to handle. Both steps, by the way, are correct and the ones the performer uses. But he adds the third step of sliding the dime out of the glass and onto his handkerchief. After drying the coin, he is able to pick it up without wetting his fingers. The performer should slide the damp coin onto several thicknesses of cloth so that he does not wet the hand holding the handkerchief.

This feat never should be attempted where damage might be done were the water spilled. While there should be no danger of such a happening occurring while the performer has the glass and plate, it always is uncertain what may occur in the experiments of others. Besides the hostess is apt to be worried rather than entertained and worrying a hostess is never the aim of a good entertainer.

Before starting this feat, the performer must make certain that the plate he intends to use is absolutely flat for not all plates are. The plate has to be flat so that there are no liquid-escaping gaps between the plate and the mouth of the glass. Otherwise when the water-filled glass is inverted the performer will find himself in the midst of a deluge and without an ark to get away in.

THE FRIENDLY CARDS

WHILE this feat is not always successful it is worth doing because it is so astounding when it does work and because the spectator believes it is his fault when it doesn't. And it is particularly good because the performer actually does absolutely nothing except talk. It even has been done by telephone.

A spectator is requested to shuffle a deck of cards and to continue mixing the cards until he feels inclined to stop. He then is asked to look at the top and bottom cards of the deck. He is told to ignore the suits and to state only the value of the cards he looked at.

"A ten and a Jack," the magician repeats, that is he says again the names of whatever two cards the spectator mentioned. The magician goes on talking, "Those are good cards. Now I want you to be kind enough to shuffle the pack again. If you stop shuffling the cards at the right instant, as I feel you will, you will have arranged the cards so that a ten and a Jack (or whatever cards were selected) are together in the pack."

The spectator mixes the cards and stops shuffling when he pleases. He then runs through the pack to see if the two cards named are together in the deck. He is likely to find they are. When the two cards named are not discovered to be together, the performer says, "Why you must have stopped your shuffle an instant too soon."

The entire stunt has absolutely nothing to do with the amount of shuffling done. Everything depends upon the law of probabilities and the chances are very favorable for finding the two cards together.

It must be remembered that there are four cards of each value in a deck of cards. Further nothing is mentioned about which card will be first in the deck. Ten, Jack may be together, but if they come in the order of Jack, ten, they are just as much together.

SPEED CONTEST

THIS feat is presented as a contest of speed and is most amusing when the contest element is stressed. As what the spectator is asked to do is impossible except by a trick, the challenge is only a gag. Making the spectator concentrate on the element of speed keeps him from discovering for some time that he can't do it at all. He will be most surprised at his inability for it appears as if it would be so simple to do. The end is hilarious when the performer shows the trick which makes it possible for him to do the impossible.

All that the spectator is asked to do is to tear a piece of paper into thirds and to do it quicker than the performer can tear another piece of paper in like manner. The rules of the contest are that the paper must be held by the opposite top corners and the grip of each hand must be maintained until the paper is torn into thirds. When the spectator is given his paper there are two tears, each about 1″ long, at the top edge of the paper. These tears are spaced so as to divide the top edge approximately into three equal parts. He is told that all he has to do is to continue both these tears until the paper is in three equal pieces. With the paper held as described, all the spectator finds he can do is to tear off one side and leave the center section remaining attached to the other side.

The performer takes another piece of paper which is a duplicate of the paper the spectator was given, even to the two small tears dividing the top edge into thirds. With his hands the performer takes hold of the paper exactly as did the spectator. The performer then grips the center of the top of the paper with his teeth. Nothing had been said to forbid such tricky action. Holding the center section in his teeth, the performer pulls each hand down and tears away the side sections of the paper. Only by holding the center of the paper can it be torn in thirds without changing the position of the hands. No spectator ever thinks of this action.

As previously mentioned, paper has grain and will tear straight with the grain. Down a newspaper page, as example, is with the grain. In most cut

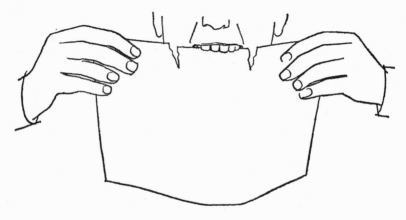

paper the grain runs lengthwise. It is only when a paper is cut into a square, as in a paper napkin, that it is necessary to investigate to know which way the grain runs. This may be discovered by testing an edge. If it is easy to tear it is with the grain. When it pulls instead of tearing, the adjoining side will be the one going with the grain. The performer, in this feat, always must be certain that he holds his paper so as to tear with the grain.

LIQUID SMOKE

A FEAT smokers will find intrigues both young and old is to make smoke seem to change to a liquid and then handle it as if it were in fact in a liquid state. It is an amusing stunt.

Cigarette, cigar or pipe smoke may be used for the feat. The demonstration begins by the smoker's taking a mouthful of smoke. The smoke is expelled into a glass which becomes filled, from the bottom up, exactly as if a liquid were being poured into it. The smoke then can be poured back and forth from one glass to another, or left to stand on the table as a glass filled with liquid smoke. For the climax, the smoke may be returned to a gaseous state or it may be shaken and then drunk as if it were a smoke cocktail.

Because dense smoke is heavier than air, all that is necessary to do this feat is to mix as little air as possible with the smoke. The smoke is drawn only to the mouth and is not inhaled. The larger the amount of smoke taken into the mouth at one time the greater will be the density of the smoke. Then, by putting the lower lip against the rim of a tumbler and opening the lips a little bit, the smoke is expelled from the mouth by raising the tongue and very slowly contracting the cheeks. The heavy smoke will pour into the glass. As the smoke goes into the glass the performer should hold his breath to avoid having the smoke diluted by the breath from his nostrils. Several mouthfuls of smoke can be put into the glass if careful, in taking the mouth away from, and returning it to the glass.

By moving deliberately to avoid making air currents, the smoke may be poured from glass to glass. The pouring should be done only after the lips of the glasses touch. The smoke cannot be kept in a dense form when the glasses are not together, for there are enough air currents even in a closed room to disturb the smoke when it is not shielded.

Smoke will stay indefinitely in a glass set on the table.

To make the smoke return to a gas form all that need be done is to blow into the glass. The blowing should be done gently and not as if trying to extinguish all the candles on a birthday cake with a single blast. The blowing should be soft, silent and protracted. It also should be aimed straight at the glass. In blowing in this manner, the performer's mouth can be as much as a yard away from the glass and still make the smoke leave the glass and rise into the air.

The smoke cocktail is made by sliding the mouth of an inverted glass over the mouth of the glass containing the smoke. Sliding one glass on to the other is essential because of avoiding air currents. One glass can not be clapped on the other. Once the glasses are mouth to mouth they are firmly held together and shaken as if they were a cocktail shaker. This will not affect the smoke in any way as the walls of the glasses keep the outside air away from the smoke. While nothing happens to the smoke when the glasses are shaken the spectators are not aware of this fact and to them it seems as if the smoke was being thoroughly mixed. Taking the glasses apart, again by sliding one off the other slowly, the performer raises the glass of smoke to his lips and drinks the smoke.

Parenthetically, a note or two about drinking smoke. First the smoke is drunk and not inhaled. In raising the glass to his lips, the performer moves at normal speed, instead of the extremely deliberate motions he had been using. About half the smoke will have been lost before the glass touches the lips. Drinking the remaining smoke will in no way affect one accustomed to smoking. That is he will not be affected provided he is dealing with the type of smoke to which he is accustomed. By that is meant a cigarette smoker, for example, should not try drinking cigar smoke. This fact I learned the hard way. While, by habit, I am a cigarette smoker, I accepted a cigar at a large dinner at which I was to do magic. Possibly I took a cigar as they were passed, to conform to the action of all the others at the head table. I was still smoking the cigar when the chairman introduced me. His introduction was very kind but he ended it with, "And, Mr. Mulholland, I hope you will begin by showing these gentlemen the feat with the liquid smoke I once saw you do." I recalled having once done the smoke business for his children and while I did not think it appropriate for a formal performance, he had liked it and wanted to see it done so I did it. At the end I drank the smoke cocktail as I usually do. However, cigar smoke is not like cigarette smoke. Fortunately I was standing behind a table which I could lean against and hold on to until the huge banquet room stopped its mad spinning.

As long as it has been noted a number of times that air currents will cause the smoke to blow away, it is undoubtedly unnecessary to mention the feat never should be attempted outdoors or in a drafty room.

THE JUMPING ARROWS

THIS is one of those confounding, ultra simple, quickly done feats which delights the very young, the very old and the intermediate ages. All that the performer has to do is to memorize the sequence of ways a two inch square of cardboard is turned over. On each side of the cardboard is drawn an arrow. As the square is turned the arrows seem to jump around to point in the same direction, in opposite direction, and up and down as well. The trick may be carried in the pocket by having arrows already drawn on a correct size piece of cardboard. The trick also may be done by cutting the cardboard and drawing the arrows in the presence of the audience.

Here is what the spectators see, not think they see, but actually see. The magician shows a square of cardboard which has an arrow running horizontally from the center of the card to, and pointing to, the center of one side. When the card is turned over the spectators see a second arrow pointing in the same direction as the first. The magician explains that the card is a small replica of a sign made to point to the entrance of a shop. The arrows point to the entrance whether the sign is seen from one side or the other. However, a rival and very unscrupulous merchant knew a wicked wizard and a hex was put on the sign. Our shopkeeper friend found that one day the arrows on the sign would point up in the air, another day they would point away from the shop, and the third day they would point toward the ground. The shopkeeper tried to get the hex taken away but he only had half success for while the arrow on one side pointed toward the shop, the arrow on the other side pointed to the ground and that is the way it is to this day.

As the performer tells about the sign, he shows one side after the other of the card. The arrows on the card keep jumping so as to point in different directions to agree with the story. Finally, giving the card to a spectator, the magician remarks that he would not like to have a wicked wizard mixed up in his business. The card can be examined indeterminately without discovering what causes the arrows to jump. The secret is a combination of confusion and an optical illusion and neither factor will be disclosed by examination of the card.

The card is stiff cardboard 2" square and blank except for an arrow drawn on each side. Each arrow runs straight from the center of the cardboard to point at the middle of one edge. The shafts of the two arrows are at right angles one to the other and point to adjacent edges. The arrows seem to jump about the card due to the fact that the card is turned over in four different ways. That the card is turned over in different ways never is apparent and would be meaningless even were it noticed because of the illusion element.

The illustration shows how one side of the card appears and, by means of dotted lines, shows the position of the arrow on the other side. The illustration also has letters a-A and b-B to designate the diagonal corners of the square. When the card first is shown, it is held between the first finger and thumb of the left with the tips on the corners a-A. The hand should be held so that the arrow points to the performer's left and the side between the letters B-A face toward the audience. By pressing down on corner B with the first finger of the right hand, the performer turns the card over. Because the card is held diagonally the arrow will again point to the performer's left when the card is turned over. Corner B again points in the same direction.

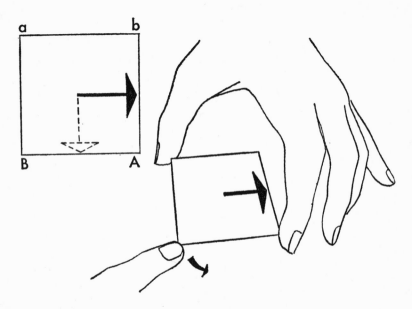

This is done three or four times so as to impress upon the spectators that no matter which side of the card is seen both arrows point in the same direction.

Then the arrow is made to jump. The performer takes the middle of the edge a-b between the first finger and thumb of the right hand and releases his left hand. Then by twisting his right wrist he turns the card over. The arrow will be pointing directly towards the performer. Again with his left hand, he takes the point of the arrow between first finger and thumb and releases the right hand. Twisting the left wrist the card is turned over and the arrow points to the performer's right. Again a switch of hands. This time the point of the arrow is taken by the right hand and the card turned over. The arrow now points towards the spectators. Again the left hand takes the card and the right hand is released. The card in this instance is held at the side opposite to the one to which the arrow points—the side which would be touched were the shaft of the arrow lengthened. Again the card is turned over and the arrow points to the performer's left as it did at the beginning of the trick. Finally, the card is gripped with the fingers of the right hand at the middle of side a-B. But this last time, the card is turned in a different way. It is turned by swinging the arm to the right. This will show the arrow on one side of the card to be horizontal and the arrow on the other side to be vertical. At this point the card is given to a spectator.

As so frequently happens the performer probably will be asked to repeat the trick. While it is a cardinal rule in magic never immediately to repeat a trick to the same audience, it is permissible in this case to ignore the rule for what is done is not quite the same. This time the card is held diagonally again but by the corners b-B. When the card is turned the arrow points in the opposite direction. While retaining hold of these corners, the card is turned over several times. The arrows will point first to the left, then to the right, left-right, left-right. Then the card is returned to the spectator.

Reading the instructions without the card in the hands will lead one to believe the trick is difficult. With the card to handle, it will be found to be utterly simple.

THE LITTLE INDIAN

THIS is a most surprising effect. Using only a white handkerchief and a lead pencil the performer forms the sculptured head of a turbaned Indian. A few folds and twists of the cloth, several marks with the lead pencil and, presto, the performer has an amazing likeness of an Indian fakir.

While making the head from a handkerchief actually is a stunt rather than a trick, it becomes rather magical when done rapidly. This is quite opposed to the general rule that a quick movement never should be used in magic. There are but a dozen steps needed to make a common handkerchief into the bust of a turbaned Indian but these steps have to be memorized in sequence and practised until they can be done deftly and quickly. The effect should be that cloth sculpturing is the easiest thing in the world.

The bust of the turbaned Indian is made from a man's handkerchief 18 inches square. It is suggested that a nice appearing but inexpensive cotton handkerchief be used.

Here are the details of the steps in making a miniature replica of a turbaned Indian from a man's cotton handkerchief. The performer lays the handkerchief on a table. The handkerchief is put on the table to form a diamond— that is, one corner is towards the performer, one corner away from him, and the other two corners at his right and left. First the lower corner and then the upper corner are folded back on top of the handkerchief. This will make the handkerchief into a wide strip of cloth and as long as the diagonal measurement (24 inches) of the handkerchief. More folding is done from the bottom and from the top until the strip of cloth is only 1½″ wide. A simple single knot is formed at the center of this folded strip and the knot is drawn taut. One side of the knot will be triangular in shape and the cloth will be smooth. This is the part of the handkerchief which, later, will be made into the face of the Indian. At the wide part of the triangle, the end of the handkerchief comes out of the knot at an angle. This is the end of the cloth used to form the turban. The end first is twisted down to make the right side of the turban. The end then is brought behind the head and folded upwards to make the left side of the turban. At the top of the turban the cloth is folded back and again brought behind the head. The short end left of the cloth is squeezed together and brought down the back of the head and is used as stiffening for the neck. That end is held against the end coming out of the lower side of the knot. Both pieces of cloth are folded back and over to form the right shoulder of the figure. The end is again folded back and over but this time to form the left shoulder. Once again the end is folded back and then brought over the right shoulder of the figure and pinned at the chest. A pin will hold the cloth securely and the job can be done quickly. However, it is possible to tuck the last end into one of the folds so as to keep the handkerchief from unfolding.

After the pin is in the cloth the head is finished by making the features on the face. These are made with a sharp pointed pencil having very soft lead. Round circles for eyes are made first. Above the eyes straight lines are drawn to make eyebrows. The nose is a short straight vertical line. Immediately below the line for the nose, two lines, one to the right and one to the left, are made to form the moustache. A beard is drawn using several lines, on the chin. A small space for the mouth, not necessary to draw, is left

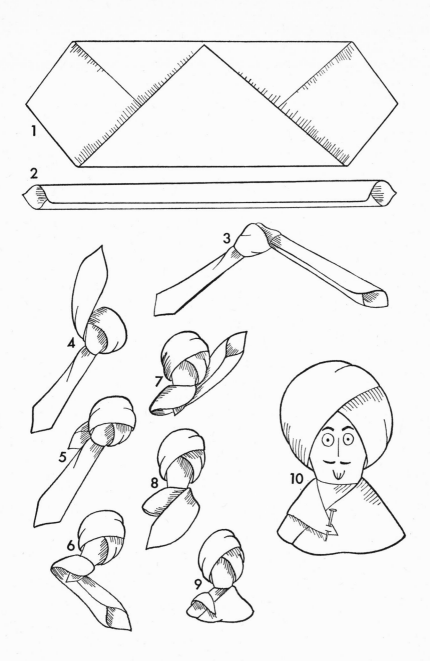

between the moustache and beard. All these lines are simple to make and require no artistic ability. Nevertheless, a little practice is needed to make the face rapidly. Such practice can be done on paper upon which have been marked triangles the size of the knot.

Many people are so intrigued with the little Indian head that inevitably someone will want to have one as a souvenir. Women and children in particular want it, as they consider it so "adorable." To be able to give away his cloth sculptures, it is suggested that the performer have in his pocket a piece of inexpensive material of the proper size (unbleached muslin is ideal) and make the Indian head with it, instead of a handkerchief.

ON THE MARK

WHILE the following is a stunt rather than a trick the magician will be credited with advanced skill for his performance. Actually no skill is required and only a drop of knowledge is needed for its success. Presented as a contest the stunt is very amusing because of the spectators' total lack of success and the performer's infallability. Both spectator and magician drop six playing cards, one at a time. The cards are aimed at a dinner plate placed on the floor. None of the spectator's cards land on the plate but all the magician's cards do. Each drops his cards from the same height—about three feet.

No preparation is needed whatsoever. The magician hands one card at a time to a spectator with the request that the cards be dropped upon the plate on the floor. When the spectator has dropped six cards, the magician, one at a time, drops six more. The spectator's cards scatter over the floor and none land on the plate. This is due to the magician's politeness, coupled with aerodynamics. The magician hands the cards to the spectator one at a time because it seems to be the courteous thing to do. Actually this kindness is due to the way the magician wants the spectator to hold the cards when they are dropped. When a card is held perpendicularly, i.e., having one edge pointing towards the floor, the card will not fall straight when dropped. The cards' uncontrollable flight is caused by ever present air currents. When a person is given a card with a flat surface facing him, he automatically will take hold of the card so that he is holding the face and back of the card. Once he has gripped the card, it is most unlikely that he will alter the way he holds it.

When the magician drops his cards he is careful to hold them flat with the face, or back, of the card facing the floor. He grips each card with the thumb on the edge of one side and a finger, or fingers, on the opposite edge. While, as was noted, no skill is required to hit the plate with each card dropped, it is advisable to make certain by private experiment what has to be done. As example, both sides of the card have to be released simultaneously or the card will twist at the start of its fall. Then, too, the aim must be straight. This is simple if the performer will bend over just enough so he can look down and align the card with the plate. The faster the magician drops his cards the more effective the stunt will be. By

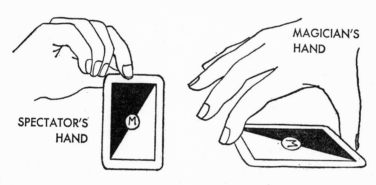

SPECTATOR'S HAND

MAGICIAN'S HAND

holding the cards to be dropped flat on the fingers of my left hand, I find it quite easy to push the cards, one at a time, so that they can be taken quickly by the right hand. I have found no difficulty in dropping all six cards in a total of five seconds. One card just reaches the plate when the next card is released.

At the start of this stunt the magician takes twelve cards from a deck—six black and six red. The black cards are those he gives to the spectator and the red cards are the ones he uses. At the conclusion the magician asks if it were noticed that the spectator was given black cards while the magician used red. He goes on to say that it probably was wrong of him for he was aware that only red cards would follow the directional beam. Such talk will serve the double purpose of giving the spectator an excuse for his lack of success and of adding to the general confusion. It also may add to the amusement for so often the spectator will demand, "Let me try again with red cards."

PERFUME—ODOR

THIS is a trick that can be done whenever conversation gets around to which political party is going to win the coming election; which of two teams is going to win the game; or which of two boxers is going to win the fight; or any similar discussion involving a choice of one of two.

It is particularly amusing when the group to whom it is shown is aware that the magician himself has a favorite side.

To perform the trick, the magician gets a piece of paper. It may be paper that he knows is available, or he feels certain can be obtained. The paper may be of any size and the kind is immaterial. However, the paper must be a piece that has four cut edges.

Taking the bottom of the paper, the magician folds it up so that the bottom edge goes on to the top edge. He then creases the fold at the bottom. He then takes this fold and brings it to the top edges of the paper and creases the second fold. The paper is to be torn on these creases so as to have four strips of paper of equal size. In order to make this tearing easier, the creases should be very sharp.

First one end of the paper is torn off and then the other end, and these two end pieces are given to one person, who is known to be on one side of the controversy. Then the center section is torn on the crease, and these two pieces given to another spectator, who is known to be on the opposing side. The first spectator is told to write on each of his papers the name of the political party, team or individual he favors. The second spectator, on each of his papers, is asked to write the name of his choice. Both spectators are asked to fold each of their papers in half and again in quarters with the writing inside. A third spectator is asked to take all four papers and to mix them. After they are mixed, they are to be handed, one at a time, to the magician. As the magician gets the paper, he holds it, still folded, to his nose and says: "I know by the perfume this is—" and names the side which he favors. If it so happens that the first paper handed up says the name of the opposite side, the magician says: "I know by the odor, this is—." The other three papers are handled in the same way, until the magician has identified all four.

The secret of this trick is unbelievably simple. The two strips of paper, torn from the ends of the paper and handed to the first spectator, each has one cut edge and one torn edge. The two pieces of paper torn from the center each has two torn edges. As the magician brings each paper to his nose, in order to smell it, he has ample opportunity to look at the edges of the paper. If the paper has been tightly creased and the edges carefully torn, it is quite easy for the magician to know the difference between the torn edges and the cut ones. However, to the spectators there is no noticeable difference.

If anyone takes exception to the word "odor," the magician quickly responds: "But, my friend, the perfume is an odor."

Four. SEEMINGLY EXTEMPORANEOUS MAGIC

ALL of the tricks in this Chapter are easy to do and most effective, and each seemingly is performed extemporaneously. However, each of these effects requires that the performer has done some prior preparation. Some of the tricks require no more preparation than providing the objects necessary for performance. Others require somewhat more preparation, but nevertheless the effect to the audience is that the magic is done extemporaneously.

THE BREAD WINNER

AT the end of Chapter 2 under the title "Coins, Paper Napkins and Olives" is described a trick in which a coin is caused to disappear while the magician is seated at a table. A moment later the coin is discovered under some object on the table such as a plate or salt shaker.

A striking variation of this trick, and using two coins as in the other version, is to make the coin reappear inside of a roll. Quarters are best to use in this trick.

One of the quarters has to be put inside a roll before the audience knows that anything is to happen. A coin is taken by the left hand while that hand is below the surface of the table. The coin is gripped between the pad of the second finger and the tip of the thumb. The right hand picks up a roll and brings the roll near the edge of the table and about 6″ above the surface.

As this is being done, the left hand, with the back of the fingers towards the spectators, is brought above the table and the magician places the edge of the bottom of the roll on the first finger of the left hand. The wrist of the left hand is then turned so that the coin is placed at the bottom of the roll. As this is done, the left thumb moves out of the way. With a very little pressure, the quarter can be pushed inside of the roll, where it will be held. The instant the coin is inside the roll, the left hand places the roll on the table about a foot in front of the magician. If the spectators notice this at all, it will merely seem as if the magician had picked up the roll with his right hand and transferred it to the left and that hand placed the roll on the table.

The duplicate coin is then introduced and caused to disappear, by dropping it in the lap as previously described. As soon as the coin has disappeared, the magician picks up the roll in which he has previously put the quarter. The fingers of both hands go underneath the roll and both thumbs press down on the roll in order to break it open.

With the top of the roll open, the magician takes his right hand away from the roll, while maintaining the grip with the left hand. With his first finger and thumb of the right hand, the magician reaches in the opening in the top of the roll and pulls out one or two pieces of the soft center of the roll, until he can reach the coin. He takes the quarter from the roll and drops it on the table.

Again taking the roll with both hands, the magician continues breaking the roll until it is in half. This is seemingly for the purpose of showing that the roll is an ordinary roll, although nothing is said about that. Actually the roll is broken in two parts to hide the opening on the bottom where the coin had been pushed in.

This trick should be performed very casually, and because it seems extemporaneous and quite unprepared, it is most surprising. After doing this trick, the reader will undoubtedly have the amusement I always have had of watching the others at the table break open rolls to see if theirs, too, were baked with coins inside.

One bit of warning. After a person has seen this trick, he will, I have found, insist that I do it again the next time we eat together. Therefore I always anticipate the request by having two coins easily available, so I am ready to start in with the trick on demand.

MONEY NO OBJECT

WHILE the previous trick, like all variations of the "Coins, Paper Napkins and Olives," requires the magician to be seated at a table, there is an excellent feat which can be done with a coin while the performer is standing. For instance, when the magician is with some of his friends at a bar or cocktail party, it will not be long before someone will say something about money or cost. This will give the magician an opportunity to say: "I recently have found something interesting about money." He takes a dollar bill from his pocket and forms it into a cornucopia. Then taking a quarter, he drops the coin in the mouth of the cornucopia. He immediately unwinds the dollar bill and shows it on both sides. The quarter has disappeared. The magician then says to one of the spectators: "Do you mind lifting that ash tray and giving me back my quarter?" Upon lifting the ash tray the spectator will find the quarter underneath.

The latter part of the trick depends upon the magician's having hidden a duplicate quarter underneath the ash tray. Of course it is quite immaterial which object the quarter is put under. It can be a bottle, a plate, or any one of a dozen other objects—whatever is available and which the magician believes will not be removed by anyone prior to his completion of the trick.

The disappearance of the quarter from the dollar bill becomes possible because the dollar bill is not as it appears to be. It is actually two dollar bills pasted together. The paste used should be of the type that is soluble in water so that after the reader is tired of doing the trick, he can retrieve his bills and with no damage to them.

In pasting the bills together, one bill is laid face up and paste is applied around the border of the bill, except at one point. No paste is put on the border above the words "The United" at the top of the bill. The second bill, also face up, is put exactly on top of the first bill, and pressed down so that the two bills are stuck together. Great care must be used in doing this so that the edges of the bills are exactly together. If this has been done properly, there is an opening between the two bills directly above the words "The United."

By grasping the edge of this double bill at the opening, the bill can be shown on both sides and will appear to be an ordinary single dollar bill. The bottom of the bill is then grasped by the first finger and thumb of each hand. The first finger of the left hand is directly over the numeral "1" at the bottom of the bill, with the thumb on the back of the bill. The position of the right hand is reversed so that the thumb is over the numeral "1" at the right hand side of the bill with the first finger on the back of the bill. It will now be found by turning the wrist of each hand towards the left that the bill automatically will be formed into a small cornucopia. When the cornucopia has been made, the first finger of the left hand still is in position over the numeral "1" inside the cornucopia. The thumb of the left hand is moved to grasp the outside of the cornucopia so that the fingers of the left hand keep the cornucopia from unrolling. The right hand then

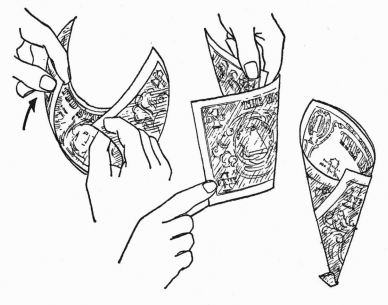

bends up ½" of the tip of the cornucopia and takes hold of the paper at this point. Before taking the first finger of the left hand out of the cornucopia, it is moved around inside the cone, as if it were smoothing out the paper. Actually something else is done which the spectators know nothing about. The nail of this first finger pulls the two bills apart where they have not been pasted. It is very easy to do this because the words "The United" inside of the cornucopia can be seen by the performer.

As soon as the two bills have been separated, the left hand is removed from the cornucopia and picks up the quarter. The quarter is then pushed in the cornucopia. Actually it goes in the opening between the two bills. As soon as this is done, the magician holds up his left hand, palm towards the spectators, so it can be seen that his hand is empty. Nothing is said, as this motion is made, which is just a gesture.

Returning the left hand to the top of the cornucopia, the two bills are grasped at the opening with the thumb on the inside of the bill and the first finger on the outside so as to hold the opening closed. When the bill has been gripped in this manner, the right hand is released, straightens out the folded tip and unrolls the bill, which is shown on both sides, folded in half and placed in the pocket.

The magician then asks one of the spectators to lift up whatever object he had used to hide the duplicate quarter, and to return the quarter to him.

This double cornucopia is very deceptive. It is so good in fact that with varying sizes of paper, it will be used in connection with other tricks in the book.

HOT MONEY

THE visitor to the Congressman was told he would have to wait as the Honorable Gentleman was engaged in practising his extemporaneous speech. Part of the effectiveness of this feat of magic is it seems so spontaneous but, as with the Congressman's speech, that is the result of previous preparation. Of course, so much of magic depends upon advance arrangement but seldom is the preparation so completely masked.

At a table the magician places a small plate on top of an empty glass. Next he wraps a quarter in a small piece of paper and puts the little package on the plate atop the glass. Lighting a match the magician ignites the paper. When the paper is nearly consumed by the flame, the quarter is seen to drop through the plate and fall into the glass. The magician can do this feat at any table where he can find a plate and a glass and he can use any piece of paper. The quarter also is just an ordinary twenty-five cent piece.

There are two parts to the working of the trick although it is not apparent to the spectators. One part is causing a quarter to disappear from the paper in which it has been wrapped. The second part is to seem to cause the quarter, actually a duplicate, to penetrate the plate.

While any paper can be used to wrap the quarter it must be cut, or carefully torn, so that it is approximately 2½″ wide and 3″ long. Prior to introducing the quarter, and in front of the audience, two folds should be made in the paper. These folds are made to run lengthwise of the paper. The first fold is made a full inch from one long side of the paper. The second fold is made by folding back the opposite long side so that the crease comes just at the edge of the first fold. The second fold will be only half as wide as the first fold. After both folds are tightly pressed the paper is opened flat again. A quarter is then taken from a pocket and shown to the audience. The coin is placed on the paper and wrapped. While this is what the audience sees and what actually is done, it is not done precisely as it seems. This is the sequence followed in wrapping the paper around the coin. As will be obvious a little further along in the description the routine must be followed carefully.

The paper is placed on the fingers of the left hand with the shorter fold toward the palm. The right hand takes the coin and places it on the center of the paper between the two creases. The shorter fold is turned over on top of the quarter and half covers it. As soon as the quarter is in place, the lower edge is gripped with the thumb and fingers of the left hand on the outside of the paper. The tip of the thumb is at the edge of the fold of the paper. Immediately the longer fold is turned down over the coin. This is the important move in this part of the trick. The longer fold is turned very slowly over the coin. It is gripped between the first finger and thumb of the right hand and the edge of the coin is gripped between the paper. As the paper is folded over, the right hand tilts the coin so that the quarter slips out of the short fold and goes on top of it and is hidden by the longer fold. As the coin is hidden by the paper, this will not be seen. If the description is read with the paper and coin in hand, it will be found that the moves are simple. The moves are easy to do but read as if they might be difficult. Therefore, try these moves with paper and coin, as they are read.

Once the coin is hidden in the paper by the two folds the ends of the paper are folded back on the coin. As the coin is still in the paper this will present no difficulty, but the folds should be made a little distance away from the coin so as not to bind it in the paper. The thumb and fingers of the left hand hold the paper and the coin. If, as suggested, these moves have been made as the description was read, it will be found that the quarter will slide out of the paper and on to the base of the fingers of the left hand the instant the pressure of the fingers of the left hand are released. This pressure should not be released until after the magician has had a spectator feel that the coin is inside the folded paper.

The left hand releases its pressure thus permitting the coin to slide into the fingers, as the right hand takes the paper and puts it on the plate. The paper is put on edge on the plate. When the fingers of the right hand release the paper the two last folds will open up enough so that the paper will stand on edge. While the right hand is standing the paper on edge on the plate, the left hand, with its hidden quarter, goes into a pocket. Inside the pocket the left hand drops the coin and takes hold of a packet of matches.

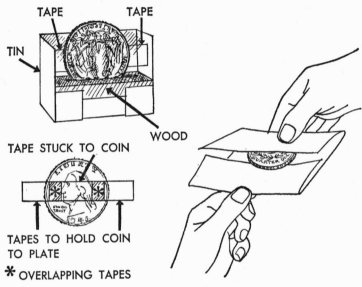

Getting the matches, which seems to be the sole reason for the left hand to go into the pocket, the hand is removed from the pocket. The magician, using both hands, opens the package of matches, pulls out one, ignites it, and touches the top corners of the paper with the flame. The paper will burn until little, or nothing, is left. The quarter, which, though the spectators are unaware of the fact, is not in the folded paper. They believe the coin is consumed in the flames. So much for the disappearance of the first quarter.

The second quarter, the one which drops through the plate, should be of the same appearance as the first one. Having them alike is the reason the magician uses his own coin in the trick rather than borrowing a quarter. The spectators believe that only one coin is used and they should not be disabused by having the coins dissimilar in appearance.

Needless to say the second quarter does not actually drop through the plate. The coin drops from the bottom of the plate to which it has been stuck. As the paper is burning, the plate is "held" on top of the glass. When the coin is to appear to go through the plate, this is done by moving the plate enough to push the edge of the coin against the edge of the glass. The slightest pressure on the edge of the coin will release it. The coin dropping from the bottom of the plate will give the effect of the coin going through the plate.

All else the magician needs to know is how, and when, the quarter is stuck to the bottom of the plate. The how is by means of cellophane tape which is cut and applied in an unusual way. The most common width of cellophane tape is ½", and such size is admirable for the purpose. This tape has adhesive on one side only. An ⅛" strip is cut across the tape. This strip is turned over and ⅛" of the sticky end of the ½" long strip is pressed against the sticky side of the end of the tape still on the roll. Again the tape is cut and another ⅛" piece stuck to the other end in the same manner. The final result should be an ⅛" strip of tape 1" long. At either end ⅜" of the sticky side of the tape is uppermost and at the center of the strip is a quarter inch having the sticky side facing down. The center portion of the strip is stuck to the face of the coin. When this is done the strip of tape should be across the face of the coin with the sticky side of each end of the strip facing away from the coin. With the coin so prepared it is laid on the fingers of the right hand, tape side up, and the hand held on the lap. The plate is picked up with the left hand and brought to the edge of the table. The right hand is raised from the lap and takes the plate. The fingers of the right hand go under the plate and the thumb on top. The plate hides the coin which is on the fingers of the right hand. The instant the coin touches the plate, and this must be done gently so as not to have a click, the fingers press the coin so as to firmly stick it to the plate. All the spectators will see is that the magician picked up a plate with his left hand and transferred it to his right. The instant the plate is held with the right hand, the left hand picks up the empty tumbler and calls attention to it by turning it upside down. The tumbler again is turned so it is right side up and placed on the table a foot or so from the edge and directly in front of the magician.

With the tumbler in place the plate is taken with both hands and gently put on top of the glass. While it is natural to be careful in placing a plate atop a glass so as not to chip the glass, it is essential in this instance so as not to jar the coin from its hiding place. Because there is twice as much tape stuck to the plate as is stuck to the coin, the tape will adhere more firmly to the plate than it will to the quarter. Therefore, when the plate is moved so that the edge of the quarter touches the rim of the glass, the coin will be released to drop into the glass and the tape will remain on the plate. When the coin is stuck to the plate, it should be in a position to go into the mouth of the glass when the plate is put on the glass, but so that it will be near the edge of the glass. This is done so that the plate need be slid but very little on top of the glass to release the coin.

The reader undoubtedly has wondered about how the coin, with its sticky tape, is safely carried in the pocket until the magician wishes to perform the feat. This is done by an especially made holder which, while making the coin easy to get, guards the tape when the coin is in the pocket. The holder is a simple open box made of tin which, at the bottom, has a piece of wood, slotted, to hold the quarter. The wood should be 1½" long, ⅜" high, and ¼" thick. The slot runs from the top to the bottom of the wood and is a full inch long and ³⁄₃₂" wide. The slot is just enough wider than the thickness of the coin so that a piece of cloth, preferably felt, can be glued along one side. The cloth will hold the coin so that it will not fall out of the slot yet permits it to be taken out easily. The tin is cut so it may be bent around the wood and leave the top of the slot open. At the back and end the tin extends ½" above the wood. When finished the tin should form a guard so that nothing can touch the tape attached to the coin in the slot. Because the holder is open at the front and on top and the tin does not go all the way to the top of the coin, it is very easy to take the coin out of the holder. As the way the holder is made is immaterial, it is not necessary to give construction details and the illustration will make clear what is needed.

Because the flame takes some seconds to consume the paper, after it is ignited, it is well to say something at this point in the trick to keep the audience interested. I have found, "Now we have seen 'hot money,' " to be a remark which will keep the spectator's attention on what is being done and yet does not lessen their surprise when the coin drops into the glass.

SOME SNAP!

THIS little stunt will delight all children and a surprisingly large per cent of adults. A rubber band is put around the first and second fingers when the hand is open and the fingers extended. The hand is closed and quite naturally the band still encircles those two fingers. When the hand is reopened the band most surprisingly jumps to go around the third and little fingers. And the rubber band is shown to be on those two fingers only. Again closing the hand and opening it, the rubber has jumped back to its original position around the first and second fingers.

Almost any rubber band can be used for this trick. However, it is easier to do if the band is large enough to fit loosely on the fingers. When the rub-

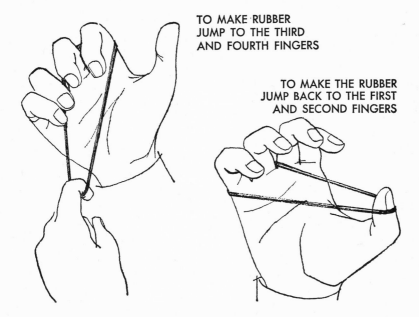

TO MAKE RUBBER
JUMP TO THE THIRD
AND FOURTH FINGERS

TO MAKE THE RUBBER
JUMP BACK TO THE FIRST
AND SECOND FINGERS

ber band is put over the first and second fingers, it is put on all the way. (Right handed people will find it easier to do the trick by putting the band on the fingers of that hand.) The magician holds his hand with the palm parallel to the floor to show the band encircling the fingers and slowly turns the hand over so everyone can see the band truly goes around the fingers. Then with the tip of the first finger of the other hand he stretches the rubber. As he does this he mentions that everyone can see it is a solid rubber band. As that first finger stretches the band, he pulls it along the palm of the right hand and a couple of inches beyond the base of the little finger. With the hands and rubber band in these respective positions it will be found that if all the fingers of the right hand are closed the tips of all four will go into the loop made by stretching the rubber. Releasing the loop of rubber, it will snap back so as to go over the nails of each of the four fingers. Upon opening the hand it will be found that the rubber band has jumped from the first and second fingers over to the second and third fingers.

It will be discovered to be very easy to stretch the rubber with the tip of the thumb of the right hand when the band is around the third and little fingers. The thumb can stretch the rubber enough so that again the tips of all four fingers will go into the loop when the hand is closed. Bending the first joint of the thumb will permit the band to slide off. Again the rubber, upon opening the hand, will jump from one pair of fingers to the other. The action of the thumb should not be seen as there is no good excuse for it. It will be found that there is no difficulty in hiding the thumb's secret help when actually trying the moves with the rubber band. It is far easier to find out what needs to be done by experimenting than it would be to attempt to follow what would have to be a lengthy description.

The trick may well be repeated in a manner to make it even more surprising. This second time the trick is done with two rubber bands. One band is put on the first and second fingers as in the first showing. The second rubber band is put over the little finger right over the second joint. The rubber is given a half twist and put over the third finger. Another half twist of the rubber and it is put over the second finger. One more half twist and the rubber is put over the first finger and released. At this point, one rubber is twisted around and connects each of the four fingers. The other rubber appears to be securely on the first and second fingers and can not be removed unless the twisted rubber is taken off. While the second rubber is impressive it does not hamper in any way doing the trick exactly as it was done the first time.

After a person has done this trick a number of times for spectators so that he feels complete assurance in doing it, there is another addition he may want to do. In this instance two rubber bands of different colors are used. One band goes on the first and second fingers and the other goes on the third and little fingers. The object is to make them change places. The way it is done is the combination of the way of making the one rubber jump over and back. It is not quite as simple to do as the single rubber, but the added effect is worth the practice required to do it well.

KIKERI, KIKERI, KI

IN his chicanery a magician has an advantage when his feat is based on fact, or what commonly is accepted as fact. Here is magic based on an ancient but fallacious belief. That the conviction is false does not diminish the effectiveness of the magic. This feat is based on an odd story and depends upon a little trickery plus the physical fact that there is a pulse in the thumb. First the background story which begins with the variations in language of barnyard fowl. Nothing, by the way, is completely disassociated from magic.

As any child knows, all English speaking roosters crow by saying, "Cock-a-doodle-do." German children are assured that their roosters say, "Kikeri, Kikeri, Ki." Called Kikeri, Kikeri, Ki, a device is sold in Germany for the purpose of determining the sex of eggs; that is, whether after incubation an egg will hatch a young hen or a young rooster. The equipment sold is simply a small wood ball attached to a length of soft string. The sales claim is that when the ball, suspended by the string, is held over an egg, it will swing back and forth if the egg is female and will swing in a circle if it be a male egg. After separation, by this method, the female eggs are hatched and the male eggs are eaten.

When the ball is suspended over the egg, the string is grasped between the first finger and thumb and the hand is held steady by resting the elbow on the table. As those who try this equipment are certain they are not swinging the ball, they are apt to think the ball must swing itself. Having reached the belief that the ball has some inner motive power, it is an easy step to accept the ball as having an ability to know the sex of an egg. So people have acted and thought for countless centuries and in many lands. In some countries, instead of a wooden ball and a string, the equipment is a wedding ring and the hair from the head of a young girl.

One feat the magician can do with the ball and string is to separate the Kings, in a deck of cards, from the Queens. The cards are placed face down upon a table and the ball is held over one card at a time, and by the way the ball swings the sex of each card is known. That is the effect. Actually four of the cards have minute markings which, while obvious to the magician, are unnoticed. Such marks and variations to the feat will be explained after this description of how the ball is caused to swing.

First it should be known that when the string is gripped tightly between the first finger and thumb, it is utterly impossible to keep the ball from swinging no matter how great the effort to keep the arm still. This is due to the pulse in the thumb. The beating of the pulse will cause the ball to start swinging. In trying out the equipment, it will be found that the ball seems to start swinging of its own volition and it will be obvious why so many have believed the ball possessed power. Once the ball starts swinging the muscles of the arm will become tense due to the extra effort to hold the arm motionless. This will cause the swing of the ball to change from back and forth to around and around and vice versa. This again seems to be solely the work

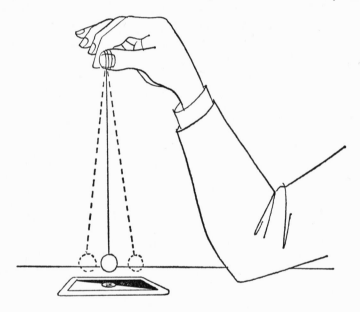

of the ball. While the ball will swing one way and then another without any effort on the part of the person holding it, the swinging is uncontrolled. It will be found possible, while expending every effort to hold the arm still, that it is quite easy to control the way in which the ball swings. It only is necessary to concentrate on the direction in which the ball is to swing. At the same time as thinking whether the ball is to go in a circular movement, or back and forth, every effort is made to hold the arm motionless. If this is done, no visible motion can be seen and yet the arm will direct the swing of the ball. It is necessary only to try this out in private to find it to be true. The longer the length of string between fingers and ball the easier it is to make the ball do as is desired. Therefore, the forearm should be held as near perpendicular as is possible and still give a free movement to the ball.

It will be found possible to mark cards by pressing the thumbnail into the back surface of the card at one edge. This should be done on a card a number of times in order to discover how small a nail mark can be made and yet be visible to the performer. Prior to presenting the trick the magician so marks each of the four Queens. After they are marked the Queens are replaced in various parts of the deck. When about to show the feat the magician requests a spectator to take from the deck four Kings and the four Queens. He is told to mix the eight cards so that he does not know which is which and to place them face down upon the table. By the marks it is easy for the magician to identify the Queens as he passes the ball over the cards.

While the ball on the string is an authentic way to follow this story, it is not as interesting as using a wedding ring and a thread. The thread is a permissible substitute for the long hair, which may be difficult to obtain and is troublesome to try to carry around. If a ring is used it is well to know that the heavier the ring the easier it will be to control the swing. Under no circumstances should a ring be used which has a setting, for the danger is too great of striking the stone and dislodging it.

ARCHES, LOOPS AND WHORLS

Such marvels are being accomplished by scientists today, that the general public has come to believe that nothing is impossible, and will readily accept as possible anything that is attributed to scientific means. This feat depends on such belief.

The magician claims that a new light ray has been discovered which will show up the arches, loops and whorls of fingerprints without the necessity of ink pads or dusting powder. He states that the compactness of the equipment is one of its great advantages, and he was lucky enough to acquire a model.

The magician shows a very small pocket flashlight and turns it on to show a very faint colored ray. He claims that this ray will make visible to the trained observer even the faintest of fingerprints.

Putting the flashlight aside on the table, the magician asks five spectators who are carrying business cards, each to take out a card. The magician takes from his pocket an envelope and a pair of tweezers. Squeezing the envelope open, he reaches inside with the tweezers and, in turn, gives each spectator a small pay envelope. He asks each spectator to put his business card in his envelope and seal it, and make certain that he alone handles his envelope. When all of the cards have been sealed in the envelopes, the magician says that he wants the envelopes put on the table in any order, and this is to be done while his back is turned. The order can be arranged any way, provided they are certain that only the owners touch their own envelopes. When they are satisfied with the order, they are to inform the magician so he may turn around again.

The magician turns to any one of the spectators who has been a subject in the test, and asks him for permission to examine his fingers and thumbs. After studying the fingers for a few seconds, the magician picks up the flashlight and turns it on, and holds it in his left hand. With his left hand, he throws the beam of light on one envelope after another. Then with the tweezers, he turns the envelopes over and with the light examines the other sides. When his examination is completed, he picks up one with the tweezers and hands it to the spectator whose fingerprints he has examined. The spectator is requested to hold his sealed envelope until the demonstration is completed. The magician goes through the same routine with two more of the spectators. When three envelopes have been picked out, the magician explains that he feels that three is enough to demonstrate the extraordinary quality of the light and he asks each person to open his envelope and verify that it contains his card.

He now turns to one of the remaining two subjects, and asks to look at his fingers and pointing the flashlight at one of the envelopes on the table says: "Your envelope is the one on the right (or left as the case may be), and will you please pick it up." Turning to the last man, he says: "The other envelope must be yours. Please make sure that I am right."

This effect is particularly strong because it is completely immaterial how the envelopes are placed on the table. The magician does not know and does not care what the order is, or whether they are placed face up or face down.

Oddly enough the magician does pick out the envelopes by examining them, as he is seen to do at the end. However, he was not looking for finger-prints as he claimed. He was looking for the secret markings on each envelope that he alone will see.

These secret markings, to be described later, permit the magician to put the envelopes in a known order. When he passes the envelopes out to the spectators at the beginning of the trick, this order has to be followed. By this means he knows into which envelope each spectator places his card. Therefore, as he knows how the envelope of each spectator is marked, it is totally immaterial in what order or position the envelopes are put on the table. As long as the first spectator has been given envelope #1, and second, envelope #2, and so on, the trick can be performed.

The envelopes used in this trick are pay envelopes which are 4¼″ long and 2½″ at the top and bottom. At the top is a gummed flap for sealing the

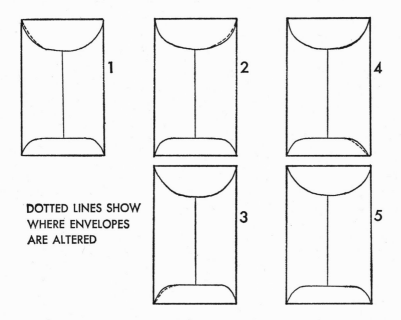

DOTTED LINES SHOW
WHERE ENVELOPES
ARE ALTERED

envelope. The bottom also has a flap which comes sealed. However the bottom sealed flap is shorter than the top flap.

Prior to the performance, four of the five envelopes have been altered in a manner which never will be noticed by the spectators but is very obvious to the magician.

Envelope #1 has a hairline of paper cut off the left hand side of the upper flap.

Envelope #2 has a hairline of paper cut off the right hand side of the upper flap.

Envelope #3 has a hairline of paper cut off the left hand side of the lower flap.

Envelope #4 has a hairline of paper cut off the right hand side of the lower flap.

Envelope #5 is not altered anywhere.

With manicure scissors, trim off just a hairline of paper being careful to follow the contour of the individual flap which is being trimmed. Since the bottom flap is sealed, it will be necessary in order to prepare envelopes #3 and #4, first to lift up, with the point of a knife, enough of the edge of the flap to be cut so that the one blade of the scissors will go under the paper. Care must be taken to cut evenly so that the cut edges will appear as smooth as they were originally. I found it easier to start cutting at the corner and cutting toward the middle of the flap. The reader will be astonished at how little paper has to be cut off for him to be able instantly to recognize the secret marking. Because it is such a slight alteration, the spectator will not notice it under the closest examination.

Because the spectators are given free rein in putting their envelopes on the table, the probability is that some of the envelopes will be face up and some back up. Even though the magician instantly will be able to know the owners of such envelopes as are back up, he must take care to lift each of the envelopes with the tweezers and study both sides so that he follows his pretense of looking for fingerprints on both sides of the envelopes.

Place a small piece of colored plastic between the bulb and the lens of the flashlight so that the light beam will be a colored ray.

WOOD OR METAL

THIS feat is entertaining because it is so simple and is a perfect optical illusion. The effect is that a piece of wood, without injury, goes through a piece of metal. All that is used in the trick is a safety pin and a small stick of wood.

The safety pin is quite ordinary and may be of any size. The stick of wood should be just a little longer than is the safety pin and about three times the thickness of the metal of the pin. The ends of the wood should have the same appearance. As example, were a match stick used for the wood it would be necessary to cut off the head. Incidentally, the shape of the stick is immaterial and it may be round, square, hexagonal, or whatever. Through the exact center of the stick a hole must be drilled. The hole should be of the exact size of the shaft of the pin. The pin is put through the hole in the wood and the pin is closed. The wood is pushed to the center of the shaft of the pin and all is ready for performance.

The stick pierced by the closed safety pin is shown to the spectators. At the time it is shown one end of the wood lies flat against the back of the pin and under the metal. That end of the wood is pointed towards the spectators.

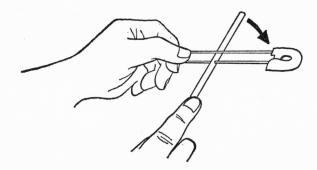

The other end of the wood points towards the performer. The pin is held by the fingers of the left hand grasping the round-spring end of the pin. The pin is held flat with the back of the pin toward the spectators. With the pin held in this manner, the performer, with the extreme tip of his right forefinger presses down on the very edge of the end of the stick extended towards him. If this is done correctly the tip of the finger will slide off the end of the stick. The instant the pressure of the finger leaves the stick the wood will revolve on the pin because of the pressure which had been exerted. What happens is that in turning on the pin a half revolution the ends of the wood are reversed so that the end now towards the audience is on top, rather than under, the metal bar of the pin. Because both ends of the stick are alike the exchange of ends is not realized. The action of the wood in turning on the pin is so rapid that it cannot be seen and the effect is that the end of the stick has gone through the metal. The illusion is perfect.

In answer to the reader's query as to my earlier statement about magic not depending upon speed, I have two more statements. I was specifically referring to the fact that the hand is not quicker than the eye and that a magician never should give the effect of performing rapidly. Mechanically, as in this case, it is possible to obtain action so rapid an eye cannot catch it but rarely is mechanics used in magic for this purpose.

When the end of the stick towards the spectators is over the back bar of the pin the magician presses up on his end of the stick, exactly as he had pressed down in the first instance, and the wood again will seem to go through the metal and back to its original position.

The reason for drilling the hole in the stick exactly the size of the pin is that the wood, while being able to move freely, must not be loose on the pin. If the hole is larger than the pin, the wood will wobble and the illusion is lost. If the hole is too tight the wood will bind on the pin.

After I have snapped the wood through the pin three or four times (which is enough) I hand the pin with its stick to a spectator. As the pin is given out, I say, "I have done this over and over and I can't make up my mind whether the wood goes through the metal or the metal goes through the wood."

THE SPOOKY KEY

THIS little feat is over almost before the spectators realize it has been done. A long shaft door key, a bit key such as is used in the lock on a clothes closet door, slowly turns over when laid on the performer's outstretched hand. The effect is weird, because the key seems to turn of its own volition, and is heightened by the performer's casual remark, "I am going to have to get a new key. This one locks the closet door every midnight."

There is nothing unusual about the key. It is an ordinary key having a ring head at one end of a long shank and the bit at the other end. The shank should be round but most such keys have round shanks. The bigger and heavier the key the greater the effect and the easier the performance. Everything depends upon the way such keys are made and no preparation at all is needed. However, the more often the magician practises the presentation the stronger will be the effect.

The magician holds the key in the right hand with the fingers on the ring head and the bit turned towards the spectators. He holds his left hand palm upwards and with fingers and palm as flat as he can make them. The right hand then places the key on the outstretched left hand. The key should lie on the crease in the palm—what the palmists call the heart line—and have the ring head extend out from the side of the hand. The bit points towards the fingers. It will be found that by an imperceptible bend of the wrist, the key will turn over so that the bit faces towards the wrist. The first few times this is tried, the key will turn over with a sudden jerk. That is because the wrist is bent too much and too rapidly. After repeating the action a few dozen times, it will be found that the key can be turned very slowly. In this practice it also will be found exactly how the left hand should be held. The wrist should be bent, prior to putting the key on the hand, just enough so that it will lie flat on the hand. But the wrist should be bent enough so that the slightest additional movement of the wrist will cause the key to turn. It will be found, if these rules are followed, that the key can be made to turn without the spectators' seeing any action by the magician.

It cannot be stressed too strongly that the effectiveness of this feat depends entirely upon its performance. It must be shown most casually with the

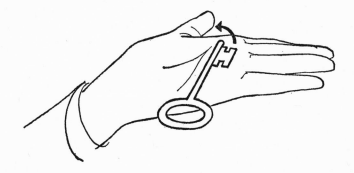

magician acting as though everything depended upon the key and that he had no part in the key's action. This is not difficult because when done properly, the magician seems to do nothing and the key seems to be endowed with a will of its own and the power to act on its whim.

THE PIRATE AND THE STRONGBOX

MAGIC which happens quickly, is completely puzzling, and where the magician seems to have no major part, will be talked about when more elaborate feats are forgotten. Here is an excellent example of such magic.

The magician tells a story about six pirates who after years of raiding had filled a huge strong box with diamonds, emeralds, rubies, and the largest of pearls. The strong box was so heavy it could not be lifted by the combined efforts of all six pirates. Being pirates, naturally, each questioned the honesty of the others. One pirate devised a plan which satisfied the others of the safety of the jewels and yet he alone would be able to have access to them. At this point in the story the magician offers to demonstrate the pirate's method.

The magician takes from his pocket six identical keys and states that he wishes five spectators to join him and to assume, as he will do, that each is a pirate. The magician drops the keys on a table. He says that the pirate had six keys made for the lock on the strong box so that each man would have a key and therefore the jewels would be equally available to all. After each of the five spectators has selected and taken one key, the magician picks up the remaining key. Each man is instructed to hold the key in constant sight as the magician holds his. The magician then reaches in his pocket, with his free hand, and takes out a closed padlock. The padlock is given to one man with instructions to try his key. The lock does not open. The padlock is passed from man to man but no one has a key that will unlock it. The magician then takes the lock and it immediately opens with his key. As the lock snaps open the magician says, "The wily pirate knew that when his fellow marauders were given a choice of six like keys each would choose one of the five wrong keys. And gentlemen, as you see it always happens."

Needed for this trick are a padlock with a key to open it and six additional keys which look like the real key. These extra six keys are just enough different in the way they have been filed that they will not open the lock.

At the start of the trick the magician has the six fake keys in one pocket and the padlock in another. The lock is in a pocket on the left side of the performer. The keys are in a pocket on the performer's right side. The seventh key, the one which opens the lock, is held in the left hand at the base of the second, third, and little fingers and with the point of the key on the little finger. The fingers are curled so that the key will be held. When the magician picks up from the table the sixth, and remaining, key he does so with his right hand. It is picked up by the head of the key—that part which is opposite to the end which goes in the lock. The hands are brought together and the point of the key just picked up is pushed between the key and the fingers of the left hand, which holds the seventh key about which the spectators are entirely unaware. What the magician does is very easy but it has to be done correctly. The instant the point of the picked up key is behind the key secretly held in the left hand, the magician looks at the spectators and says: "Each of you has had a choice of keys. And each of you is holding the key he selected." While this is being said the magician, because everyone is looking at his face, can with safety, and with no difficulty, take, with his right hand, the key he had had in his left hand and leave the key he picked up from the table. The key is taken with the tips of the fingers of the right hand and held in the air. The instant the key is taken by the fingers of the right hand, the left hand goes into the left pocket, drops the key held, and takes out the lock. As this is being done, the magician holds up his key and asks each of the other key holders to hold their keys in the same manner.

The magician is able, indetectibly, to substitute keys by following the very simple manipulative procedure and by making his statements simultaneously. Every day of his life the reader will go through the same hand movements in selecting the proper coin from the change he holds in his hand. Manipulatively there is absolutely no difficulty in changing keys. As the substitution of keys is done within the hands there is nothing for the spectators to see. As the magician talks as he changes keys, the audience is interested in, and pays attention to, what he says rather than what he does. The reader, in order to free himself of the fear that he will be caught changing keys, should substitute one key for another, in private, a number of times in order to discover how completely unsuspicious is the exchange.

At the end of the feat the magician may find the audience are amused by the following:

"You may have been surprised because this is a modern lock. Perhaps I failed to tell you they were very modern pirates. And you realize that only a very up-to-date pirate would have majored in psychology while in college."

Finally it should be noted that while it is quite immaterial which kind, or make, of lock is used the magic is more impressive when using a better lock. By better lock is meant one having tumblers and a fluted, rather than a completely flat key. One reason is that the six false keys can be made more nearly like the genuine key so that they appear identical. Another reason is that people have less faith in a totally flat key than they do in the more elaborate type. Finally a more complicated lock fits better with the story the magician tells.

In this presentation the magician's role is completely unobjectionable for he, seemingly, has had no part in the feat for the spectators had a free choice of keys. The magician only took what the others did not want.

Five. THE HUNGRY JACKASS

THE story of the unusual appetite of a jackass is the basis for several of the most amazing mysteries to be performed with cards. Not only are the card tricks astounding but it seems incredible that the magician can be doing anything to cause them to happen. The general effect of these several tricks is that the magician has a magical and complete control of each individual card in the deck. And everything is caused by the story of the jackass.

This story, when memorized, gives a system for arranging the cards in a deck so that it is easy for the magician to know the location of every card. First you must know the story which is told in telegraphese. Here it is:

> Jackass ate live tree
> King intends to fix
> Several for benign Queen

You will find it a sort of doggerel easy to memorize. But before you commit the story to memory you first should know the meanings of the words in connection with cards. The card meanings will be clearer if you say the words aloud. Jackass stands for two cards; first a Jack, and second an Ace. *Ate* has the same sound as *eight*. *Live* and *five* sound quite alike, as does *tree* and *three*. King still is read as King. *Intends* has a few two many letters but those spelling *ten* are among them and are the ones accented in pronunciation. *To* has the same sound as *two*. *Fix* and *six* sound almost the same. *Several* starts off like the word *seven*. *For* is like *four* in sound. *Benign*, forgetting the first syllable, has the same sound as *nine*. Queen means Queen. You have, therefore, in the story a word which sounds like, or at least will remind you of, the value of each card in the deck. These are the key words for all the thirteen cards of each suit and run, seemingly, without any order.

As there are four suits in a deck, there is one other word to know. This word is *chased*. The consonants in CHaSeD are the first letters of the four

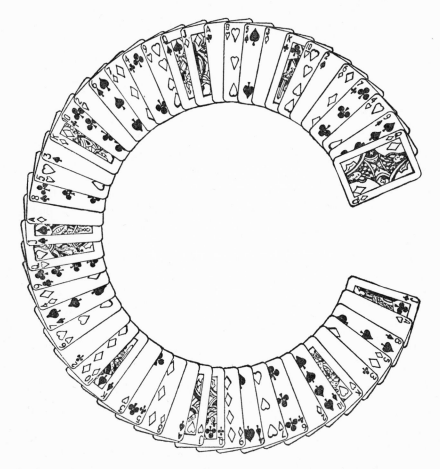

suits in a deck—Clubs—Hearts—Spades—Diamonds. The word not only puts the suits in an easily memorized order but it alternates the colors.

Using the Jackass story and the word "chased" together the cards can be arranged in an order known to the magician while to the spectators the deck, apparently, is thoroughly mixed. To arrange the deck the Jack of Clubs is put, face up, upon the table. On top of the Jack is placed the Ace of Hearts. Then the 8 of Spades, the 5 of Diamonds, and the 3 of Clubs are put down one after another. So each card of the deck goes on the table by following the Clubs, Hearts, Spades, Diamonds rotation of suits and the Jackass story. When arranged the deck would look like and be in the order of the cards in the illustration.

Before describing the tricks which can be accomplished with this pre-arranged deck (called "stacked" in card parlance) I want you to remember that the audience must never know that the cards are in a known order. The explanation for the way the audience is kept from suspecting that the cards are arranged will be given after the instructions for the following several tricks.

TO KNOW WHICH CARD HAS BEEN SELECTED

THE deck may be spread out on a table, or the magician may fan the cards in his hands. A spectator is permitted freely to choose any card. All the magician has to do is to cut the deck at the place where the card was taken. Cutting the deck in this way will put the card which had been above the selected card upon the bottom of the deck. The magician will know instantly which card was taken by looking at the bottom card and mentally recalling the story of the Jackass and the word chased. For instance the card on the bottom of the deck is a 9 of Hearts. Recalling "benign Queen" the card will be known to be a Queen. Thinking of CHaSeD the suit after Hearts will be known to be Spades. Therefore the chosen card must be the Queen of Spades and the magician announces this fact. When the Queen is returned to the magician he merely places it on top of the deck.

Here, perhaps, it should be pointed out that cutting the pack does not alter the order of the cards. Please refer again to the illustration of the stacked pack which purposely was drawn in a circle. It will be seen that pushing some of the cards around the circle will put the break in a new place but that each card remains in the same relative position to the other cards. It is exactly as if one were to lay a watch face up on a table and, by pushing the stem, turn the watch. A different number would then be nearest you but nothing has been done to the order of the numbers on the dial. Perhaps with cards the confusing point is that the card after the bottom card of the deck is the top card. If that is remembered all else should be clear.

TO KNOW BY SOUND WHICH CARD IS MISSING FROM THE DECK

As in the previous trick a spectator is permitted to make a free selection of one card from the deck. However, in this instance the spectator is instructed to take great care that absolutely no one, including himself, knows which card has been chosen. The magician cuts the cards and glances, secretly, at the bottom card. Of course, at this point, he is aware of the value, and suit, of the card but he says nothing. Instead he holds the deck to his ear, as if it really meant something, and runs his thumb along the corner of the deck. This motion with the thumb is the same as is done in one form of shuffle and is called riffling. The sound produced is something like "burrr." The instant the noise is over the magician says, "I can tell by the sound that the card missing from the deck is—" and he names the selected card.

TO KNOW HOW MANY CARDS ARE TAKEN FROM THE DECK

THE magician asks that several cards be taken from the deck. A spectator is instructed to take the cards from one place in the deck and to keep the magician from knowing even the number of cards selected.

The magician can know the number of cards taken by cutting the deck and looking at both the bottom and top cards. All he has to do is to "say his piece" from the card after the bottom card to the card before the top one and count the words. For instance the bottom card is a 3 (at this point the suit may be disregarded) and the top card is a 4. After 3 (tree) comes "King intends to fix several" and the magician stops, for the next word would be the top card. "King intends to fix several" stands for exactly five cards and the spectator is told that he has withdrawn five.

The trick does not stop there for the magician then asks for the cards to be given back to him one at a time as he calls for them. Now the suits of the top and bottom cards also are taken into consideration. It is advisable to ask for the cards out of order as it makes the trick, while no harder to do, more confusing and impressive. The easiest way to do this is to start with the end cards held by the spectator and work toward the middle.

THE FORTUNE TELLING CARDS

THE magician tells the audience that he is almost convinced that there is something to fortune telling with cards. He then turns to one spectator and says, "You know how the fortune teller always has the deck divided into three piles on the table." Irrespective of what the spectator says the magician instructs him to cut the deck into three piles on the table. When that is done the magician asks the spectator to slide the top card of each pile upon the table and to keep those cards face down so that no one can know which cards those are. The spectator next is asked to turn each pile face up on the table. The magician names aloud the card, face up, on one of the piles and through it works out the name of the card taken from that pile. By "works out" is meant to give some pseudo fortune telling talk directed to the spec-

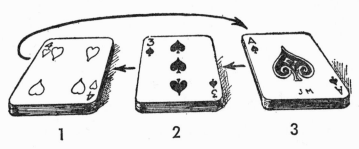

tator. Hearts can mean friends; Diamonds, wealth; Clubs, work; Spades, trouble; a black King, a dark man; a red Queen, a blonde woman; etc. One's ability to extemporize counts greatly in making this trick impressive and amusing.

There is an unexpected secret in this trick which can be best explained by numbering the piles. Let us call the cards from the bottom of the deck pile 1; the cards from the center pile 2; and the cards from the top of the deck pile 3. The cards face up on the bottom of each pile actually do indicate which cards have been selected but in the order as shown by the arrows in the illustration.

The card from pile 3 is the one in the memory code after the card showing on pile 1. The card from pile 2 is indicated by the one showing on pile 3. The card from pile 1 is given by the card face up on pile 2.

Of course, in the patter the magician talks about the card showing on pile

3 when he describes the card selected from pile 3 and so on. Remember that he only talks about the cards in that combination and that he gets his information from the other piles.

There is a small trick in replacing the selected cards so as to pick up the piles and have the deck still in order without being obvious about the matter. Perhaps the easiest way is for the magician to take each card after it has been named correctly. When he has finished announcing the names of the cards and has all three in his hands he calmly lays one card on top of each pile and puts the piles together. He must be certain that the card taken from the top of pile 3 goes face up on pile 1. The card from pile 1 goes face up on pile 2. And the card from 2 goes on pile 3. This is a little confusing on paper but one learns to do it quickly and naturally by practice. Such practice, please remember, should be done before attempting to do the trick.

Before going on with the next trick, and seemingly while squaring the deck in his hands, the magician runs through the pack until he comes to the Queen of Diamonds. He cuts the pack at this place in order to bring the Queen to the bottom of the deck. The cards are now, you will notice, in the same order that they were when first stacked.

A CORRECT PROPHECY

THE magician puts the pack face down upon the table and stands back a couple of paces. He asks one of the spectators (picking out one in order that he will get but one answer) to name any number from one through fifty-two. The magician suggests, to make the trick as impressive as possible, that the spectator does not select the first number to enter his mind but rather to choose a number which already has a meaning to him and which the magician cannot possibly know. When the number is announced the magician writes on a small blank card which he has taken from his pocket. As he starts to write he says, "I shall write a prediction." On finishing writing he steps nearer the table, reaches out, and drops face down on the table the card upon which he has written.

The spectator is asked to count cards from the deck, face down upon the table until he reaches the number he has chosen. As the card at that number is reached the magician says, "Please put your selected card face down upon my prediction." The spectator is asked to count the cards once again to make certain that there has been no error. This recount, while making the trick more impressive, actually is done to put those cards back in order. Counting the cards one at a time upon a table reverses the order. Reversing the reverse puts the cards, of course, as they were. The magician then picks up the pack and the extra cards and puts them together but not evenly for he wants the break held where he is to replace the chosen card.

1 J♣	11 4♠	21 2♣	31 3♠	41 A♣
2 A♥	12 9♦	22 6♥	32 K♦	42 8♥
3 8♠	13 Q♣	23 7♠	33 10♣	43 5♠
4 5♦	14 J♥	24 4♦	34 2♥	44 3♦
5 3♣	15 A♠	25 9♣	35 6♠	45 K♣
6 K♥	16 8♦	26 Q♥	36 7♦	46 10♥
7 10♠	17 5♣	27 J♠	37 4♣	47 2♠
8 2♦	18 3♥	28 A♦	38 9♥	48 6♦
9 6♣	19 K♠	29 8♣	39 Q♠	49 7♣
10 7♥	20 10♦	30 5♥	40 J♦	50 4♥
			51 9♠	52 Q♦

If the reader does not wish to trace this chart to use in his shows it can be reproduced quite inexpensively by a photostat company (see local telephone directory).

On the table are left the prophecy and the selected card. The spectator is told to turn them over and he finds that they agree and the prophecy is true.

Actually in taking the little white card from his pocket the magician takes several cards. This is a perfectly natural thing to do for one card would not be stiff enough to write upon. One of these cards is a key card which gives the name of each card according to its number in the deck. As soon as the chosen number is announced the magician glances at this key. He does this as he holds up, for everyone to see, the blank card on which he is going to write his prediction. The trick is made more impressive if the prophecy is written in full as—"I predict that the chosen card will be the six of Hearts."

The effectiveness of this trick lies in the fact that, as no one in the audience knows why the number is chosen or knows the location of any card in the deck, the magician seems to write his prediction before a card is selected. This idea will be strengthened in the minds of the spectators if the magician, after laying down his prophecy, will say to the one spectator, "You have a number in your mind? Please take the pack and count cards face down upon the table until you reach the number of which you are thinking." This emphasis upon "in your mind" and "thinking" makes everyone forget that the magician knew the selected number before he wrote his prophecy. The fact that the prediction was written also adds to the effect.

As soon as the magician receives the selected card and it is properly placed in the deck he puts the bottom five cards on the top of the deck. This will leave the 2 of Spades on the bottom. The deck is placed on the table.

DEALING THE WINNING HAND

As an introduction to this trick the magician reminds the audience that a real magician should have no difficulty, except a moral one, giving himself winning hands in a card game. He calls attention to the fact that the deck is on the table and asks whether his demonstration is to be for a game of Poker or a game of Bridge. That choice actually is given as it makes no difference which is chosen.

If the selected game is Bridge the magician merely picks up the pack and deals the cards. It is suggested that instead of dealing the cards around the table as is customary that the hands be dealt near one another at the center of the table. When the deal is finished the magician calmly picks up all the hands except his own. As he does this he steps back and says, "Please look at the hand I dealt myself." While the cards in his hand are being turned over and discovered to be thirteen Spades the magician "absentmindedly" shuffles the remainder of the deck, and while he is shuffling the cards, the magician casually remarks, "The chance of being dealt that hand, for anyone other than a magician, is one in more than 635 billion."

If the selected game is Poker the magician announces, as he picks up the deck, "A six-handed game is fun." He then deals six hands, of five cards each, in the usual way; one card at a time, five times around.

The magician then picks up the first and second and the fourth and fifth hands dealt and puts them together and places them back on the deck. As he does this he says, "These hands are uninteresting but (speaking to the person nearest to the third hand which remains on the table) I believe you will like your hand." The spectator is given time to pick up his hand and to discover that he is holding a "straight." The magician then reminds every one that he has promised to deal himself the best hand and he asks that it be looked at. The magician's hand also will be a straight but a much better one.

The reason for not leaving all the hands on the table in either game is that the other cards might give someone the idea a system is used. The deals are completely convincing even though the extra hands are discarded.

There is no trick at all to the dealing. Everything was figured out when the story was written about the Jackass, and the cards are arranged in the proper order to deal either a superb hand of Bridge or of Poker, provided only, the magician makes certain that the 2 of spades is the bottom card of the deck before he starts to deal.

BY NUMBER

OTHER tricks may be performed with the stacked deck such as knowing the location in the deck numerically of any card mentioned by a spectator. This can be done either by mental arithmetic or by having made a secret card which gives this information at a glance. The illustration shows how to make such a card.

Other tricks will come to anyone who uses the stacked deck frequently but these tricks, if used, should be substitutes for the ones previously described rather than added to the number of tricks with a stacked deck shown at one time.

	♣	♥	♠	♦
A	41	2	15	28
2	21	34	47	8
3	5	18	31	44
4	37	50	11	24
5	17	30	43	4
6	9	22	35	48
7	49	10	23	36
8	29	42	3	16
9	25	38	51	12
10	33	46	7	20
J	1	14	27	40
Q	13	26	39	52
K	45	6	19	32

If the reader does not wish to trace this chart to use in his shows it can be reproduced quite inexpensively by a photostat company (see local telephone directory).

SHUFFLING THE DECK AND A TRICK IN CONNECTION THEREWITH

THE one weak point in handling a stacked deck is that the cards cannot be mixed. In order to overcome this weakness here is an excellent trick to use in introducing a series of tricks with a prearranged deck.

For this trick the magician needs a second deck which must be identical with the first. The magician brings forth this deck and several different spectators are asked, one after another, to shuffle the cards. It makes no difference how much the cards are mixed except that everyone must be certain, when the shuffling has been finished, that the cards are in no known order. This point should not be mentioned by the magician but must be clear in the minds of the spectators.

Once the deck is very thoroughly mixed the magician asks that the cards be spread out face down on a table. He then asks one spectator to select one card and to remove it from the pack. When this has been done the magician gathers up the cards. This is the first time he has touched the cards since he gave the pack to be shuffled. He then says that he will turn away while the person who holds the selected card looks at it and also shows it to several of the other spectators.

There is the crucial point of the trick, for the magician exchanges the cards which have been shuffled for the duplicate and stacked pack in his pocket. I prefer using a side pocket of my coat but it makes little difference which pocket is used provided the pocket is easy to get into, and to get out of, and is empty except for the cards. All the magician has to do is to put his hand in his pocket and to leave the much shuffled deck as he takes out the stacked cards. This substitution will not be noticed, for the magician, pretending to turn away while the spectators look at the selected card, stands so that his body hides his action. There is but one thing to remember: the action of putting the hand in, and out, of the pocket must be done slowly. The magician has ample time to exchange decks for everyone will be looking at the selected card and not at him.

Having the stacked pack the magician asks that the chosen card be replaced anywhere in the deck and the deck placed on the table. Another spectator is asked to cut the deck for the announced reason that no one then could know the location of the card in the deck. The magician asks all who saw the card to make a picture of it in their minds and to concentrate on that picture.

The magician runs through the deck looking at the faces of the cards. He picks out one card as "matching" the spectators' mental pictures. Naturally it proves to be the selected card. What he actually does is to go through the deck, starting at the top, silently repeating the Jackass story. When he comes to the card which is out of place, in the story, that is the extra, and selected, card.

Of course, as this selected card has a duplicate in the deck it must be got rid of before any other tricks can be done. The easiest way to do this is to have a Joker in each of the decks. The Joker is in the first deck merely so that were anyone to examine the deck, as it is shuffled, the Joker would be found among the cards. In the stacked deck the Joker is put on top of the deck; that is on top of the Jack of Clubs which takes it out of the Jackass story. After the selected card is found and shown to the audience it is put on the bottom of the deck. The magician says, "I wonder if there is a Joker in this deck?" He then looks through the deck and takes out the Joker which he shows to the spectators. This card, too, he puts on the bottom of the deck. Then, as an afterthought, he says, "Perhaps it would be better not to have the Joker in the pack." As this is said he takes both the Joker and the extra card, as if they were one single card, and puts them in his pocket. The deck is then ready for the tricks requiring a stacked deck but the audience is quite satisfied that the deck has been most thoroughly mixed.

Unless the specific trick forbids it the magician should cut the cards several times and most obviously whenever the deck is in his hands. Cutting a deck seems to almost everyone to mix the cards and, while you know better, it is very nice that they think so.

Six. FURTHER MYSTERIES

ALL the tricks in this Chapter need some preparation and some also require simple pieces of equipment to be made. Nothing is difficult to prepare, or to make, and the time spent in secret preparation is very well worthwhile both to audience and to magician. Even though a part of each trick has not the innocence the spectators expect, there are several of them which may be presented in a most off-hand manner. That must be qualified by noting that those tricks may be presented extemporaneously on any occasion when the magician has the necessary parts in his pockets. All the tricks are astounding mysteries and excellent entertainment.

MATCHES ON PARADE

THIS is an excellent example of magic requiring prior preparation and which occurs so spontaneously when performed.

Three matches are torn from a packet of paper matches by the magician. He asks a spectator to hold one end of a piece of paper while he holds the other end. The paper is held flat as if it were a table. The three matches are placed on the paper so they appear like soldiers lined up for inspection. The matches are placed some distance apart so they look like this: 1   1   1. The magician holds his end of the paper with his left hand. Slowly the matches begin to close ranks. One deliberately moves alongside of another and together the two go over to join the third. In close order formation all three travel to the edge of the paper and into the performer's right hand.

The feat takes but a minute to do and what happens is so unexpected that always it is amusing.

There are two parts to the preparation. First the staple is carefully taken out of a packet of paper matches. After the wire staple has been removed the two rows of matches can be taken from the cover. By cutting out two or three matches of the back row, there will be space for a small flat magnet. Adding the magnet to the packet, the matches are put back in the cover and pasted in place. Pasting will be found quicker and easier than attempting to replace the staple and will make a neater job. Then one match is torn from the packet. Into the bottom end of the match is inserted a short needle and the needle is pushed into the match until it is entirely hidden.

In presenting this feat the magician first finds a piece of paper. It should be no smaller than 8½" x 11" which is the size of typewriter paper and most business letterheads. A piece of newspaper may be used, or a menu, provided it is not printed on heavy cardboard. Having the paper or having noticed where it is readily available the magician is ready to begin.

From his pocket, the magician takes a packet of paper matches (the previously prepared packet), opens the cover and tears off three matches. He has the piece of paper held at one end by a spectator and he takes the other end in his left hand. He grasps the paper with his fingers underneath and his thumb on top. The packet of matches is under the paper, backside up, resting on his fingers. The three paper matches he still holds in his right hand are placed in their proper positions on the paper. The magician must be certain that the match containing the needle is placed furthest away from him. This match, by the way, having previously been torn out of the packet, was only stuck under the cover, where it was held by pressure. The magician pretends to tear this match loose, though he actually does tear out the other two.

The magician reaches under the paper with his right hand and takes the packet of matches away from where it rests on the fingers of his left hand. This action should be without the knowledge of the spectators. This easily can be done if the matches had been placed properly on the left fingers. The packet should be lengthwise on the second and third fingers and with the top of the packet near the tips of the fingers. The packet is back up so that the magnet is towards the paper. The thumb and first finger of the right hand go to the sides of the fingers of the left hand, grasp the packet of matches and slide it off the fingers of the left hand.

The right hand can then so manipulate the packet, with its magnet, that the match with the needle will move wherever desired. By pulling the match against another match both will move. When the two are slid against the third match, all will move together.

When the three matches have been brought to the edge of the paper, the packet is returned to the left fingers by reversing the move by which it was taken away. The right hand goes to the edge of the paper and puts the thumb on top of the paper, and on the matches, but leaves the fingers under the paper. Squeezing the matches, the right hand slides them off the paper. The paper is discarded.

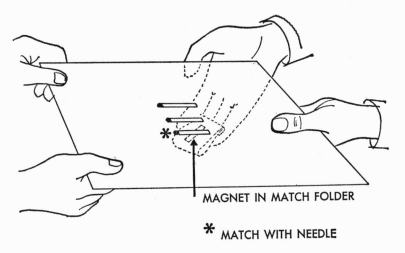

MAGNET IN MATCH FOLDER

* MATCH WITH NEEDLE

Igniting the three matches, blowing them out and tossing them aside, is the proper finish for the feat. But it means using another needle next time this magic is performed. The packet can be used over and over by having all three matches loose at the start of the feat.

RETURN FIRE

Another surprising effect which needs a little advance preparation also is performed with paper matches and it, too, can be shown anytime and anywhere. It has a double climax which adds greatly to its entertainment value.

The magician takes a folder of paper matches from his pocket. He raises the cover, pulls out four matches and drops them on a table, or, if no table is available, on the outstretched hand of a spectator. He closes the cover of the match packet, picks up one match and lights it. Putting down the folder he picks up the other three matches and ignites them from the lighted match. Then all four matches are extinguished by blowing on them. When the matches are cool he puts them down again and takes a handkerchief from his pocket. He opens the handkerchief and drapes it over his left hand. Picking up the matches and holding them together the magician pushes the ends of the matches against the center of the handkerchief. The matches press a little pocket in the cloth. The matches are pushed down into the pocket formed in the handkerchief until they no longer are visible.

As soon as the matches are out of sight, the magician takes hold of one corner of the handkerchief with his right hand and jerks it away from his left hand. He shakes the handkerchief, crumples it and returns it to his pocket. The burnt matches have disappeared. The magician says that he will cause the matches to return to the folder so that they can be used again. He asks someone to open the cover of the match folder to make certain the matches have obeyed. Inside the packet are seen the four burnt matches. They are again attached exactly as if they never had been torn from it.

The magician takes the folder, tears out one of the burnt matches, strikes it and, as it bursts into flame, holds it up so everyone can watch it burn. As he looks at the flaming match the magician says, "Ah! Return fire."

Blowing out the match, the magician hands it and the folder of matches to a spectator. Human nature being what it is that spectator, or another, will attempt to relight one, or other, of the burnt matches. He will have no success whatsoever for, as the magician explains, "Without magic it is impossible to relight a burnt match by striking it."

The handkerchief is quite ordinary and nothing is done to change its condition. The folder of matches, too, is ordinary but it has been prepared for the trick. Besides the handkerchief and the match packet of which the audience are aware, there also is needed a common rubber band about 2" long. The audience never knows of the existence of the rubber band. The folder of matches should be a new one from which no matches have been taken. The feat is more effective if the match heads are red, or yellow, so as to make a clear contrast with the burnt matches. A second match packet, having similar matches, also is needed to supply the four extra matches required for the trick. The new folder of matches is prepared by lighting and blowing out three of the matches but not taking them out of the folder. A fourth match, also left attached to the folder, is made to simulate a burnt match, by painting its head black with india ink, or black shoe dye. The four extra matches are stuck in the front edge of the folder. These are the matches the magician uses at the beginning of the feat.

Prior to explaining how the matches are caused to disappear, a few additional details about the preparation and use of the matches should be noted. A new folder of matches seems to have four rows of matches because of the bulging head of each match. While the twenty matches each packet contains are cut from two pieces of cardboard, the alternate matches of each piece of cardboard are pushed forward to allow space for the large heads. Therefore, there are only five match heads pushed forward of the ten

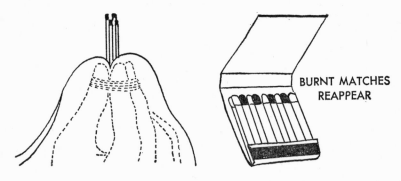

BURNT MATCHES
REAPPEAR

matches attached to the front piece of cardboard. Because a right handed persons tears off the match on his right first, and thereafter goes from right to left as he takes matches, the trick is designed to aid the right handed. The second match from the right is the first one having its head pushed forward. That is the match which has its head painted black with india ink. The match, at its base, is bent forward and away from the other matches so the head is colored on all sides. No more ink should be used on the job than is necessary to blacken the entire tip. The match must be allowed to dry thoroughly, which will take several minutes. After the ink has dried, the fourth match from the right of the front cardboard, that is the second of the front row of heads, is bent forward and the cover closed behind it. Every packet of matches carries on its cover the warning, "Close cover before striking match." This admonition must be followed in this trick. With the match bent away from the packet, it is lighted from the flame of another match and then blown out. Before opening the cover and bending the burnt match back into position with the other matches, make certain that the head no longer is hot so as to avoid igniting the entire packet. One at a time the third and fourth matches in the first row of heads are burnt in the same way. When this is done, the four extra matches are put in the folder under the cover. These are pushed between the base of the matches in the folder and the stapled lower flap of the cover. Each match goes into the space provided by the alternate match which is pushed back. The magician takes these matches from the folder so that it appears as if he were tearing each loose. This is not difficult acting for the way they are pushed in the folder makes removing one of them or tearing out a match almost an identical action.

Now the details about making the matches disappear. Prior to beginning the performance of the feat and even before anyone is aware that one will be done, the magician loops the rubber band around the tips of the first and second fingers of his left hand. The rubber, according to its length, is wound two or three times around the fingers. The rubber band is in place when the routine begins. The rubber is kept hidden by keeping the fingers of the left hand curled and always having the back of the left hand toward the spectators. When the four matches are taken from the folder, it is held between the left thumb and the side of the first finger. The top of the back of the folder goes on the side of the second joint of the first finger. In this position, the folder and the hand will cover the rubber from almost all angles. A few trials will demonstrate how to act to keep the rubber hidden.

When the four matches and the folder all are out of the hands of the magician, the left hand is dropped to the side and the right hand gets the handkerchief. The handkerchief should be folded when it is brought from the pocket, not only because that proves that it is not soiled, but also that it is unprepared. This latter fact should not be mentioned for it puts questioning ideas in the minds of the spectators. The handkerchief is opened and spread on the left hand. As the cloth covers the hand, the fingers and thumb are brought together and, by turning the hand, pointed towards the ceiling. Once covered, the fingers bound by the rubber, are spread enough so that the thumb also can slip into the loop. When the matches are pushed against the handkerchief, the thumb and fingers are spread to allow cloth and matches to be pushed between them and into the double loop of rubber. When the matches are pushed so far into the folds of the handkerchief that they no longer can be seen the right hand takes one corner of the handkerchief. Just as the right hand grips the cloth, the thumb and first and second fingers are bent simultaneously. This will let the rubber band slide off the fingers and go around that part of the handkerchief in which the matches are pushed. When the right hand shakes the handkerchief, no matches fall out. The handkerchief should be shaken two times which is enough to show the matches have disappeared. The movement of the handkerchief, plus the ways the cloth will fall into folds, will keep anyone from seeing the pocket in the cloth where the matches are hidden or the rubber band which holds the pocket closed. As with everything else a magician does, this should be tried a number of times in private before trying it publicly to insure having all the details clear in mind.

SCIENTIST'S DOLLAR DINNER

ABOUT the period when George Washington was learning to become a surveyor, magicians in England and the continent, as well as in the American Colonies, began attributing to scientific causes all the magic they performed. The brighter and better educated people, those who then and now attend magic shows, had outgrown the belief that magic was accomplished by the use of special words or the connivance of a familiar spirit. Magicians discontinued their claims to occult powers and offered the idea that they were learned in all the sciences. As few people then, or even today for that matter, were aware of just what was scientifically possible, they were willing to accept anything they saw, but did not understand, as being the result of science. As they were mystified by the performances of a magician, they were ready to acknowledge magician's self-bestowed title of Professor of Physics, Professor of Chemistry and, the more comprehensive, Professor of Science. Professor, as a title for a magician, was usual for nearly two centuries. Finally, when scientific marvels became common objects in every home, magicians had to drop their claim to a superior knowledge of all sciences. However, science still can be used as a background for many mysteries. While extremely few magicians could convince an audience of their scientific superiority for any length of time, they can claim to have scientists as friends. They merely have to be careful to keep their statements within reason when quoting their friends and to base their talk on some discovery the public has, or thinks it has, heard.

Here is magic with just that sort of a scientific twist. The magician begins by reminding his audience how many different foods are sold as concentrates and how many foods are enriched before being put on the market. There seems to be no limit to what the food scientists can do. They are working now, according to information received, the magician states, on a tablet which will contain every element found in a nine course dinner. Imagine nothing to prepare, no cleaning up after a meal, and the time saved in eating. The magician exhibits a tablet which he claims is one of these full dinner concentrates in its prototype form. The scientists, he says he was told, now are working toward reducing the cost and the firm planning to distribute the tablet dinners are worrying about how to package them. The magician says he believes he has solved the packaging problem and would be interested to discover if the audience agrees.

The magician asks a spectator to help with the packaging. The magician has a small tray, upon which, beside the tablet-form dinner and a pair of tweezers, by which the tablet had been held when shown, are two vials, and several small pieces of absorbent cotton. One of the vials is small enough to go inside the other. Both vials have removable tops. The smaller vial is given to the spectator with instructions to remove the top. He then is told to put a little cotton in the vial and to use the tweezers to do so. He then is to put the tablet in the vial, continuing to use tweezers, and finally to put in more cotton before he replaces the cap. This vial is taken from the assistant who is given the larger vial. Again he is asked to take off the top. He is given a small paper label the magician takes from his pocket. On the label is written either the elements contained in the tablet, or the day of the week in which it is to be eaten. This label is put inside the vial so the lettering can be read from the outside. The assistant is told to put a little cotton in the bottom of the vial, and on top of the cotton, to drop the smaller vial which already had been packed and then add more cotton to fill the vial. Finally, he is asked to replace the top and to hold the vial in his hand and where everyone can see it.

The magician asks if one of the other spectators will be willing to lend a dollar bill for a few minutes. Going to the person offering to make the loan the magician takes the dollar, folds it and starts to put it in a small envelope he has taken from his pocket. He stops this action and says he would like to have the last four numbers of the bill memorized as he reads them off. The bill is then pushed into the envelope and the flap is moistened and sealed.

Holding the envelope so everyone can see it, the magician returns to stand near, but not too near, the assistant who is holding the nest of vials containing the tablet.

The magician tells the audience, "The scientists expect that these dinner tablets will cost a dollar each when they are in production. At present this is the situation. My kind assistant has the dinner I am to have, and I have the dollar to mail to the company. Because I feel that here is a case where the scientists have gone too far, as they are taking away the pleasure of eating, being a magician, I have a plan. To carry out my plan I snap my fingers. That may not be too scientific but snapping the fingers is required by the rules of magic, and it always works. Now, in this envelope is the tablet and the dollar is in the vial packed in cotton. The company will get back its tablet and the dollar is saved. We had better see if the magic worked."

The magician tears open the envelope and out slides the tablet. The assistant opens the larger vial and takes out the small one. Opening that, he finds the dollar bill wrapped in cotton. When the bill is returned to the lender he finds the numbers he memorized on the bill. The magic is effective, and amusing. The best part is that the magician has so little to do during the performance for almost everything is the result of prior preparation.

Obviously, there are two parts to this feat. The first is exchanging the dinner tablet in the smaller vial for a dollar bill. The second is exchanging the dollar bill for the tablet within the envelope. The first part is simple for the magician to accomplish. The second part is done almost automatically.

Prior to the performance the magician has rolled a dollar bill in cotton and both bill and cotton were inserted in a vial which is identical with the smaller vial of which the audience is aware. Before wrapping the bill in cotton, the magician has noted and memorized the last four figures of the serial number of the bill.

Also prior to performance, the magician has altered the envelope into which, during performance, he puts the borrowed dollar. The envelope used is one which opens at one end. These envelopes, commonly called pay envelopes, usually are 2½″ wide and 3¼″ long. About ¾″ of the top of a second envelope is cut off with scissors. The top is that part which is open and has the gummed flap. While the flap, too, is cut off it is not open when the measurement is made. A duplicate of the tablet is dropped into the whole envelope. Then the shortened envelope is pushed inside the intact envelope. The top edges of the cut envelope are pasted to the inside of the whole envelope. An envelope prepared in this way appears to be quite ordinary. The dollar bill is folded and pushed inside the envelope and the flap is closed and held shut by the gum which had been moistened. By tearing off the bottom end the tablet is free to slide out but the dollar bill is secretly held inside the inner section. After the tablet is out of the envelope, the envelope is crushed and set aside. During the performance all that the magician is required to do is to note, upon tearing open the envelope, which is the top and which the bottom. As, in appearance, they are quite unalike

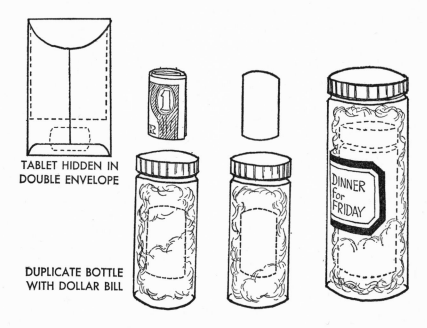

TABLET HIDDEN IN
DOUBLE ENVELOPE

DUPLICATE BOTTLE
WITH DOLLAR BILL

DINNER
for
FRIDAY

this presents no problem. He also has, when pretending to read off the last four figures of the borrowed dollar, to recite the four numbers he memorized of the dollar in the vial.

Prior to performance the magician has put the vial with its cotton wrapped dollar in the left side pocket of his jacket. He also put in the outside right side pocket of his jacket the little label. At the point in the trick where the magician takes the tablet-packed small vial from his assistant he does so with his right hand as with this same hand he hands the larger vial. As holding two vials would occupy both the assistant's hands, it appears merely to be courteous to relieve him of one. As the exchange of large vial for small vial is being made, the magician, with his left hand, takes the duplicate vial from his jacket pocket. The vial is held, and hidden, inside his clenched fist. As the magician tells his assistant to take off the top of the large vial, he seems to transfer to his left hand the small vial taken from the assistant. Actually, bringing his hands together, he lets the one vial slide into his right hand so the fingers can close around it and hide it, as the left hand is opened to disclose the duplicate vial. This action should be made by the magician as if everyone were watching him, for some individual may actually be doing so. The likelihood is that the attention of everyone is on the assistant to see what he is doing. The right hand, with its hidden vial, goes into the jacket pocket and brings out the small paper label and, though undoubtedly unnecessary to mention, leaves the unneeded vial.

The words written on the label give an excuse for having the label and, as well, can add a touch of humor. A label could have a list of mouth watering delicacies and the magician would read them off—wait a second—and say, "So that is what is in the tablet." Or on the label might be "Dinner for Friday." After reading these words, the magician would say, "That's fine! I always liked fish." Because of the incongruity either caption will be found to be mildly amusing.

The vials best to use in this feat are the plastic pill and capsule vials druggists use and, usually, are willing to sell. The smaller vial I have is $2\frac{1}{8}''$ long and $\frac{13}{16}''$ in diameter. Two vials of this size are required. The larger vial is $3\frac{1}{8}''$ long and $1\frac{1}{16}''$ in diameter. These seem to be standard sizes. The smaller vial easily can be hidden in the closed hand.

As a brand new product the tablet should not have the appearance of anything on the market and, in particular, it must not seem to be medicine of any kind. By sawing a flat bone game counter in half, I made a tablet which always has been accepted as being exactly as claimed. The sawing also gave me a tablet and the necessary duplicate. The flat tablet is $\frac{5}{8}''$ wide, $1''$ long, and $\frac{1}{8}''$ thick. The sides are parallel and straight. The ends are slightly rounded. The bone is tinted an appetizing dark cream color. Of course, substances other than bone may be used to make the tablet, but it helps the trick if the material is not recognizable. It would be well to follow the size and shape noted. Such a size goes easily in the vial and, because it stands on end, is hidden better in the cotton.

The tweezers should be at least $4''$ long and have pointed tips. Actually they are needed only to remove the dollar bill from the vial at the end of the trick. But they are in keeping with the idea of not touching food with the hands and, because few people can use tweezers well, it makes the feat seem more incredible that the magician could substitute the dollar for the tablet so rapidly that no one could see it. This isn't what happens and speed is not used but why not aid and abet the spectators' delusions which they so enjoy?

An additional suggestion, probably unnecessary to mention, is that the vial containing the dollar bill has to have the same appearance as the vial containing the tablet. The magician will have to experiment to see how best to wrap the bill. He also, in his experimenting, will learn the proper size to make the wads of cotton, which he gives to the spectator.

Earlier in this book the advice was given that the magician should perform his mysteries in a convincing manner. While I stand by that statement I would like to hedge just a little. The magician should make his audiences believe he does what he claims, but should not convince himself. I am loathe to admit how many envelopes containing dollar bills I have thrown away. Like my audience, I was satisfied that the dollar returned to the spectator actually was the dollar he permitted me to borrow. Such an attitude is costly. In short, be convincing but always remember, after the show, to retrieve the dollar in the torn and crushed envelope.

STRING FOR A PARCEL

THE magician reminds his audience how annoying it is to attempt to re-tie a package with the string originally used. Either the string is not long enough to go around, as usually happens when the package was opened by cutting the string, or the string is full of knots and impossible to use. The magician then suggests that the difficulty may be overcome by a slight knowledge of magic.

"Here is a loop of string—or rather, two pieces of string tied together here, and here, with knots. Of course, what we want is one neat and knotless string and that is where magic comes in. In order to join the two pieces of string together, it is necessary to have nice, fresh, clean cut ends and these scissors will do that. A snip and one knot is out of the way. Put those fresh ends together, say the magic word 'rat-atar,' blow on the knot, and we have one fine, straight, knotless piece of string. And, by the way, if the string isn't long enough—stretch it."

The magician most convincingly seems to do exactly what he claims he does. However, there is a bit more to the mystery than blowing on a knot and pronouncing the magic word.

First there is the preparation of the string which is not quite as it looks to be. The string should be at least three, and preferably not longer than four, feet long. A piece three inches long is cut off the string. The long string is doubled and the loop at the center is folded back and grasped with the thumb of the same hand, which holds the string. This doubling back will make two loops. The short string is threaded through one of these loops and

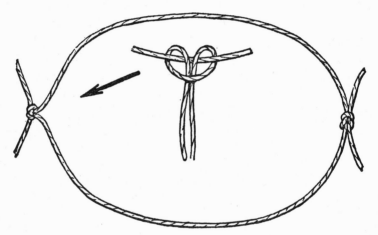

brought back through the other (see illustration). Both ends of the short piece of string are put together, with the free hand, and pulled. The other hand continues to hold the doubled, long string. This will make the string look exactly as if it were two pieces of string of equal length, tied together. The actual ends of the string are tied together with a real square knot, which will look so much like the imitation knot already made that the magician must remember to keep in mind which is which. The string will seem, when so prepared, that it is two pieces of string tied together in a loop.

The magician, after exhibiting the loop of string by holding it up and sliding it around in his hands, takes hold of the doubled string just below the fake knot. With a pair of scissors in the other hand, he snips off the real knot. He puts down the scissors, or pockets them, and with the same hand takes one of the real ends of the string. He takes hold of the string between the forefinger and thumb and with the tip away from, not towards, the second finger. The tip of the string must be hidden between the fingers. The string is held by the pads of the fingers and not the tips. Holding on to the end of the string the hand is raised and the thumb and forefinger, like a clothes pin, go over one end of the short string. Immediately that that end, too, is firmly gripped, the other hand lets go of the string and picks up the other end of the long string. That end is taken with precisely the same grip as the first was picked up in the other hand, except that the tip is allowed to protrude an inch or more. That hand, with its end, is raised so that the forefinger and thumb may clip on to the faked knot.

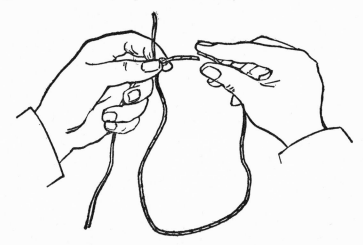

With the hands holding the various parts of the string as described, the magician is ready for the final moves while the audience has lost track entirely of which end is which. If the directions have been followed, the hands will be back up and the thumbs together. The hand, the fingers of which hold one end of the long string and one end of the short piece, pulls the short piece free of the faked knot while the other hand makes this possible by holding the knot. As this is done, the hands are lifted towards the face and the magician blows his breath on the knot. Immediately both hands are turned palms up and the arms outstretched to the full extent of the string. The audience will believe the short piece to be a part of the string for both one end of the long piece and one end of the short are held—and hidden—between the fingers.

In pulling out the string, it should not be pulled taut and the elbows must be kept in towards the body. On the second pull to give the appearance of stretching the string, a pretense of strength is made, the elbows brought out, and the string pulled taut. It is entirely a coupling of suggestion with the optical illusion caused by the change in position of the arms. The string does not stretch at all, but it looks as if it did.

The magician now has arms outstretched and a long piece of string—plus a short piece—held in his hands. He first drops the string from the hand which held only the end. The other hand he sticks into a pocket as though

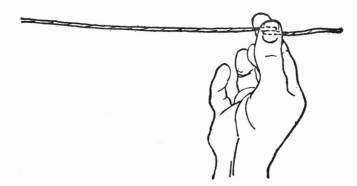

he were starting to put the string away. In making this motion, all but the end of the string will be in plain sight of the audience, as it hangs out of the pocket. No sooner is the hand in his pocket than the magician, still holding the string, takes it out again. The instant the hand goes into the pocket the magician releases his hold on the short piece of which the audience never has been aware. He puts his hand in his pocket only to get rid of this secret short piece of string. In bringing his hand out of his pocket, the magician, as if the idea had just occurred to him, says, "Perhaps someone would like to have a piece of string which has been mended magically." He winds the string around his fingers and hands some spectator the neat coil.

There is nothing in this trick which requires an unusual use of the fingers, but, because he is aware of the short piece of string, the magician is apt to try to hurry in performing the trick. The audience is not aware of the short piece, nor of the faked knot, and there is nothing for anyone to see which will explain the mystery, and it is much more effective if done slowly. It is almost impossible to perform the trick too slowly, for when done in a slow manner, the audience knows that the string has not been substituted, that the hands are empty except for the string, and that everything is absolutely fair. With the audience convinced of these things, the trick becomes completely impossible—and, therefore, good.

BY THE SENSE OF TOUCH

EVERYONE has heard about people who have developed the sense of touch to a high degree. While remembering having heard accounts of what can be done, few people can recall any particular incident. The magician can depend upon his spectator's being particularly interested in this unusual card trick because of their confused recollections regarding accounts of exceptional touch sensitivity.

After a spectator has divided a deck of cards, which may be borrowed, into three heaps, he and two others each look at one card from his separately assigned heap. Each person puts his card back into his third of the deck and shuffles those cards. The three heaps are put one on top of the other and the entire deck is shuffled. The magician, up to this point, obviously has done nothing except to explain to the spectators what he wanted done. Next the magician calls attention to his inside coat pocket and shows it to be empty. He puts the entire deck into this pocket and tells the audience what has been done and what he is about to do.

"Three cards have been chosen by different people and all that anyone can know about the cards, after all that shuffling, is that they are somewhere in the deck, which is in my inside coat pocket. What I propose to do is to see how quickly I can discover each card using only the sense of touch. Of course, before I can do that it is necessary for me to know the names of the three chosen cards. Will you please tell me your card? The eight of Hearts? Thank you. And which card did you select? The Jack of Clubs? Thank you. And yours? The three of Diamonds? Excellent. Now I shall see how quickly I can find those three cards—the Jack of Clubs, the eight of Hearts, and the three of Diamonds. Here is the first one, the Jack. The second card, the eight. And finally the three of Diamonds. I doubt if it took me twenty seconds to locate all three cards in my pocket, entirely by the sense of touch. Perhaps you would like to see how long it takes to find these particular cards, and take them from the pack, even when you can look at the deck. I shall put these cards back in the deck so you can try."

After the magician puts the three cards back into the deck one at a time, he takes the deck from his pocket. If anyone does try to discover how long it will take to find the three selected cards, it is unlikely he will beat the speed of the magician's sense of touch.

That is the effect of the trick and the presentation, and it is most astounding to the audience. Amazing as is the feat, it presents no difficulties for the magician.

Although they are not aware of the fact, the spectators do not select their cards and their choice is controlled by the magician. He puts the three cards he wants the spectators to have on the bottom of the deck before he begins the trick. It will be found quite simple to shuffle the deck without disturbing the location of the three bottom cards and while shuffling adds to the general effect, it is not essential.

When the spectator is given the pack, he is instructed to take off a quarter, or so, of the deck and put those cards on the table in a pile. Next he is to take off cards for a second pile. Then to take cards for a third pile. The remaining cards he is told to deal on to the three piles, one card at a time, on one pile after another. While the dealing is being done, the magician in a tone of complete satisfaction states, "And that further mixes the cards." Of course, actually the dealing puts one of the three bottom cards on top of each pile.

The three piles of cards on the table the magician assigns, one pile apiece, to the one who did the dealing and two other spectators. He then instructs these spectators to look secretly at the top card of his own pile and then thoroughly to shuffle his cards. The three piles are put together and after the entire deck is shuffled, the magician puts the deck into his empty inside coat pocket.

In order to convince everyone that the pocket is empty, which it actually is, the magician should have something—perhaps a letter or even a pencil —in the pocket which he has to take out and put into another pocket. It may seem silly, but the fact that something had to be taken from the pocket before it could be claimed to be empty, is the most acceptable proof that nothing more can be inside.

The top of the inside coat pocket is practically even with the top of the upper vest pocket (a fact of which few are aware) and if the fingers are put into the coat pocket, the thumb will slide into the vest pocket without awkwardness. This presumes that the hand is put inside the coat as it normally hangs, without being held away from the body with the other hand.

When the thumb goes into the vest pocket, it draws out one of the three cards, of the same value as those the spectators had "chosen," which the magician had put into the pocket in preparation for the trick. The cards are in the pocket face out, that is with the backs of the cards next to the body, and when withdrawn face the audience. As soon as the thumb draws one of the cards part way out of the vest pocket, the fingers grasp the other side of the card. As the hand is brought out of the coat, it continues in an arc which turns the card end for end but keeps the face of the card toward the audience. The other hand takes the card and the second card is gone

after. The faces of the cards look so much alike that the substitution will not be noticed. The only difference that will attract attention is a difference in size. If the deck the magician is given is of a different size than his cards, he doesn't do the trick.

At the conclusion of the trick the magician's three cards are replaced, one at a time, in his vest pocket and the deck is taken from his coat pocket and given back to the audience. The deck may be examined 'til doomsday, and likely will be, and no one can discover how the magican can tell one card from another by the sense of touch.

FURTHER MYSTERIES

BEELZEBUB'S LETTER

THIS is a really fantastic trick with a borrowed coin. It is a trick which magicians classify as a "transposition effect." As the name implies, an object mysteriously travels from one place to another. Actually, of course, such a trick is a combination of two tricks; first, a disappearance; second, a production. Please remember, as you read the description of what the audience sees as one trick is actually a combination of two.

The magician asks to borrow a quarter. When one of the spectators indicates his willingness to lend the money, the magician gives the person a small blank gummed label and a pencil and asks that the label be marked and stuck on the coin in order later to identify the quarter. The magician puts a pocket handkerchief over the coin and asks another spectator to stand, and, with his thumb and first finger, to hold both the handkerchief and the coin. Instructions are given to the person not to release his grip.

The magician walks a little distance away and tells the audience about a number of letters he had received through the mail from someone signing himself "Beelzebub." Whoever "Bub" may be, he seems definitely to have an amazing power, the magician tells his audience as he takes "Bub's" latest letter from his pocket. The magician calls attention to the envelope and shows that it still is sealed. The envelope is placed on an inverted tumbler so that it remains in plain view of everyone.

The magician walks back to the person holding the quarter inside of the handkerchief and inquires if the quarter still can be felt. Immediately after he is told that the quarter still is in the handkerchief, the magician says: "Then watch," as he takes one corner of the handkerchief and jerks it free of the spectator's fingers. No quarter falls to the floor and the magician shows the emptiness both of his hands and the handkerchief.

The magician then tells his audience that the reason he feels that Beelzebub is a remarkable person is that regularly Bub has mailed letters yesterday, containing things which have disappeared today. The magician goes to the envelope, tears off one end and pulls out a rather thick card. The card is held up for the audience to see. At one end of the card is a hole with a cross of tape over it and between the strips of tape can be seen a quarter. On the other end of the card is written, "Here is the quarter you are going to borrow tomorrow. Regards. Beelzebub."

The magician takes hold of one end of the tape and pulls it free of the card. The tape with the quarter sticking to it is returned to the lender. The quarter proves to be the borrowed, marked quarter.

First comes the disappearance of the quarter. For that trick, the magician must get an ordinary metal washer of the size of a five-cent piece. Any hardware store will have them in stock. The reason for using a washer the size of a nickel, rather than a quarter, is that it is a better size for the trick and no one can feel the difference in size through a handkerchief. The washer must be cut in half. Sawing a washer in half with a hack saw is but a two-minute job, provided you have access to a hack saw and a vise. If you haven't, you very probably can make arrangements with the hardware store man to do the job for you. He will think you crazy for it ruins the washer, but what difference does it make? You then take an ordinary white pocket handkerchief which has a hem about a quarter inch deep. Into this hem is pushed one half of the washer. The washer is pushed into the hem until it is completely out of sight, but only that far. It is unnecessary to sew the washer in place, for it will be a rather tight fit and will not fall out.

While the donor of the quarter is marking the gummed label and sticking the label securely on the coin, the magician takes his prepared handkerchief from his pocket. When the handkerchief first is brought forth, it should be folded just as if it were fresh from the laundry. The magician opens out the handkerchief and runs his fingers around the hem until he locates the hidden washer. The next steps are the important ones. Holding the handkerchief with the right hand and by the corner with the washer, the magician spreads the cloth over the palm of his left hand so that the center of the handkerchief is over the center of the palm. That done, the magician folds back the corner he holds in his right hand until he can drop the corner, washer and all, on the center of the handkerchief. He then takes a new grasp of the handkerchief with his right hand—right at the center of the fold. Thus holding the handkerchief he drops both hands to his sides.

During the time the magician has been getting the handkerchief ready, he has been talking—not incessantly but as needed—to the man with the quarter suggesting that he be careful to make a mark he will be able to recognize; to make certain the label has been securely stuck on the coin; and to note the date on the coin as further identification. The handkerchief may be gotten ready most deliberately for nothing suspicious is being done and there is nothing to see. If anyone should notice the magician getting out his handkerchief, he will think the magician merely is taking the proper precautions to make certain there are no holes in the material.

Once the coin has been marked, the magician holds out his left hand for the quarter. He does not touch it with his fingers, but has it placed on his outstretched hand. The magician holds his hand near several different spectators so that each can see how the coin is marked.

Then slowly and deliberately the magician covers his left hand with the handkerchief and verbally calls everyone's attention to the fact that he is

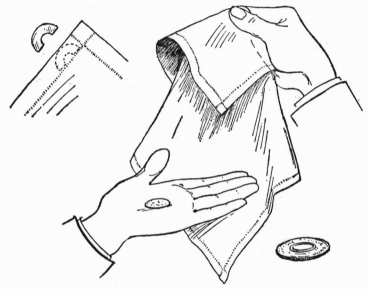

The corner of the open handkerchief
above the open hand has the hidden half-washer

doing so. The covering is done, at waist height, by bringing the handkerchief up over the fingertips and drawing the handkerchief along until the half-washer is about over the base of the middle finger. The magician then lets go of the handkerchief and it hangs over his left hand. With the announcement that he is picking up the quarter, the magician takes hold of the washer and lifts the handkerchief up. Turning towards some spectator who has not previously entered into the trick, the magician says, "Will you please stand." Just as this is said, the magician closes his left hand, still hidden by the handkerchief, and, holding on to the marked and borrowed quarter, drops the hand to his side. There is no reason for a death grip on the quarter. Merely close the hand, it is natural to do so, and the quarter will be both hidden and safe.

When the spectator stands, the magician asks that, with the very tips of his finger and thumb, he take hold of the quarter. The spectator will hold the washer with complete satisfaction not only that he is holding a quarter, but the particular marked quarter. The sense of touch is most untrustworthy.

To finish up this first trick, all that is necessary to cause the quarter to disappear is to take hold of one corner of the handkerchief and jerk it from the spectator's fingers. It even is possible to have someone else jerk the corner of the handkerchief to make the coin disappear, provided the magician gets the handkerchief before it is handled too much. There is nothing suspicious to see about the handkerchief but it is possible to feel the half-washer.

The second trick depends first upon the envelope to back up the story. All that is necessary to do this is to mail an envelope to yourself. On the face of the envelope write your name and full address only. When it is returned to you, write the "sender's" name in the corner—Beelzebub, % General Delivery, and the city. When mailing the envelope, stick down only the very tip of the flap so that it may be opened easily and without tearing.

The card which has the hole for the coin and the message is not quite as it seems. Really it is a piece of cardboard but very little thicker than a quarter. At one end of the card is a hole the size of the circumference of a quarter. From the opposite end the card is cut to the hole, so that the card has a U-shaped slot running almost the entire length. On each side of the card are pasted pieces of paper. On only one side is the paper cut and a hole is cut in it to match the hole (but not the slot) for the coin. The illustration will make clear how the card is made. Crossed over the hole in the paper are two narrow pieces of adhesive plaster. The reason for using surgeon's tape is that the sticky substance remains sticky and does not need to be moistened or otherwise treated. The card is finished once the message of Beelzebub is affixed.

It will be obvious that if the quarter is dropped into the slide in the card it will run into the hole and, the moment the adhesive is touched, will be stuck in place.

The prepared card is put into the envelope and the end of the envelope is marked at the spot where the slide comes in the card. After the envelope is marked, the card is removed until the marked part of the end of the envelope is cut away with scissors. The cut need be no more than a sixteenth of an inch deep. The card is put back in the envelope. The card, by the way, should be about three-eighths of an inch shorter than the envelope. The card is pressed up against the cut out end and the hole in the envelope aligned with the slide in the card. To hold the card in this position an ordinary paper clip is stuck about three-quarters of the way on the envelope and right at one side of the hole. The envelope is securely sealed.

After the envelope with the card is prepared, it is put in the inside pocket of the magician's coat and clipped with the paper clip to the top of the pocket. The paper clip not only holds the envelope so that the magician

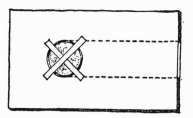

Beelzebub's message was left off the card in the illustration to show the construction of the slide more clearly

knows exactly where it is, but it acts as a guide for dropping the coin into the slide.

When the spectator is left holding the half-washer in the handkerchief, the magician walks away from him. As he walks, he brings his left hand, which holds the marked quarter, inside his coat. The quarter is dropped down the slide. All the time necessary to do this, and there is no reason why it should take long, is "covered" by the magician's story about the mail he has been getting from Beelzebub. It is even permissible for the magician to hold his coat away from his body with his right hand and to look inside his coat as he drops the coin into the slide. The looking will be thought natural, for the magician wants to see that he gets the right envelope.

Once the coin is down the slide, the envelope is taken from the pocket and immediately squeezed so as to stick the adhesive onto the quarter. The paper clip probably will fall off as the envelope is taken from the pocket. If it doesn't fall off, calmly take it off and discard it. The paper clip is neither suspicious nor of interest.

After the envelope is exhibited and put where everyone can see it, but likewise out of everyone's reach, the magician causes the coin to disappear. Returning to the envelope the magician taps it so that the card slides to the end opposite the cut and tears off the cut end. He takes the card out and exhibits it. In exhibiting both envelope and card, the fingers are over the open end. The adhesive is pulled loose from the card and with the coin sticking fast handed back for identification. The trick is somewhat better if the magician will remember to drop the coin in the slide so that the sticker side is away from the adhesive. If this is done, the coin can be identified while still fast to the adhesive.

There are the two tricks which, in combination, make a most entertaining and completely confounding mystery.

If you are a stickler for perfection, have a second card identical with the first except for the slide. After the coin is removed from the one card, put that card in your pocket and take out the other one. Then both card and envelope can be examined time without end with nary a suggestion as to the secret of Beelzebub's letter.

THE FLIGHT OF A COIN

First marking the coin with a gummed label, upon which he writes his initials, a spectator lends a twenty-five cent piece to the magician. The magician puts the money into a pay envelope and seals the flap. The magician announces that he is going to burn the coin and lights a match in preparation. Before igniting the envelope, the magician holds the flame behind it and calls attention to the fact that by the flare of the match the form of the coin may be seen. The envelope is burned until nothing but the ash is left and the coin has disappeared most mysteriously.

The magician then calls everyone's attention to a very carefully wrapped and sealed package which he never even has been near. A second spectator is asked to examine the package. He finds it tied with string and the knots of the string covered with sealing wax. Gummed paper strips are stuck over the folds and the overlap. A knife has to be used to cut off both the string and paper. Inside the paper is found a box which also is tied with a string which has sealing wax covering the knots. The string is cut and the box opened. Inside the box two slotted pieces of cardboard divide the box into thirds. An envelope is stuck into the slots of the cardboard, but otherwise the box is empty.

The magician asks the spectator assisting him to take the envelope from the box and to feel it. "You seem to find something in the envelope," inquires the magician. "What does it feel like?" The object in the envelope is said to be the size and shape of a quarter. The assistant is told to notice how

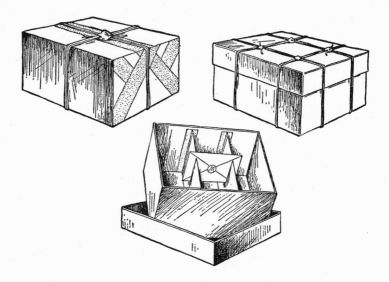

the envelope is sealed. Not only is the flap glued securely, but the envelope also is fastened with sealing wax stamped with a crest.

The envelope is torn open, the quarter slid out upon a plate, and the plate given to the spectator who lent the coin. The spectator identifies the coin as the one he had lent and marked.

The trick is easy to perform and, while some bother to prepare, well worth doing for it is very entertaining and astounding.

The initial preparation is in the pay envelope. First the bottom crease of the envelope is slit half way across with a sharp knife. Next a totally opaque piece of paper is cut into the size of a twenty-five cent piece. The easiest way to do this is to lay a quarter on the paper and carefully cut around it with a pair of scissors. The paper disc, with a dab of paste, is stuck inside the envelope in the bottom on the side not slit open.

Before the magician drops the coin in the envelope, he first holds up the envelope in one hand and the quarter in the other and says, "A pay envelope and what the Treasury Department leaves in it." As he finishes his sentence, the magician drops the coin in the envelope. The envelope is held with the flap side towards the audience and on a slant so that the quarter drops to the half of the bottom still closed. The magician moistens the flap and seals the envelope. As, with his right hand, he presses the flap to make certain it sticks, he holds the envelope with his left hand. The left hand has the fingers on the side of the envelope towards the audience and the tips touch the paper about an inch above the coin. The thumb is in the same position on the side next the magician. In squeezing the flap, the envelope is tilted and the coin drops onto the palm of the left hand. The instant the coin is in the left hand, the right hand lifts the envelope a foot higher in the air. The left hand, closing enough to hold the coin, goes into the left coat pocket, drops the coin, and immediately brings out a paper of matches. The paper disc in the envelope will be assumed to be the quarter, when the light of the match shows the form. Opaque paper, sold at stationery stores, should be used rather than cardboard, which does not burn so readily and which may interfere with the coin's sliding out of the envelope.

After the envelope is ignited, it should be held so that the "quarter" is consumed at once. When the paper gets too short to hold, it may be dropped on a plate to finish burning, or held with tweezers.

The box, in which is the sealed envelope with the coin, is made exactly as described above and shown in the illustration. There is nothing tricky about the cord, the wrapping, the box, or the envelope. That is, there is absolutely no trickery except that the coin in the envelope is not the borrowed coin. The box illustrated is the size to hold two pounds of candy. The envelope is the size ($2\frac{1}{4}$" x 3") used for calling cards.

While all the examination of the package, and the unwrapping and string-cutting is going on, the magician never gets near the spectator who is doing the work. When finally the box is opened, the magician asks that it be held so that the audience may see inside, and then steps closer to the assistant as if he, too, wished to look. The spectator is instructed to take the envelope from the box and is asked if he seems to feel something inside. Upon being told that there seems to be a quarter in the envelope, the magician takes the envelope.

There is the crucial part of the trick. The magician some moments previously, while he had nothing to do but watch the spectator, had retrieved the borrowed coin from his pocket. He holds the coin at the base of his two middle fingers by closing his hand until the coin is gripped. When he takes the envelope in the right hand, he turns it flap side up and lays it over the coin in his left hand. If the envelope is held over the left hand, and brought

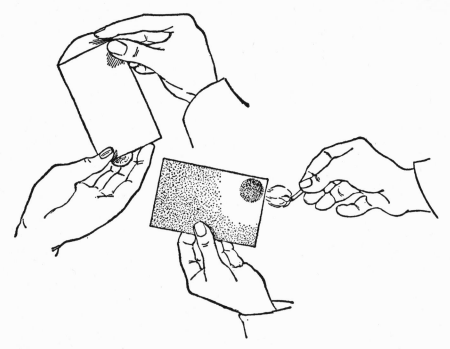

down as the left fingers open, it will mask the existence of the borrowed coin. There is absolutely nothing to these moves except to watch the timing so that they synchronize.

As soon as the envelope is over the coin, and while the magician talks about the sealing wax and wonder whose crest is impressed on it, the magician presses his left thumb on the envelope and over the coin. The magician then bends up one of the fingers upon which the coin is resting. This lifts the coin and the envelope off the other fingers so that the magician can get his right thumb under a part of the coin. As soon as the right thumb touches the coin, the right fingers close on the envelope and so holding the envelope tilt it until it is vertical. The left hand takes hold of the envelope at one end—the fingers go on the side towards the audience and the thumb on the back over the quarter. The coin on the back of the envelope may be shifted from thumb to thumb as the magician goes on talking about the crest, or the manner in which the envelope is sealed. He need remember but four things: (1) he can be perfectly natural for the moves appear to be so and the audience knows nothing about the coin behind the envelope; (2) the spectator must not stand behind the magician; (3) the coin inside the envelope must be slid to the right end; (4) the two coins finally must be in

the position so that the quarter inside the envelope is gripped by the first joint of the right thumb and the quarter on the outside pressed with the tip of the pad of the same thumb.

The magician, with his left hand, tears off the end of the envelope, to his left, and then picks up a plate with the same hand. The envelope is held over the plate and tilted and the outside coin only released. It will seem to the audience as if the coin dropped out of the envelope. As the magician takes the plate to the owner of the quarter, he pockets the envelope. The coin is identified and the trick, except for the amazement of the audience, is over.

When the magician takes the envelope, his manner should be that of calling attention to the way the envelope is sealed, rather than that he wanted to touch it himself. Once having the envelope in his hands, he "notices" the crest which gives material for patter and the patter will focus attention on the envelope rather than the coin. It is amazing how many objects around the house, when pressed in hot sealing wax, will make excellent and odd crest seals.

Instead merely of pocketing the envelope, when returning the borrowed coin on the plate, it is a better idea to pocket it only long enough to drop out the "other" quarter. There may be someone who wants to examine the envelope and that may be done to his heart's content once the extra quarter is removed.

One final point: the magician must remember in preparing for the trick that having matches in that left pocket is most important.

Seven. EXCEPTIONAL MAGIC

THE tricks in this Chapter are particularly effective and can be shown with the audience near, as in a parlor, and yet also are excellent even for stage presentation. Each trick requires equipment but nothing needed is difficult to make. Each trick, too, has multiple details of performance and, while nothing is hard to do, or to learn, extra practice is necessary to memorize these details to assure a smooth and interesting performance. The time spent in preparation and practice of these tricks will be repaid a thousand fold in satisfaction to the magician and in the delight of his spectators.

For various feats described from here on, in this book, mention is made of tables being needed for the performance. These are a prop (short for properties) table and performance tables (usually termed "side tables" by magicians). The prop table holds whatever is required for the show until actually used in performance. The performance tables, generally two are used, are for displaying the tricks to better advantage. More about the tables will be found among the notes in the final chapter.

A BOY AND A BOX OF CANDY

THIS is amusing magic which delights children and is equally entertaining to an audience of adults in which there is at least one boy 8 to 10 years old. The boy is needed to "assist" the magician in the trick. The boy is shown a box of candy and is promised that if he does his part properly the candy will be his. Whether or not the boy will receive the candy is part of the humor of the trick—at one point the box of candy disappears and the boy becomes involved with yards and yards of silk. However at the conclusion of the magic the box of candy reappears and is given to the boy for his work as assistant.

The humor arises from the situations which occur. Of course, the magician does not ridicule the boy which would be unkind to him and distasteful to the audience. The magician's role is that of sympathetic friend to one having difficulties. Naturally the magician is aware that there will be difficulties but he must act as if he never could have imagined that such things could happen.

The magician begins by saying that for his next mystery he is going to choose a bright and well mannered boy to help him. It cannot be stressed too strongly that the magician says he will *choose* one boy. He does not ask for a volunteer which is apt to cause an uncontrollable stampede in his direction. By the way, the magician is wise always to select the person he wishes to act in the trick rather than asking for a volunteer. With an adult audience the magician can pick the person he believes to be the most suitable rather than getting a volunteer who, by the very act of volunteering, is apt to be somewhat of an exhibitionist. With a children's audience it is entirely essential, in order to maintain order, never to ask for volunteers.

Having selected a boy and having him walk forward, the magician asks the lad if he is familiar with the game of "Truth or Consequences." The boy will say yes and the magician continues talking and says that he is certain then that he is just the right person to help in the magic. From the start of the trick to the end the magician addresses every remark directly to the boy and while speaking loud enough for everyone to hear, he seems to ignore his audience. The magician states: "Now here is your question. Do you know the alphabet?" To the boy's "sure," "yep," or even a formal "yes, sir," the magician, as if gratified that he has picked the right boy, says, "That's fine."

The magician then explains to the boy that he will receive a box of candy if, without error, he recites the alphabet in 30 seconds. The magician then points to a nicely wrapped and ribbon tied box of candy standing on end on one of his tables. He tells the boy he feels so certain that he will win that he will put the candy box in a paper bag so it will be all ready to take home. Picking up a flat brown paper bag the magician opens it up and stands it on the table alongside the box of candy. The bag is just large enough for the box to go in easily. The box is picked up and dropped into the bag with a thud. The top of the bag is closed by twisting the paper.

The magician then holds up his watch. The magician tells the boy, "You are to start when I give the signal. You have a full 30 seconds to recite the alphabet. And you know you have to say it backwards. Go!"

Usually, the boy will just stand speechless. If he does, the magician will appear surprised and say, "You don't know the alphabet backward! My goodness, what sort of teachers do they have in your school?" Putting the blame immediately on the teachers takes the onus from the boy and at the same time gives him an unanswerable question which takes more time. If by then the 30 seconds have not passed another question can be asked. "Would it be easier for you to say the alphabet in Latin?" At the end of the 30 seconds the magician says, "Oh, that's too bad. I don't remember if I told you that if you didn't answer correctly the candy would disappear." Picking up the paper bag the magician crushes it in his hands until it is just a little wad of paper having no space for a box of candy.

Even before he puts aside the wad of paper he is holding, the magician expresses regret to the boy that the candy has disappeared and thanks him for having been so kind as to come up but announces that for his consequence he will have to be his unpaid assistant. Continuing, the magician expresses the hope that the boy will enjoy helping with the next feat. This should be said in such a way that the boy is assured that the magician really wants him, that his troubles are over, and that he really is a pretty fine fellow. The manner and tone of voice of the magician is as important as his words. It should be said in a man to man manner and never as adult to child. Treat the boy as if he were the man he would like to be. This not only pleases the boy but the adults as well.

The magician goes on to tell the boy that the next feat only can happen when the magic whistle is blown. The boy is given the magic whistle (the cheapest kind of a small whistle) to hold and to protect. The magician shows a cardboard box to be empty and displays the cover of the box. He puts the cover on the box and stands aside. He tells the boy if the whistle is blown properly that the box will become filled with beautiful silk. The way to blow the whistle is to blow two long blows first and then two short blows. "Like this," and the magician puckers his lips and whistles—pheweeee, pheweeee, phet, phet. He tells the boy to blow on his whistle. No matter how the boy blows the magician says, "That is absolutely perfect. Let's see if the silk has arrived."

EXCEPTIONAL MAGIC

Opening the box, by taking off the cover, the magician reaches in the box and pulls out a piece of silk which he holds as high in the air as he can reach. Turning to the boy, the magician says, "You see the whistle worked. Now I'll give you the silk as I take it from the box. You hold it and take care that none of it gets on the floor." The magician hands the end of the silk to the boy, goes back to the box and rapidly pulls silk from the box. The silk is in one long piece. Without looking at the boy, the magician keeps tossing the silk to the youngster who will have extreme difficulty in holding all the silk he has and catching more. This has to be done carefully so it is not obvious that the magician is making the boy's task difficult. As the silk is all in one piece, at the end the boy is as entwined in silk as is a kitten who has found a spool of thread to play with.

When the magician has taken the last of the silk from the box, he turns to the boy and announces, "You have done your job so well that what do you think has happened—the box of candy has come back." Taking the candy from the big box the magician says to the boy, "Here is the candy. You give me the silk and I'll give you the candy." After the boy divests himself from his silken wrapping, the magician takes the silk and gives the boy the box of candy. The silk is stuffed back in the box which it more than fills.

As the boy starts back to his seat, the magician calls out, "Just a minute, son. Next time you go to school ask your teacher if she can recite the alphabet backwards—in 30 seconds."

The feat of making the candy box disappear is very surprising and is as simple to perform as it is striking in effect. The wrapped "candy box" never leaves the paper bag, after it has been dropped inside, because it is so made that it can be crumpled up with the paper bag. This never occurs to the audience because they not only see the box of candy but are assured of its solidity by hearing the thud when the box is dropped into the bag. The "box" actually is only a narrow piece of cardboard formed to the same size rectangle as makes the sides and ends of the real box of candy. The rectangle has a metal weight attached to it. Fancy wrapping paper is folded around this cardboard form and the edges secured with cellophane tape. Around this empty package, ribbon is tied and the ends made into an attractive bow. The actual box of candy is wrapped in like paper, with the same folds, and tied with matching ribbon and bow. The real box and the pseudo box must be identical in appearance.

This is the way the disappearing box is made. First is formed the inner cardboard frame. The cardboard is cut 1″ longer than the combined length of the four sides of the rectangle and this extra inch is bent and pasted, at the inside corner of the rectangle, to the other end of the cardboard strip. When pasted the rectangle will hold its shape if no pressure is put on it. In the center of the cardboard at one end of the rectangle is punched a small hole. This hole is only large enough to permit the arms of a split paper fastener to go through. To the cardboard, on the inside of the rectangle, is placed a metal block with a hole drilled through it. By means of the

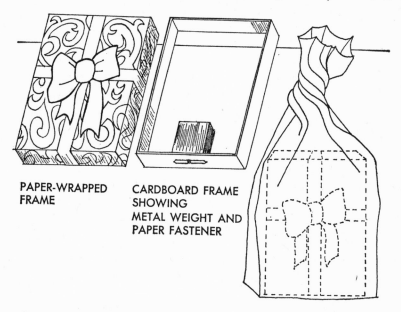

PAPER-WRAPPED
FRAME

CARDBOARD FRAME
SHOWING
METAL WEIGHT AND
PAPER FASTENER

paper fastener the weight is attached to the cardboard, at the center of one end. The block of metal should be approximately 1¾″ long, 1¼″ wide, and ½″ thick. Such a block, made of any heavy metal, will weigh about 6 ounces which is heavy enough to hold the box upright when stood on end and will make a thud, quite like the sound of a box full of candy, when the pseudo box is dropped into the paper bag. The metal weight is small enough so that the space it takes up, when bag and "box" are crushed, never will be noticed.

When the weighted cardboard frame is wrapped and tied the "box of candy" may be handled as if it were a real, filled box. All that has to be remembered is always to take hold of the box at an edge and grasp it so the fingers are on top of the box and the thumb on the bottom. Actually, it is the edges of the inner cardboard which the fingers press against. The paper, with which the cardboard form is wrapped, gives enough body to the package so that it will hold its shape though it will not allow pressure except against the edges of the cardboard. At the beginning, as will be recalled, the pseudo box stands on end on the table. The weighted end is next to the table and the top of the box, with the bow of ribbon, is toward the audience. The box is picked up, when needed, by grasping the top end. The fingers go on the top of the box and the thumb on the bottom and both thumb and fingers take hold of the edges of the cardboard form.

Once the pseudo box is in the paper bag the top of the bag is twisted so as to close the bag. While this is a normal thing to do, it is necessary in this instance so that when the bag is crushed no part of the box or ribbon is disclosed. Because of its construction, the box will crumple up inside the bag with very little pressure. The bag first is flattened from top to bottom and then is squeezed into a crumpled ball of paper. Care should be taken to put the bag aside casually, but carefully. It is not to be dropped on the table for the weight still inside the paper would be heard.

Two final details on the disappearance of the box inside the paper bag. The magician has told the boy that his inability to recite the alphabet backwards from Z to A would cause the candy to disappear and he crushes the bag to show that the disappearance has occurred. The magician is careful not to act as if he were making the candy disappear. The magician has nothing to do with the vanishing of the candy in his actions and he must act as if he were as sorry as the boy at the loss of the candy.

The other detail is that the magician may find a boy who can recite the alphabet backwards within 30 seconds. To be prepared for this most unlikely situation it is essential that the magician himself has learned the alphabet in reverse. Parenthetically, this is a mnemonic task of only a few minutes provided the letters be written in groups of 3—zyx—wvu—tsr—etc. and learned in that manner. If the magician knows the reverse alphabet he probably will catch an error and an error probably will be made. If, however, no error is made and the recitation is completed within the half minute the plot of the trick changes. Then the magician compliments the boy on his ability and picks up the paper bag holding the candy box. As he starts to hand the bag to the boy the magician says, "You realize that this is magic candy and has to be treated in a certain way—never squeeze it like this or it will disappear."

Holding the crushed bag in his hands, the magician looks most sad and says, "Just look, I've done just what I told you not to do. You must help me to get your candy back." The trick then proceeds in exactly the same way as if the boy hadn't been so smart. That is, the magician claims that the box will reappear inside the cardboard box which has just been shown empty as soon as the boy properly blows the whistle. The magician says nothing at all about the silk this time and appears to be both surprised and a little annoyed when he finds the silk upon opening the box. As he holds up the end of the silk the magician tells the boy that there seems to be something else in the box and he asks the boy to hold the silk as he looks for the candy.

The cardboard box is one sold as a container in which to pack a gift. Such boxes are made to enhance the appearance of the present and often are covered with colorful paper of attractive design. (Most variety stores sell such gift boxes). What seems to be one of the standard sizes is a box 12″ long, 7″ wide and 6″ high. The cover of the box fits over the top and extends about an inch down the sides. A box of such a size, or approximately so, is admirable for the trick. The box should be covered with paper of bright colors and with some involved pattern. Of course, any well made cardboard box, with a separate cover, can be used and it is quite easy to paste gift paper of suitable design to the outside of both box and cover.

Starting with a cardboard box of the right size and appearance, the magician transforms it into a trick box. As everyone is familiar with cardboard boxes and how completely untricky they are, it never occurs to anyone that any cardboard box could be responsible for the magic. The box is tricked by having two doors which open into the box and leave a large hole. The doors are made in one of the long sides of the box and open like a double barn door. Due to the design of the fancy paper covering the box, the doors, when closed, are not visible when the box is shown to the audience as just an empty cardboard box.

In preparing the box the first thing that is done is to cut a hole in one side of the box. In the size box mentioned, the hole is 8″ long by 4⅝″ high. The top of the hole should be even with the bottom of the part of the cover which comes down the side of the box. The bottom of the hole should be exactly at the inside level of the bottom of the box. The cutting of the box must be done with extreme care so that each corner is entirely straight. The cutting should be done with a razor-like blade and made from the outside of the box to insure that the paper covering the box is not torn. Wood should be held against the inside of the box as the knife is used to make certain of a clean cut. The utmost care must be used when making the bottom cut so as to have it exactly even with the inside surface of the bottom of the box. Care also must be used to have the piece of the box which is cut out left in perfect condition. Once it is removed from the box, that

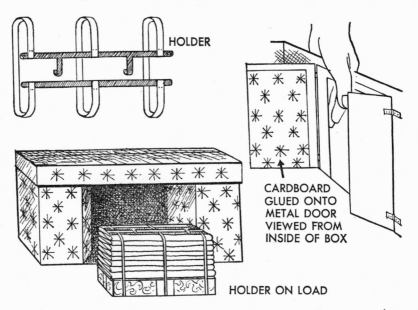

HOLDER

CARDBOARD
GLUED ONTO
METAL DOOR
VIEWED FROM
INSIDE OF BOX

HOLDER ON LOAD

piece has to be cut precisely in half lengthwise so as to have two pieces 4″ long.

The next step in preparing the box is to cut a piece of tin of a size to fit snugly inside the box and completely covering the entire side where the hole has been made. Then the tin is cut to the form of an arch. The opening of the arch is ¼″ bigger at each side and ¼″ higher than the hole in the box. Two doors are cut of tin the same thickness as was used in making the arch. These doors are hinged to the sides of the arch. Small hinges (no bigger than ¾″) are used and are attached to the tin by very small rivets. To use small rivets, holes have to be drilled of the proper size. The screw holes found in most hinges are too large to use. When the arch of tin with its hinged doors is glued inside of the box it will be found that the doors will close but cannot be pushed through the hole due to their being larger than the hole in the cardboard. The next task in finishing the box is to glue the pieces of cardboard which were cut from the box to the tin doors. This is done while the doors are closed in order to get the cardboard exactly in position. The last thing to be done is to cover the exposed surface of the tin inside the box with white paper. After the paper is attached it is cut so as to permit the doors to open.

In presenting the trick, the box, with its doors closed and with its cover in place, stands on another table about 3″ in front of a package of the candy box and silk which later are mysteriously produced, and hides them from the audience. First, the cover is taken off the box and stood on its side behind the box, but in front of the candy and silk. It is held upright by the left hand and masks the silk and candy. The right hand takes hold of the back of the box by placing the fingers on the inside against the top of the doors, and the thumb on the outside just above the doors. Holding the box in this manner precludes any chance of the doors opening inadvertently. The box is lifted in the air and, by twisting the wrist, given a quarter turn. Swinging the arm to the right shows the audience the inside of the box. The box is turned back so that it can be placed back on the table. In showing the box which looks like, and the audience believes to be, an ordinary empty cardboard box all the magician has done is to show the box to be empty. He does this quite rapidly for there is no need to take any appreciable amount of time to demonstrate anything quite so obvious. When the box is back on the table the cover is replaced on top of the box. The cover is put on first at the back and brought down to cover the front. As the front of the box is being pressed in place the right hand on the cover pushes the box toward the back of the table. Simultaneously, the left hand goes behind the hidden package and pushes it into the box. This is not noticed by the audience for all the magician seems to be doing is fitting the cover on the box.

In mentioning the candy box and silk it has been called a package and if these two items are to be handled easily they have to be made into a package. The package has to be so made that it will take the smallest possible space, hold together firmly, and yet easily and instantly made ready to take out of the box. Assuming that the candy box is 4″ x 6″ and 1½″ deep (a standard size) the silk is pleated so as to go on top of the box. In other words the silk is pleated to 4″ x 6″ and placed on top of the box. The silk is held to the box by three bands of elastic. These pieces of elastic not only hold the silk to the box but compress the silk so that it takes up the least possible space. Pure silk should be used because it not only will compress into a smaller space than is possible with any other material but, when released, looks better as it shows fewer wrinkles and creases. The silk should be of the sheerest quality. It will be found that 10 yards of such thin silk, which usually comes 29″ wide, will compress into a bundle small enough to be used in the trick. When permitted to expand that amount of silk becomes spectacularly large. (See illustration.)

In order that there is no fumbling, the elastic bands which hold the package together have to be made so they can be released easily and instantly. By the term elastic is meant that fabric made elastic by rubber woven into it. Such elastic may be purchased in varying colors and widths. As it never will be seen the color is immaterial, but the width should be at least ½″. One and a half yards of elastic should be sufficient. The elastic is cut into 3 pieces of equal length. The release is designed not only to detach all three bands simultaneously but also to help compress the silk while the bands are in place. The release is made of two strips of metal 6″ long and approximately ¼″ wide and 1/16″ thick. To one of the strips two hooks are soldered. These hooks have shanks 1¼″ long and are made of the same metal as are the strips. The hooks are soldered at right angles on to the strip and 3″ apart —that is each hook is 1¼″ from the end of the strip. Both strips have small holes drilled at the center. To one of the strips the 3 pieces of elastic are sewn—1 piece of elastic is sewn at one end of the strip, another piece at the center and the third piece at the other end. The end of each piece of elastic is wrapped around the metal strip and sewn together. The elastic, through the holes drilled through the metal, is then fastened to the strip. (See illustration.) That strip is placed on top of the pleated silk which is on top of the candy box. The strips of elastic are wrapped around the package and looped around the second bar which has been hooked to the first. Each elastic is pulled almost, but not quite, as far as it will stretch and marked so that it can be taken off the package and sewn to the strip. It will be seen, because of the long shanks of the hooks, that the strips are ½″ apart when hooked. Because of this separation all that has to be done to release the hooks—and the 3 elastic bands—is to press the strips together. The pull of the elastic will disengage the hooks when the pressure is applied.

A final note. Although the candy box and silk are hidden from the audience until both are produced, the candy and silk package could be seen by the boy. He will not notice it during the alphabet and vanishing candy routine for there is nothing to call it to his attention. While the magician shows the box to the audience he has the boy stand so that the magician's body hides the package from the boy.

MAGIC DYE

WHILE being an excellent effect as far as the mystery is concerned, this effect has the extra qualification of being very amusing. It is amusing because of the way in which it is presented and also due to the audience's belief, at one point, that the magician has been detected in his trickery. When he proves that he wasn't caught that too causes laughter.

At the spot in his program where he is about to introduce the feat, the magician, in a most serious manner, says:

"Were this a program on TV, or radio, it would be interrupted at this point for a commercial. As others do so, I feel it permissible for me, too. However, I am not going to advertise the product of anyone else. I am introducing my own new product called, 'Magic Dye.' This dye is by far the best on the market because it is possible to have exactly the colors you want and it is so, so very easy to use. And so clean to use, no liquid, no mess. And, finally, it takes but seconds to do the job. But let me prove my statements by a demonstration."

The magician picks up a carton having a label with the words "Magic Dye" in two lines of large, heavy letters at the top and his name in smaller, lighter letters at the bottom. He states the carton contains the magic dye powder which does all the work and that all the purchaser needs to do is to open the carton and push in the material. As this statement is made the magician opens the top of the carton. He then picks up a white silk handkerchief and pushes it in the carton. When that is completely inside the carton, a second white silk and, finally, a third are treated the same way. As the handkerchiefs go into the carton, the magician continues talking in the non-stop way announcers have.

"While in this demonstration I am using pure silk, the dye will give equally good results when used for cotton, wool, or any one of the synthetic materials. Nor is this dye limited to cloths of small size. For those who wish to color large pieces of material there also are the large economy size carton, and the super-bargain size carton."

By the time this is said the silks will have been put into the carton. The magician continues, "Now all that has to be done is to reclose the carton (this is done), to decide upon the color, or colors, wanted, and to shake the magic dye powder over the cloth."

When properly acted and spoken the spectators are not certain whether, or not, the magician is serious until he makes the statement about deciding on the color, or colors to be used. This ridiculous claim puts everything back into the realm of magic. The magician continues in speech and action to be most serious and as if he expected to be believed.

"Let me see," the magician goes on talking, "I believe I have put three silks into the box. Now the colors I want are a beautiful orange, a deep gorgeous red, and a navy blue. Now all that has to be done is to shake the powder all over the cloth." Taking the box between his two hands, he slowly waves, not shakes, the box back and forth in the most completely listless manner possible, as he says, "You can see how easy this is."

Having held the box with both hands, it is very easy to turn the box around so that when it is again taken and held in the left hand, the box is upside down. The magician must not look at the box as this is done. He is looking at and talking to the audience and inverting the box must seem to be inadvertent.

"The dying is completed and all that needs to be done is to open the carton and take out the material." As the magician says these words, he opens the bottom of the carton, which now is uppermost, and, with his right hand, takes out the first silk. "A perfect orange," the magician announces as he shakes out the first silk. This he slips under one of the fingers of the left hand which is holding the box. Reaching into the box he pulls out the second silk. "A magnificent red." This red silk is put with the orange one. As he brings the third silk from the box, the magician says, "And the navy blue. Each silk exactly the shade I wished for." The orange and the red silks are taken back into the hand holding the blue and all three put under the left arm, which holds them squeezed between the arm and body.

Unless every member of the audience is unbelievably reticent, one or more persons will gleefully call the magician's attention to the very obvious fact that the carton is upside down. This would seem likely to have something to do with the change in color of the handkerchiefs. If not too many mention the inverted position of the box, the magician ignores those who do call out. If so many speak out that they can't be ignored, the magician merely states, "That makes no difference," and goes on with his sales talk. In either instance, once the handkerchiefs have been taken from the carton and are tucked under his arm, the magician says, "I seem to have been awkward and turned the box upside down. It really makes no difference whether the box is top end or bottom end uppermost." As this is said, he quickly closes the bottom, turns the box over, opens the top and peers inside. He goes on talking, "It really makes no difference for, you know, the only purpose of the carton is to hold the magic dye powder. Once the dye has been used, there is no further need for the carton." With these final words, the magician tears the carton a number of times and lets the pieces flutter to the floor. This may be done, for the carton is needed only to hide the working of the magic and is devoid of trickery.

The carton I use is yellow cardboard without any printing on it. It is 8¼" high, 6¼" wide, and 2¼" deep. It is a standard size. While I purchase the cartons I use in lots of 500, those who perform infrequently may wish to make their own. The easiest way to do this is to buy some food, or household product, packed in a carton of the requisite size. The carton is carefully opened and used as a pattern to cut colored cardboard, which is sold in stationery stores. The overlap, running the height of the box, is glued. The top is folded and held in place by cellophane tape of the same color as the cardboard. The bottom likewise is folded and taped.

I had a label 6¼" high and 4¼" wide printed on gummed paper. When the label is pasted on the face of the box it has a 1" margin of box all around it. Whether the labels are hand drawn, or printed, is immaterial but the design is most important. It has to be very obvious when the label is upside down.

The three white handkerchiefs, the orange one and the red one are exactly as they appear to be; that is, 18" hemmed squares of silk. The blue silk is of the same size but an addition has been made to it. This addition is a tube 4" long and 2" in diameter. I used a plastic tube though it may be made of metal. Whatever the material of the tube, it should be both light in weight and rigid. At each end of the tube the edges must be rounded and completely smooth so that there can be no possibility of a silk being caught. Around one end of the tube, a number of holes are drilled. These holes need be only large enough for a needle and thread to pass through. To this end of the tube is sewn a conical shaped piece of silk. The cone is made of material identical to that of the handkerchief. The cone is 2" in diameter at its base, or just large enough to slip over the outside of the tube. The silk is pushed on to the tube ½" and is sewed to it. From the tube the silk cone tapers to a sharp point. The silk cone is 9" long. The point of the tube is sewed to one corner of the blue handkerchief. In order to have the tip of the cone sewed in the proper position, the handkerchief should be laid flat on a table. The cone and tube then are put on the handkerchief. The tip of the silk cone is put at one corner of the handkerchief and the bottom opening of the tube should point towards the diagonally opposite corner of the handkerchief. The handkerchief then is folded over the cone and tube until the two other diagonal corners meet. When this is done, the cone and tube are hidden inside the folded handkerchief. The tip of the silk cone then is sewed to the folded corner of the silk so that the folded corner and cone tip are securely fastened together. Finally, in a line halfway between the center fold of the handkerchief and its double edges, the two thicknesses of the handkerchief are sewed together. From the corner where the tip of the cone had been attached, the sewing runs for 1' down the handkerchief. It will be seen by holding the handkerchief by the corner, where the tip of the cone is attached, that the silk hangs diagonally in natural folds and hides the tubing completely.

When the magician introduces the carton of magic dye, the three colored silks are inside it. He claims the carton contains a quantity of magic dye powder. There is no need to amplify this statement by showing the powder nor the inside of the carton where the powder is said to be. Therefore, the colored handkerchiefs are safely in the carton for they are unseen and their existence unsuspected. The colored silks have to be put into the carton in a particular manner. Both ends of the carton are open when the silks are put inside.

This is the way the silks are arranged before they are pushed into the carton. All of the blue silk which hangs below the lower end of the tube is pushed back until at least an inch of the tube is exposed. The silk which is pushed back is bunched about the tube and held. Tube and bunched silk are held so that the open end of the tube points up and the corner of the silk, where the tip of the cone is sewed, hangs down. The two silks of the other colors are then held against the tube. One corner of each silk must hang down as far as the hanging corner of the blue silk. Then the rest of each of these silks is bunched around the tube. At this point, the tube and bunches of the three silks are held with one corner of each silk hanging

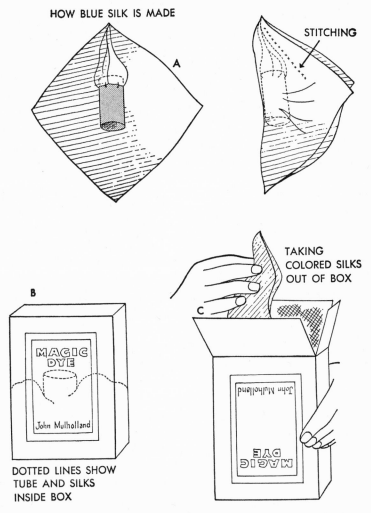

HOW BLUE SILK IS MADE

A

STITCHING

B

TAKING
COLORED SILKS
OUT OF BOX

C

MAGIC
DYE

John Mulholland

DOTTED LINES SHOW
TUBE AND SILKS
INSIDE BOX

down. Retaining hold of tube and silks, the three corners are inserted in the top of the carton. Once in the carton, the corners, reaching into the open bottom end of the carton, are pulled through the carton until they extend a couple of inches. The corners are then pushed back into the carton and the bottom folded and fastened with tape. While these things are done the tube and silk continue to be held with the hand inside the carton. After the bottom is sealed, the tube and silks are released. The silks probably will be at the bottom of the carton, and at the side of the tube and with the open end of the tube exposed. If it happens that any silk covers the mouth of the tube, it should be pushed aside. The top of the box then is folded, closed, and taped. In sealing the box with tape, it is most important to remember to turn under a quarter inch of one end of the tape, sticking it to itself. This will make a small tab by which the tape can be pulled free of the carton instantly and without fumbling. The carton, with its colored handkerchiefs, is ready for performance.

When the magician has reached the point in his "sales talk" where he opens the top of the carton, he first pulls on the tape. The tape is pulled only far enough so the carton may be opened, but the one end is left attached to the back of the carton so the tape is in position to reseal the top after the white handkerchiefs have been inserted. In opening the top of the carton each of the four flaps are folded back so that they stand up straight. In doing this, the magician looks into the carton for the position of the tube. He sticks two fingers in the tube and raises it almost to the top of the carton. Due to the dimensions of the carton and the size of the tube, a little extra pressure on the outside of the carton will hold the tube firmly in place. When the white handkerchiefs are put into the carton, they actually are pushed into the tube. As the second and third handkerchiefs are pushed into the tube the first handkerchief goes through the tube and inside the cone of silk. Due to the silk pocket and the size of the tube, the handkerchiefs go in so easily that the magician seems, as he says he is doing, merely to be putting the white silks into the carton. After all the handkerchiefs are inside the carton, and the tube, the top of the box is closed and resealed.

The reason the magician holds the carton with both hands as he "shakes the magic dye powder over the material" is it makes it easier to invert the box without his seemingly being aware that he has done so. Opening the bottom of the carton now uppermost, the magician takes hold of the corner of the orange silk and pulls it out. After showing the silk he slides it under the fingers of the hand holding the carton. The corner of the red silk is taken and it, too, withdrawn, shown, and transferred to the other hand. Finally the corner of the blue silk is grasped. As this handkerchief is taken from the carton, the silk will fall over the tube and hide it and the white handkerchiefs it contains. There is no worry connected with this action for if the silks were packed as described, it cannot help happening. The hand holding the blue silk takes back the orange and red handkerchiefs and puts all three under the arm. The box is torn into pieces. The handkerchiefs are taken from under the arm, crushed together and put aside. Put the handkerchiefs aside, do not drop them, for the tube might clunk if it hits the table.

The prepared silk has to be of a dark color so that neither tube nor white silks will show through. The other two silks may be of any shade as long as the colors are strong and of great contrast.

ANOTHER CENTURY

BEYOND the Biblical years of three score and ten the plot of this colorful piece of magic has been popular with audiences. In the last century, it was felt that the idea was so advanced it was named "The Twentieth Century." During the years since it was originated, magicians have devised dozens of methods for doing it. Some of the methods required difficult sleight-of-hand. The simpler ways for performing it either became too well known or did not appeal to me. The method about to be described requires no sleight-of-hand and I like it—not because it is mine but because it is popular with audiences. It is so popular with audiences that very possibly it will be shown for "another century."

The simplicity of the plot makes the magic easy to follow and the colorful silk handkerchiefs used in the feat are most attractive. The mystery is particularly good because the climax of the magic occurs in the hands of the spectator.

This is what the audience sees. The magician shows two silk handkerchiefs alike in color, and gives them to a spectator to hold. Taking another handkerchief of a different color, the magician walks several feet away from the spectator and causes his handkerchief to disappear. The magician then instructs the spectator to shake out the handkerchiefs he is holding. It is discovered that the handkerchief which had disappeared a moment before is now tied in between the two handkerchiefs held by the spectator. The surprise of the audience is surpassed only by the spectator who is the assistant.

While this is an accurate description of what the audience sees, it is a digested version. To make the secret things the magician does easier to follow, it will be well to know in detail all the audience can see.

The magician picks up from his prop table a tray which he carries over to one of his performance tables. Hanging down from the front of this tray are three silk handkerchiefs. The tray is placed at the front of the table so that the handkerchiefs hang over the edge of the table. The two handkerchiefs of the same color are on either side of a third and different colored handkerchief. On the tray there also are two tumblers and a paper tube which has been flattened. After calling the attention of the audience to the three handkerchiefs, the magician picks up the silk of the different color, crumples it and sticks it into one of the glasses. This is done most casually as if the magician merely wanted to get that handkerchief momentarily out of the way. As this is the fact it therefore requires no acting on the part of the magician. The magician picks up one, then the second silk of like color, crumples them and puts them in the second glass. This glass he immediately picks up and gives to a spectator whom he asks to come forward. The spectator is instructed to hold the glass in a way that the audience can see it, and the handkerchiefs, at all times. The spectator is asked to stand some distance away from the performer's table.

The magician removes the single handkerchief, the one of different color, from the glass, straightens it out, and shows it to the audience. He explains that in order to do the magic it is necessary to have four knots tied into the handkerchief. He puts the handkerchief on the table, folds it into a strip and, using two diagonally opposite corners, ties four single knots into the handkerchief. Picking up the knotted handkerchief, the magician puts it back into the glass. He picks up the flattened paper tube and opens it. The tube is an inch higher than the glass and just big enough in circumference so that it slips over the glass easily. The tube is put over the glass so that the handkerchief is hidden. Still standing by the table, the magician, with his left hand, picks up the tray with its covered glass. With his right hand, he takes the tube and its glass from the tray. He puts the tray, upside down, back on the table.

The magician then puts the glass and tube on the palm of his outstretched left hand as he tells the audience what is about to happen. The magician says that he is going to cause the (naming color) silk in the glass he is holding to go over to the other glass. He also, he says, is going to demand that the handkerchief use the knots which have been put in it to tie itself in between the other two handkerchiefs. He then most fairly and quite deliberately takes the tube off the glass. The handkerchief, most obviously, is no longer in the glass which is put back on the table. The tube is held up so the audience can see through it, flattened, and dropped back on the table. The assistant is requested to pull the silks out of his glass. The handkerchiefs come out in a long string and with the third handkerchief tied between the other two.

Besides the tray, two glasses, paper tube and three handkerchiefs of which the audience is aware, a duplicate of the different colored silk is required. The secret preparation and devices needed will be explored in the order in which the action of the trick takes place.

An oblong tray 5″ x 8″ is an excellent size for this feat. The tray should be of considerable weight. The reason for the required weight will be apparent in the description of its use. Two small screws are put into the top and along one narrow side of the tray. The screws are put near the corners of the tray and about an inch from the edge. Over the heads of these screws is stretched a rubber band, so that the two strands of elastic will cross the top at one end of the tray. This edge will be termed the front of the tray. The rubber band is used to hold the corners of the three handkerchiefs when they hang over the front edge of the tray.

Three of the handkerchiefs (two of one color with the different color between) are tied together using square knots. (Square knots are best to use in tying silks because they will not slip, and yet to separate the handkerchiefs all that has to be done is to pull on one of the corners extending from the knot and then pull on the handkerchief and the corner will slip right through the knot.) The corner of one of two handkerchiefs of like color is tied to a corner of the silk of different color, and the second silk of the first color is tied to the diagonally opposite corner of the silk of different color. The silks should then be placed on a table in a row and spread out so they form three attached diamonds. The handkerchiefs are in a horizontal row directly in front of you. The handkerchief to the left, we will call handkerchief 1; the handkerchief of different color, to which it is tied, we will call handkerchief 2; the next handkerchief which is of the same color as handkerchief 1 and is also tied to handkerchief 2, we will call handkerchief 3. One corner of each handkerchief is pointed away from you. The diagonal opposite corner is pointed toward you. The other two corners of each handkerchief are to your right and left. To make this description easier to follow, we will call those corners at the top of each diamond—those corners away from you—A; the corners to the right, B; the corners at the bottom of the diamond—those toward you—C; and the corners to your left, D. In this position, corner B of handkerchief 1 is tied to corner D of handkerchief 2 and corner B of handkerchief 2 is tied to corner

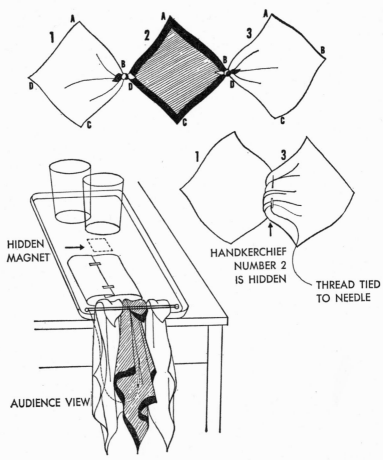

D of handkerchief 3. The handkerchiefs should have been placed on the table so that the sides of the knots with the protruding ends will be uppermost.

At this point, corners A and C of handkerchief 2—the center handkerchief—should be pleated each toward the center. After this has been done, corner B of handkerchief 2 is pleated toward corner D. Since corner B of handkerchief 2 is tied to corner D of handkerchief 3, this also will bring handkerchief 3 to the left. The pleating is continued until the entire handkerchief 2, along with the corner D of handkerchief 3, is over corner B of handkerchief 1. Then continue to pleat the bundle to the left in corner B of handkerchief 1 just enough so that it is entirely covered—i.e., handkerchief 2 is now completely hidden between the corners D of handkerchief 3 and B of handkerchief 1. The silks are held securely in this position by means of a needle which is used as a pin. The needle is put into the material from the bottom of the bundle toward the top, so that the eye of the needle is pointing downward. A black silk thread is put through the eye of the needle and tied, leaving a couple of feet of thread hanging down. I use a # 7 darner's needle.

Now lift up handkerchiefs 1 and 3 by grasping corner A of each and bring them to the tray. It appears as if there were only the two handkerchiefs of like color because the bundle of handkerchief 2 is completely hidden in the folds of the handkerchiefs 1 and 2. The corner A of handkerchief 1 is pushed under the rubber band at the left corner of the tray. Corner A of handkerchief 3 is pushed under the band at the right corner of the tray. Corners A, prior to being put under the rubber, should be folded over about 1". This will leave the corner in a position to be grasped easily and, as it is pulled, the handkerchief automatically will be free from the band.

The loose end of the black silk thread is tied to one of the screws holding the rubber band. The thread should hang loosely with the handkerchiefs.

A corner of the duplicate different colored silk is put under the rubber at the center of the tray so that handkerchief hangs between the other two. When this silk is picked up, as it obviously is not attached to the other handkerchiefs, it is most convincing evidence that the other silks also are separate. As these handkerchiefs appear to be separate and, seemingly are picked up separately, it will never occur to anyone that they might be other than separate. The way these attached silks are picked up is, with the right hand, to pull free of the elastic the corner of the silk at the right. Holding firmly to this corner, the hand is brought up an inch, or so, and brought partially in front of the other silk. The left hand pulls that corner free and the two hands are brought together, both being raised several inches, and the corner in the right hand is transferred to the left hand so that both corners are held together. The right hand goes loosely around both silks as the left continues to be raised slowly and, as it is lifted, is brought back over the tray. When the silks have been raised through the right hand until the bundle of hidden silk is inside the hand all the silks are gripped tightly with the right hand. Now, with both hands, as the silks are raised still higher, the black silk thread attached to the tray will pull the needle out of the silks. (Because of the weight of the tray, there will be no difficulty in freeing the needle.) As the right hand keeps the hidden silk from the sight of the audience, the left hand brings to the right hand all of the silk outside the hand except a corner of one silk. This should be the corner D which is diagonally opposite the corner which is tied to the hidden handkerchief. All the rest of the silk goes into a bundle which is pushed into the right hand. The bundle then is put into the empty glass. The bundle so goes into the glass that the one free corner is on top in a position for the spectator to take hold of it at the climax of the feat. The rest of the trick is exactly as described in what the audience sees. The silk filled glass is given to a spectator who holds it until he is asked to pull the silks out of the glass.

Going back to the table, the magician, with one hand, takes hold of the handkerchief in the glass (the duplicate different color handkerchief) and begins slowly to pull it out. The other hand slides the needle, which had been dropped on the tray, so that it goes under the rubber bands where it will be held. By the time the needle is in place, the handkerchief will be free of the glass. The magician then grasps the handkerchief with both hands and holds it by two corners of one side of the handkerchief so that the audience can see it is just an attractively colored silk handkerchief. It is an attractive silk handkerchief, but, as advertisers are wont to say, something has been added. This is a disc of steel, or iron, about 1″ in diameter, and 1/16″ thick. (An iron washer of the proper size can be used.) The silk I use for the trick has a border of solid color and with a piece of silk of matching color a pocket was made sewing the disc near one corner of the silk. When at the beginning of the trick, and later when the handkerchief is shown to the audience, the corner of the handkerchief having the disc always is held in the hand. After the handkerchief has been shown to the audience, the magician announces that the magic requires that four knots be tied in the silk. As he makes his statement the magician lays the handkerchief flat on the table. The corner with the disc is put toward the audience, but not released, and the diagonally opposite corner points towards the back of the table. In an action which is continuous, the handkerchief is placed on the table and the corner with the disc brought back and put on the center of the handkerchief. As this is done with one hand, the other picks up the lower corner and places it over the disc. The other two corners of the handkerchief are then taken, one in each hand. These corners are tied with a simple knot and the knot pulled quite tight. Three more knots, one at a time, are rapidly tied on top of the first. The result should be a little bundle of silk having at its bottom (through two layers of silk) the steel disc. The silk bundle, disc side down, is pushed all the way back into the glass. The paper tube is shown to the audience and put over the glass.

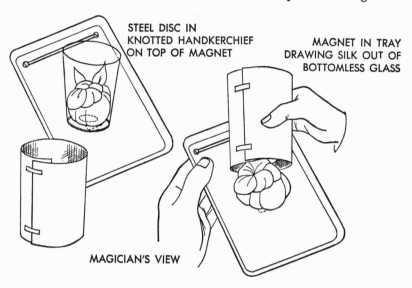

STEEL DISC IN
KNOTTED HANDKERCHIEF
ON TOP OF MAGNET

MAGNET IN TRAY
DRAWING SILK OUT OF
BOTTOMLESS GLASS

MAGICIAN'S VIEW

It is time for the reader to know two things of which the audience is never aware. The first is that this glass has no bottom. The second is that a flat magnet is embedded in the tray. It is suggested that both tumblers used in the trick should be of the transparent plastic variety. They should be identical in appearance for the one handled by the spectator convinces the audience that its mate, which is the same in looks, is the same in fact. It is simple to remove the bottom of such a tumbler by drilling a small hole and then through that hole using a coping saw, or a jeweler's saw, to cut around the edge of the bottom. The magnet should be square, or round, and no thicker than the bottom of the tray. The surface of the magnet should be a little larger than the steel disc in the handkerchief. A hole should be cut in the bottom of the tray and the magnet glued in place so that the top of the magnet is exactly flush with the surface of the tray. The hole should be centered in the bottom of the tray. The magnet is painted to match the rest of the tray.

It will be obvious that when the steel disc, inside the handkerchief, is put into the bottomless tumbler and the tumbler is placed over the magnet that the disc will stick to the magnet. Upon raising the glass, the handkerchief will be pulled out of the glass, because it too is attached to the tray. This may be done quite easily and without the knowledge of the audience. It will be recalled that the glass is covered with a paper tube. Because of that covering the audience cannot see when the handkerchief is or is not in the tube. When the magician lifts the tube covered tumbler off the tray, he does so with the right hand. The left hand has hold of the left side of the tray. That hand tilts up the front of the tray as the tumbler is raised from it. The tray is raised until the bottom of the tray is towards the audience. The tray is lowered until an edge is on the table and then dropped, back up, on to the table. Because of the flanges of the tray enough space will be found under the tray to hide the handkerchief. The move of tilting the tray as the glass is raised should be tried out in front of a mirror to find out exactly how each hand should move so that the handkerchief never is disclosed.

When the tray is on the table and the magician steps forward holding the glass, the trick actually is done. However, the degree to which the magic is effective depends upon his speech, actions, and manner at this point. When he speaks about the knotted handkerchief he holds he looks into the top of the glass. When he states, "I will make this handkerchief leave the glass I hold," he points at his glass. In other words it is the sincerity of the acting at this part of the trick which makes it a miracle rather than merely an excellent bit of magic. The manner in which the magician takes the tube off the glass and shows the tube to be empty is part and parcel of this acting.

At the end of the trick the magician, after thanking the assistant, takes the glass and the three handkerchiefs from him. The magician goes back to the table on which are the rest of the properties he used in the trick. He places the glass on the table. He very loosely bunches up the three handkerchiefs and puts them on the tray which he turns right side up. The three handkerchiefs are used as a shield to keep the audience from seeing the fourth handkerchief as the tray is turned over. The silks are placed on the tray so as to cover the fourth handkerchief when the tray is right side up. After returning the two glasses and the paper tube, the tray is picked up and put back on the prop table.

Whereas, in this feat, there is no sleight-of-hand and nothing the magician is required to do is at all difficult, it is he, after all, who has to do all that is done. First of all, therefore, he must be certain that he knows exactly what has to be done. Then he must do the trick in its entirety until he can do each part easily, confidently and, almost, automatically. The practice need not be lengthy, once the magician really knows what is required, for the routine is quickly learned.

THE OBEDIENT COLORS

THIS feat of magic appeals to men because of its impossibility; women like it because it is attractive and colorful; and children find it interesting because it is done with objects with which they are familiar. The trick will fit into any program as it takes little time to perform and the effect is unusual.

The magician makes a number of colored blocks rearrange themselves in a box to form a color pattern chosen by a spectator. Nine cubic wooden blocks are used. Each face of a cube is painted a different color. The same six colors are used on all nine blocks. The box used to hold the blocks is just large enough for the purpose. There is nothing tricky about the box and each cube is solid wood. At the beginning, the empty box is shown and filled with the colored blocks. The audience can see that the colors on the faces of the blocks are in no particular pattern and quite as chance might bring. A cover on the box is closed and the box set aside. A spectator chooses 3 of the 6 colors and also chooses the sequence of those 3 colors. After the color selection has been made, the box is reopened to show that the blocks have rearranged themselves to show only the 3 chosen colors and to show them in the order designated.

The colors used on the blocks are: red, white, blue, green, yellow and black.

The box, as has been said, is without trickery in its construction. It is merely a frame large enough to hold 3 rows of blocks with each row containing 3 blocks. The frame has the depth of a block. To the sides of this frame two doors are hinged—one at the front and one at the back. The doors are hinged on opposite sides of the frame. The front door swings to the right and the back door swings to the left. When the box is turned around back to front the door then at the front will swing to the right exactly as before. In short, whichever way the box is turned it will have the same appearance. The inside surfaces of both box and doors should be covered with felt in order to keep the blocks from rattling inside the box. At the top of the box is a handle.

The wooden cubes should be about 2 inches square. They can be made from a dressed piece of 2 x 2 lumber which actually is $1\frac{7}{8}''$ to a side. Or suitable blocks may be found in a store selling toys. In either instance, the blocks have to be colored properly.

The principal secret of the trick is the manner in which the blocks are painted. Whereas each block is like the other blocks inasmuch as the same six colors are used on all the blocks, the relationship of one color to the colors on adjacent sides varies. This difference never will be noticed for it is extremely difficult to attempt to keep track of the relationship of the six sides of a cube. As example, it is the very rare person who could tell how dice are numbered. This is true even among those who know that the opposite sides of a die will always add up to seven. It is even harder to keep track of colors as they cannot be added. The relationship and sequence of the colors on each cube will be given after a description of the routine followed in handling the blocks.

At the start of the magic the performer introduces the box which is on a table. He picks it up by the handle. He opens the front door of the box and shows the nine cubes which fill the box. Leaving the door open, the box is turned around and the back door, which has been brought to the front, is opened. The magician, after having shown the back of the blocks again, reverses the box and places it on a table. The doors are left open. By pressing on the back of a block with the finger of one hand, the magician pushes the cube out of the front of the box where it is taken with the other hand. All six sides of the cube are shown and attention called to the six different colors. The block is placed on the table to the magician's right and a distance in front of the box. One at a time the other blocks are pushed out of the box, casually shown, and placed on the table in a line from right to left across the table.

When the box has been emptied, the back door is closed and the box is tilted over so that it lays on its back on the table. The magician, using both hands, rapidly picks up the blocks and puts them back into the box. The right hand picks up one block at a time from the right end of the line of blocks. The left hand also singly takes the blocks from the left of the row. When all the blocks are in the box the magician stands the box upright, calls

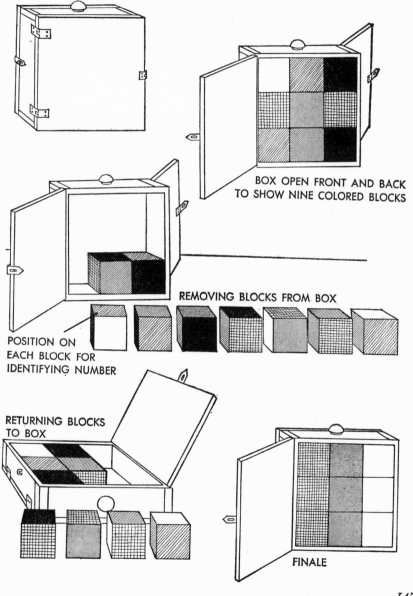

BOX OPEN FRONT AND BACK
TO SHOW NINE COLORED BLOCKS

REMOVING BLOCKS FROM BOX

POSITION ON
EACH BLOCK FOR
IDENTIFYING NUMBER

RETURNING BLOCKS
TO BOX

FINALE

attention to the confusion of colors on the blocks, and closes the door. Picking up the box, again by the handle, the magician turns the box around and shakes it. He calls attention to the fact that the blocks fit so tightly into the box that they not only can't move around but they don't even rattle. The box is replaced on the table.

At this point a spectator chooses in sequence, three of the six colors. In order for the feat to be successful the choice has to be controlled without the knowledge of the chooser or any other member of the audience. The method used for the control of choice will be divulged shortly. At this moment it is sufficient to know that the choice and sequence of colors will be—RED, BLUE, WHITE. The magician opens the door of the box to disclose that the blocks are now arranged in vertical rows with the 3 blocks forming the first row showing their red faces. The three blocks in the next row are blue and the final three blocks are white. As the climax, the box is tipped forward so that all the blocks can spill out on the table.

The seeming ability of the blocks to move inside the box so as to form a chosen color pattern is due to three things: 1. The fact that the box has a front door and a back door which are identical in appearance. 2. That, while each block is painted with identical colors, the order in which the colors are put on varies with each block. 3. That in handling both box and blocks the magician follows an exact sequence. Actually there is nothing difficult to do and what is done is the natural thing to do in the circumstances. When, prior to the show, the blocks are properly put into the box the magician will find the actual performance almost automatic. And as each block is numbered there is little chance of failing to put the blocks properly into the box.

In order to describe the order in which the colors go on each block it is necessary to be able to designate each surface by a name. It seems easiest to use the terms front, top, back and bottom. As the colors which go on the remaining two sides are those not used on the other surfaces, and as it is immaterial which side gets a particular color, there is no purpose in differentiating the sides. The block is placed on a table with one surface facing you. That is termed the front. The surface upon which the block rests is called the bottom. The one opposite the bottom is the top and that opposite the front is the back. Each block has a minute numeral written on the upper right hand corner of the front. Following will be given the number of the block and the color which must be used on each of the four named sides. In order to simplify the description, the front of the block will be called A, the top B, the back C, and the bottom D. These are the colors and their order for each of the 9 blocks:

1. A-white, B-green, C-yellow, D-red
2. A-green, B-yellow, C-blue, D-red
3. A-black, B-blue, C-white, D-red
4. A-red, B-black, C-blue, D-white
5. A-blue, B-red, C-black, D-white
6. A-red, B-yellow, C-green, D-white
7. A-green, B-white, C-red, D-blue
8. A-yellow, B-black, C-green, D-blue
9. A-black, B-green, C-red, D-blue

The two sides of each block not mentioned above are painted respectively with one of the 6 colors not used on the block. Those colors are: 1-black, blue, 2-black, white, 3-green, yellow, 4-green, yellow, 5-green, yellow, 6-black, blue, 7-yellow, black, 8-red, white, 9-yellow, white.

The task of painting the blocks is made materially easier if, before starting to paint, on each side of each block is written in pencil the color to go on that side. After all the painting is finished the number of each block should be written on face A as small as possible. These numbers are needed only to facilitate preparing the trick prior to performance. If the blocks are put into the box in sequence with numbers 1-2-3 making the top horizontal row, 4-5-6 forming the second row, and 7-8-9 as the bottom row, the trick is ready to begin. It will be found that looking at the blocks from either the front or back of the box that, like the coat of Joseph, there are many colors but no design or pattern.

When the magician has shown the blocks with both doors of the box open he, as previously noted, pushes each block out of the box, one at a time starting with block number 1 and going in sequence through block 9. The blocks are put in a row on the table with the first block at the right. It will be found that red is the color on the bottom (side D) of blocks 1-2-3. The bottom color of blocks 4-5-6 is white, and blue is the bottom color of blocks 7-8-9. After all the blocks have been put on the table, the box is shown to the audience. Then the rear door is closed and the box is placed, on its back on the table. Laying the box on its back gives the box a quarter turn from its upright position. Therefore, if the blocks are picked up, and without twisting put into the box they will show different faces than those shown when they previously were in the box. The faces at the front will be pattern-less and varicolored. Those at the back will show only the colors of red, white and blue. When the blocks are put back into the box they are arranged in vertical rows. Blocks 1-2-3, the red ones, are picked up with the right hand from one end of the row of blocks on the table and put in the box along the side opposite to the side to which the door is hinged. As the right hand works with the blocks at one end of the row, the left hand picks up the blocks at the other end of the row (the blue ones) and puts them in the box in a vertical row alongside of the first row. The last three blocks (all white) make the third vertical row in the box. The box is then raised to an upright position and the audience can see that the blocks are in no color order and apparently are just as they were before having been taken out of the box. The front door is closed and the box is picked up by the handle. The box then is shaken for the stated purpose of showing that the blocks fit into the box so tightly that they cannot twist, turn, or even rattle. While the shaking makes the feat more impressive the major purpose in the action is to turn the box around so that the back door becomes the front. Turning the box back to front will not be noticed if the edge of the box is turned toward the audience when the box is shaken. When the door is opened it will show the blocks in vertical rows of red blocks, blue blocks and white blocks.

Perhaps the easiest way to make the box and have it attractive is to use ¼" plywood for both frame and doors. Angle brass is used at the corners of the frame and held to the wood with screws. The hinges and the hasps to hold the doors shut also are of brass. The handle, too, is brass and is a small-size drawer pull. It must be remembered to make the box enough bigger than is needed to hold the blocks so that it can be lined with the felt which keeps the blocks from rattling. It is suggested that the box be stained so as better to show off the colors on the blocks.

While the description of the way to make the blocks and their box neces-sarily has to be lengthy, the trick may be done easily and rapidly. It will be found the trick is so effective that it is well worth the bother of making it.

The choice of colors also is simple to perform.

The magician uses sixty cards for this choice, a paper bag, a needle and a length of ribbon. One side of each card has three colored stripes. Each card is different and the stripes are varying combinations of the six colors used on the blocks. The cards are shown to the audience and it is pointed out to the spectators that the combination of colors on each card is different.

A new paper bag is opened and the magician drops all of the cards into the bag. He takes hold of the mouth of the bag and holds it closed. He then shakes the bag up and down in order, as he explains to the audience, to mix the cards thoroughly. Picking up the needle, through which the length of ribbon is threaded, the magician holds it against one side of the bag and steps up to one of the spectators. The spectator is asked to thump the bottom of the bag and, as this is done, the magician pushes the needle through the bag. The spectator is told that he was asked to thump the bottom of the bag so as to knock a card up in the bag in order that the needle could go through it too. The magician goes on to say that he is certain the needle has pierced a card and adds that the card is completely a chance selection for no one can know which card it is. The magician continues pulling on the needle until the ribbon is halfway through the bag. He then takes the needle off the ribbon and asks two spectators each to take a tight grip on one end of the ribbon. The magician takes hold of the bottom of the bag and slowly pulls down. The ribbon will tear through the walls of the bag and when the ribbon is completely free of the bag everyone can see that one card is hanging from the ribbon.

The ribbon goes through the card near one end. The magician points out that had the ribbon gone through the other end of the card, the colors would have been reversed, and so make a different color combination.

The magician announces that the blocks are very obedient and that he is going to ask them to rearrange themselves in the box so as to show the same colors and in the same order as are the colors on the card chosen by chance by the spectator. The magician opens the box to show that the blocks are rearranged and do show exactly the same combination of colors as is on the selected card.

There is nothing tricky about the yard of ribbon used. The ribbon should be of an attractive color, be quite strong, and one half inch wide. The needle has to be sharp-pointed and with an eye large enough for the ribbon to go through easily. (These needles are purchasable at notion and variety stores and are the kind used for sewing with heavy yarn.)

The paper bag, however, is not exactly as it seems to be. It is a quite ordinary # 6 brown paper bag such as grocers use, but within it there is a secret pocket. The pocket is made of the same kind of paper as is used in the bag. A piece of paper from a second bag is used for this purpose. The pocket is pasted inside the back of the bag and the top of the pocket is 3″ from the top of the bag with its mouth toward the top.

One side, at the top, of all grocery bags is cut down a fraction of an inch in order that the bag may be opened more easily. The cut down side is the front of the bag and it almost always carries the name of the manufacturer of the bag and the size.

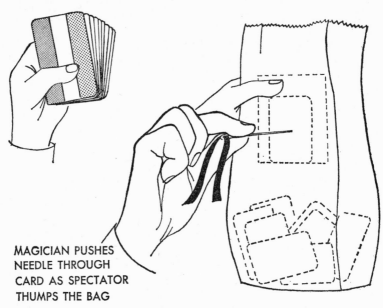

MAGICIAN PUSHES
NEEDLE THROUGH
CARD AS SPECTATOR
THUMPS THE BAG

The pocket is made just large enough for one of the cards to slip in easily. The mouth of the pocket is left open and the other three sides are carefully pasted to the inside of the bag. To paste the pocket inside, the bag must be opened but this should be done carefully so as not to crinkle the bag, and after the paste is dry the bag should be carefully refolded.

Into this pocket is put a duplicate card which the audience knows nothing about. This card has stripes of red, blue and white, the same colors in which the blocks have been rearranged in the box. In putting this card in the pocket, care must be taken to put the side having the colored stripes so that they face toward the outside of the bag and with the red stripe at the right hand side of the pocket.

Sixty cards are used for the trick. Excellent cards for this purpose can be made by cutting in half, lengthwise, ordinary plain white 3 x 5 index cards, so that the cards used are 2½″ x 3″. Each card has three stripes of different colors running lengthwise. While there are 120 possible combinations of three of the six colors used on the blocks, it is necessary only to make 60 cards, because each card gives two combinations by turning the card rightside up or upside down. Each stripe is ⅓ the width of the card. Water colors, India ink or crayons can be used to put the colors on the cards. The chart showing the combination of the colors which appears on each of the 60 cards can be found on the next page.

In performance, the magician shows the color-striped cards to the audience and points out to them that the same six colors are used on the cards as were used on the blocks. He tells them of the possible combinations of these colors. He also notes that the order of the colors is changed when a card is turned upside down. He gives all the cards to one of the spectators and instructs him to mix the cards.

The magician then gets the paper bag and holds it with his right hand at the mouth with his fingers on the inside and his thumb on the outside of the back of the bag so that the edge of the bag is at the crotch of his thumb. The tips of the fingers will then be in position to hold the top of the pocket closed and keep the card concealed in the pocket. With the bag held this way, it will be found that the rush of air will open the bag, if the arm is quickly moved in a sweeping motion.

As soon as the bag is forced open, turn it upside down, which will convince everyone that it is empty. Then maintaining his grip on the bag, the magician takes hold of the front of the bag in the same manner with the other hand and, holding the bag open, asks the spectator to drop all the cards in the bag.

The magician then releases his left hand from the mouth of the bag and puts the fingers of that hand on the face of the bag and the thumb on the back of the bag. Squeezing the bag between the thumb and fingers will flatten it, so that the right hand can push it over into the crotch of the left thumb. The left hand should now be in the position, on the outside of the bag, so that the top of the hidden card in the bag can be felt between the thumb and the first finger. When the left hand is in this position, the right hand is released and the bag is now held by the left hand.

The magician then starts to jiggle the bag up and down with the explanation that he is doing this in order further to mix the cards. As he jiggles the bag, he walks to his table and picks up the ribbon threaded needle. He

RED WHITE BLUE	RED YELLOW GREEN	WHITE RED BLUE	WHITE GREEN BLUE	BLUE WHITE BLACK	YELLOW WHITE GREEN
RED WHITE YELLOW	RED YELLOW BLACK	WHITE RED YELLOW	WHITE GREEN YELLOW	BLUE YELLOW GREEN	YELLOW WHITE BLACK
RED WHITE GREEN	RED GREEN WHITE	WHITE RED GREEN	WHITE GREEN BLACK	BLUE YELLOW BLACK	YELLOW BLUE GREEN
RED WHITE BLACK	RED GREEN BLUE	WHITE RED BLACK	WHITE BLACK BLUE	BLUE GREEN YELLOW	YELLOW BLUE BLACK
RED BLUE WHITE	RED GREEN YELLOW	WHITE BLUE YELLOW	WHITE BLACK YELLOW	BLUE GREEN BLACK	YELLOW GREEN BLACK
RED BLUE YELLOW	RED GREEN BLACK	WHITE BLUE GREEN	WHITE BLACK GREEN	BLUE BLACK YELLOW	YELLOW BLACK GREEN
RED BLUE GREEN	RED BLACK WHITE	WHITE BLUE BLACK	BLUE RED YELLOW	BLUE BLACK GREEN	GREEN RED BLACK
RED BLUE BLACK	RED BLACK BLUE	WHITE YELLOW BLUE	BLUE RED GREEN	YELLOW WHITE BLUE	GREEN WHITE BLACK
RED YELLOW WHITE	RED BLACK YELLOW	WHITE YELLOW GREEN	BLUE RED BLACK	YELLOW RED GREEN	GREEN BLUE BLACK
RED YELLOW BLUE	RED BLACK GREEN	WHITE YELLOW BLACK	BLUE WHITE GREEN	YELLOW RED BLACK	GREEN YELLOW BLACK

puts this needle against the back of the paper back at a point immediately below the tip of the left thumb, and he goes to a spectator whom he asks to thump the bottom of the bag. The instant that the thump is made, the magician jabs the needle through the paper bag. At the time the needle is pushed through the bag, the magician must take the precaution of having separated the second and third fingers of the left hand to avoid jamming the needle into his fingers. When the needle has been pushed through the bag properly, it also will have gone through the hidden card and near the top of that card. The magician continues pulling the ribbon through the bag until half the ribbon is on either side of the bag.

The magician then removes the needle from the ribbon and asks two spectators each to take a firm grip of one end of the ribbon. It is advisable to instruct each spectator to wind his end of the ribbon around his fingers to avoid the possibility of one or other spectator letting the ribbon slide through his fingers. At this point, the magician informs the audience that the reason he asked the spectator to thump the bottom of the bag was to knock one of the cards up in the bag so that it could be pierced by the needle.

The magician then takes hold of the bottom of the bag with both hands and pulls it down slowly so that the ribbon the two spectators hold will tear through the paper walls of the bag. When the bag has been pulled free of the ribbon, it will be seen that one card is pierced by and suspended from the ribbon.

The magician then points out to the audience that if the ribbon had gone through the other end of the card, the colors would have been reversed. He calls attention to the colors and names them, and to the order— red, blue, white. He tells the audience that the blocks in the box are very obedient and he is going to ask them to rearrange themselves to show just the three colors which the spectator has selected, and in the order the spectator chose.

The magician walks over to the table upon which is the box of blocks and, dropping the paper bag with the rest of the cards on the table, he picks up the box. He opens the door of the box so the audience can see the blocks have been rearranged. Holding the box so everyone can see it, he walks to the spectators who are still holding the ribbon. He takes hold of the card and he asks the spectators to release the ribbon. He holds the card alongside the blocks so that everyone can see that the colors on the blocks are those of the colors on the card, and that the blocks have been truly obedient.

Because the card which is strung on the ribbon has a hole punched through it, a new card has to be made for each performance. With the blocks painted as described the trick only can be done with the colors red, blue and white. However, the order in which these three colors appear in the box can be changed, and this should be done if the trick is performed on another occasion before the same audience. There are six possible combinations with these three colors and besides the rows of color may be made either vertical or horizontal.

Since there is nothing about either the blocks or the box which would prohibit them from being examined, the performer may, if he wishes, at the end of the trick, drop all the blocks out of the box and let the audience not only look at them, but handle them.

THE BOTTOMLESS BOXES

This feat is a magical way to introduce gifts to present to everyone in the audience. The magic also may be used with a single object to be presented to the guest of honor. This is a wonderful way to discover candy for the children who, because they are certain it must be magic candy, always believe it to be unusually sweet. Over the years I have used the Bottomless Boxes to discover a variety of objects by magical means. On one occasion neckties embroidered with the organization's insignia were found for each guest. Hundreds of cigarettes were produced and passed around at another time. And at a different show, souvenir lighters were the magic gifts. Any small objects can be used in this trick and the variety I have been asked to use is great. On one, single, solitary occasion the object to be mysteriously found was a diamond necklace valued at a quarter of a million dollars. It is suggested that it is inadvisable to wait to learn this feat until someone wants a diamond necklace given away, for here is magic which can be used for so many other purposes.

The story the magician tells is that he saw two handsome boxes in a shop window but when he went in to purchase them he discovered they were without bottoms. The clerk assured him that bottomless boxes are the best kind and suggested that he take them on trial. The magician goes on to say that he agreed with the clerk and that he bought them because he never had found any boxes like them. The boxes are shown and the production made. At the very end the magician explains that he has found bottomless boxes to be best because more can be put into them.

The magic is done with two attractive brass trimmed wooden boxes. The boxes are of identical height but one box is just enough smaller than the other so as easily to fit inside. Neither box has a bottom or a top. When the boxes are introduced to the audience, one is nested inside the other. Each box is shown to the audience and, as they lack bottoms and tops, everyone can see there is absolutely nothing inside either.

After the boxes have been shown, so that there is no question of their innocence and emptiness, the larger box is put on the table with one open end facing the audience. The smaller box is put on top of the larger one. Reaching into the top of the smaller box, the magician brings forth whatever object, or objects, he had been asked to use, and was given, prior to his performance. The boxes I made, and long have used, are not large. The outer one is only 8″ square at the top and bottom, and 11″ high. The inner box is the same height but only 7″ square. From these boxes, after they are shown to be empty, can be taken 6 to 10 pounds of candy. The weight will vary according to the kind of candy used. Over 800 cigarettes will pack into the same 270 cubic inches of available space where, until wanted, they are invisible to the audience.

While it is quite possible to construct the Bottomless Boxes either smaller or large than the sizes mentioned, there are disadvantages in doing so. Small boxes will not have space to contain contents which are impressive when produced. The larger the boxes, the greater will be the weight of the boxes and of the hidden contents. Weight plays an important part in one's actions when it comes to trying to mask that the weight exists.

The trick depends upon the use of a container about which the audience knows nothing. The container holds the "load." A load is the term in magic for whatever is to be produced mysteriously. The load container is made of thin sheet metal and is 8″ high with a square top 6″ x 6″. The sides are made of one piece of metal 8″ x 24″. This metal is bent so as to form the four sides. The corner where the two ends of the metal meet is soldered. Because of the bent and soldered corners even quite thin metal will have sufficient rigidity for easy handling during performance. In order to increase this rigidity, as well as to make an easy way to put a bottom in the container, it is suggested using ½″ angle aluminum. The aluminum is cut into 6″ lengths. One flange of the angle goes inside the box and the other extends along the inside edge of the bottom. The bottom flanges have to be mitered at each corner to fit properly. The angles are riveted to the sides of the container. A square of metal is made to go inside the container and lay on the bottom flanges of the angles. The metal square should be cut of such a size that it will be held in place by friction. At the top of the container, on two opposite sides, are soldered wire loops. These loops extend 1¼″ above the centers of the sides. At the points where the wire leaves the

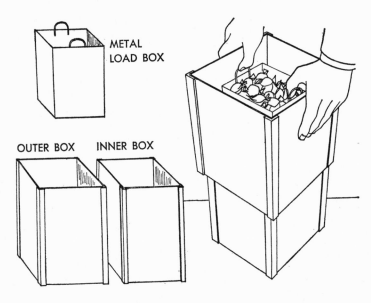

wall, the sides of the loop are 2″ apart. Each end of a wire loop extends 1″ inside the container and is soldered to it. The outside, bottom and sides, of the container is covered with felt in order to deaden sound when the container is handled inside the boxes.

Most attractive boxes can be made from ⅛″ thick plywood. Mahogany, or other hardwood, enhances the appearance of the boxes enough to warrant the extra cost. The corners of the boxes are ornamented with ½″ angle brass, 1/16″ thick. The angles are attached to the wood with flat-head machine screws. The heads of the screws are inside the box. The angle brass is tapped so that the brass is screwed right to the wood. The screws are filed flush with the outside of the brass. While the use of screws make the boxes strong, it is possible to glue the brass to the wood with a plastic glue instead of using screws. In finishing the boxes the wood should be stained and polished.

Both boxes are 11″ high as was noted. The larger box is 8″ square on the outside. The inside, using the thickness of wood and brass suggested, is 7⅝″ square. The outside of the smaller box is 7″ square. The inside is 6⅝″ square. The container is 6″ square. These measurements allow for a full ¼″ of space between each side of the container and the inside walls of the smaller box. The smaller box inside the larger one also has a full ¼″ of clearance on each side.

Handling the boxes so as to show both to be empty and yet hide the container is surprisingly easy as will be found after the equipment has been made. At first only the inner box and container should be used in order to learn how to handle both together. The magician puts box and its nested container on a table. He stands in back of the table. The wire loops of the container should be at the performer's left and right. He takes hold of the box with both hands, one at each side. His fingers go on the outside of the box and his thumbs go on the inside. If the box is grasped at the center of the sides, it will be found that the tips of the thumbs will go into the wire loops. Bending the thumbs will raise the container. The container is made 3″ shorter than the boxes so that in handling it can be raised and eliminate the possibility of the audience's catching a glimpse at either top or bottom of the box. The box, when lifted, actually is held by the pressure of the fingers on each side. The fingers go down on the side until the crotch of the thumb is at the top edge of the box. The thumbs handle the container. After it has been found how easy it is to handle a box and the hidden container together, both are put inside the larger box. When the inner box is halfway down in the larger one, the tip of each thumb is pressed against the inner wall of the box enough to hold the weight of the box. This permits releasing the pressure of the fingers on the outside of the smaller box so that the fingers can slide on the outside of the larger box. Retaining the thumbs in the wire loops, press the fingers against the sides of the larger box. It is amazing to find upon lifting the larger box that the container sneaks right out of the smaller box and comes up with, and hidden by, the larger box. If the larger box, and container, are placed on the table, the inner box may be put in the outer box from the top and right over the container. When enough experimenting has been done to be satisfied that it is very easy to handle the boxes while keeping the container hidden, it is time to learn the sequence used in showing the boxes to the audience.

At the very beginning of the trick the magician picks up the two boxes as one, with, of course, the hidden container, and places them on the table where he is going to perform his feat. That table at the time, naturally, should be bare. The boxes, prior to performance, may have been placed on the prop table or on the seat of a chair, whichever is more convenient. This first time that the boxes are picked up only one hand is used. The hand goes on the boxes as has been described and with the thumb in the loop of the container. The inner box is held by the pressure between outer box and container. When boxes and container are on the table and while the magician is telling his story about the boxes, the outer box is slid a very little on the top of the table. This sliding is done to center the container inside the inner box. Picking up all three objects in one hand puts the container off center where it is not quite so easy to handle with two hands.

Now the sequence used for showing the boxes. As this is being done nothing should be said about the boxes being empty. The magician merely shows the outside and the inside of two nesting bottomless boxes which, to the audience, quite obviously are empty. Mentioning anything obvious is not only unnecessary but is apt to create suspicion where none would exist. First the outer box alone is lifted above the smaller box and tilted just enough so that the magician can call the attention of the audience to the lack of bottom on the box. The larger box is put back over the smaller box as the magician notes that one box fits inside the other. The larger box no sooner touches the table than it is raised again. In lifting the outer box this time the container is brought with it. The inner box now actually empty is raised and tilted so that the lower end is toward the audience. The magician calls attention to its, too, being without a bottom. As the magician speaks about the absence of a bottom in the box he runs his free hand through the box and wiggles his fingers when they are out of the other end of the box. While seemingly he merely is demonstrating that the box is without a bottom, he is, without mentioning it, also convincingly showing that the box is empty. Having shown the smaller box the magician repeats his statement that one box fits inside the other and puts the smaller box into the bigger one and (though the audience does not know it) the smaller box goes over the container. The instant the smaller box is on the table, the magician raises the larger one and puts it back on the table on its side so that the audience can see right through the box. The smaller box (and container) are taken from the table and placed on the upper side of the larger box. The production is then made.

In the event that the audience is so large that 10 pounds of candy is not enough to go around, there is a very tricky way to circumvent this difficulty. When the candy is brought out of the bottomless box, it is put in a large metal bowl prior to distribution. Handful after handful of the candy is taken out of the bottomless box and put into the bowl. It does not occur to the audience, then or later, that the bowl was half full of candy at the beginning. Remember to insist that each piece of candy to be produced is wrapped individually. Not only should anything which is passed out to be eaten be clean, and obviously so, but both magician and equipment also will be kept clean if the candy is wrapped. A magician never should be stuck up—even with candy.

Eight. ESPECIALLY FOR CHILDREN

THE magic in this Chapter particularly appeals to children though there is nothing childish about any of the tricks. It is merely that each feat conforms to the more exacting requirements of the reasoning of childhood. The complete enchantment of magic is granted only to the young or to those who, like children, are willing to accept the impossible as both sensible and logical.

A BALL, PAPER AND NOTHING

THIS feat is based on that quality of reasonable illogic found in a fairy story. Primarily, it is magic designed to appeal to children but, provided not more than half the audience is adult, the trick will fit well into any program of magic.

When children transpose 3 signs they cause a ball, a handful of confetti, and a quantity of nothing to follow invisibly the movement of the signs. The stated purpose of the signs, as each is introduced, is to help the spectators remember what the magician does.

The magician begins by putting a rubber ball into a small glass which is standing on a table. He covers both with an empty paper tube. The magician tells the audience, "You have seen me put a ball into a glass and cover it with a tube." At this point he raises the tube high enough to show the ball and puts the tube back on the table. He then picks up a board with "BALL" lettered on it. As he holds up the board he continues his talk. "Here is a sign. What is on it?" Some of the children will inform the magician of the word on the board and he agrees with them. "That's right—ball. This sign is to help you keep track of where the ball is." The magician tells one child to come and hold the sign. The child should be old enough to read the word.

The magician then crosses to another table on which are a second glass, a paper bag and a small silk handkerchief. He picks up the glass with his left hand and reaching into the paper bag, with his right hand, pulls out a pinch of confetti and releases it slowly so that it flutters back into the bag. Then putting the glass into the paper bag he fills it, shows it and pours the confetti back into the bag. He fills the glass a second time, places it on the table and sets the paper bag aside. Picking up the handkerchief he covers the glass of confetti. As these things are being done the magician explains that confetti is the proper name for the tiny pieces of paper he takes from the bag to fill the glass. When he picks up the board, which he has a second child hold, he says the board wasn't big enough to put the word confetti on it so he just had the word PAPER printed on the sign. For children paper is the better word.

Finally the magician shows a small plate on both sides. The plate obviously is empty but the magician claims, as he holds the plate right side up, that he is putting a handful of nothing on it. Then in order to keep the nothing from falling off the plate which, he explains, he doesn't want to have happen, the magician shows a metal cup which, mouth down, he puts on the plate to cover the nothing. The covered plate the magician puts on the seat of a chair placed between the two tables. He then calls for the third child as he picks up the third board which is entirely blank. He shows both sides of the board to the child and asks, "What do you see written on this sign?" To the reply of "Nothing," the magician says, "That is exactly right. This is the nothing sign. You hold it here by the plate filled with nothing."

The magician walks over to the first child and asks what is on the sign he is holding, and upon being told "ball" the magician agrees that is correct and proves it by raising the tube so the ball may be seen. The same routine is followed with the child holding the "paper" sign and the child holding the "nothing" sign and the magician shows both paper and nothing.

The magician announces that all he has to do is to have the signs moved to change the positions of the hidden objects. He escorts the child holding the nothing sign over to where the ball is hidden. The child holding the ball sign is taken to where the paper is and the child holding the paper sign is moved to where nothing has been. The magician, pointing toward where the ball had been placed, asks the audience, "What is over there?" Some of the children will say "ball" and some, going by the sign, will say "nothing." The magician ignores their divergent answers and pointing to where the confetti had been he asks the same question. This time he seems to notice that the children's answers do not agree and says to the audience that he thought he had told them that everything moved when the signs were moved and that he would prove it. The magician lifts the tube and where the ball was is nothing. Taking off the silk the ball is in the glass rather than confetti. Lifting the cup off the plate discloses a pile of confetti where nothing had been.

In concluding the magician says, "Now that should prove to you that you should always pay attention to signs—particularly traffic signs."

So much for what the audience sees and what the magician does openly. Secretly the magician does three things. He gets the rubber ball out of one glass. He substitutes a rubber ball (a duplicate) for the confetti in the second glass. And, finally, he puts a quantity of confetti on the empty plate. Prior to describing the methods used it is necessary to describe some of the articles used. All three tricks depend upon the glass used in changing confetti to a ball to decide the sizes of all the other objects required. The glass easiest to use is one no more than 3" high and with only a little taper to the sides. Such glasses generally are used to serve liquor, tomato or orange juice. The glass may be smaller, or if the performer is willing to do a little more preparatory practice, it may even be larger. The size of the ball must be at least ⅜" less in diameter than is the inside diameter of the bottom of the glass used. The size of the ball is regulated by the means used to change the confetti to the ball.

The secret of the disappearance of the ball is that it is pulled out of the glass and carried away hidden inside the tube by means of a thread. The thread, about which the audience is unaware, and which is invisible to them, is extremely fine black silk thread. Because of the way the trick is made, it is very easy to do. Prior to describing how the thread is utilized, it is necessary to describe the tube which is used. The tube should be twice the height of the glass and with the inside circumference large enough to go over the glass easily. The glass should be identical to the one used to hold the confetti. The tube must give the effect of being a simple paper tube. While it is merely a tube and can be made of paper, the walls of the tube may not be flexible. A rigid tube easily can be made from a large-size cardboard mailing tube, or from a tin can, of the proper dimensions, which has had removed both the top and bottom. Inside and out the tube is covered with paper. The tube is completed by drilling an extremely tiny hole ⅛″ from one end.

The silk thread should be put through the tiny hole in the tube. The end of the thread, extending from the inside of the tube, is attached to the ball. The easiest way to do this is to push a needle straight through the ball and, by means of the needle, pull through the thread. With a solid rubber ball this is not difficult and such a ball is best to use in the trick for, being rubber, it is silent in use. After the thread is through the ball a knot is made in the

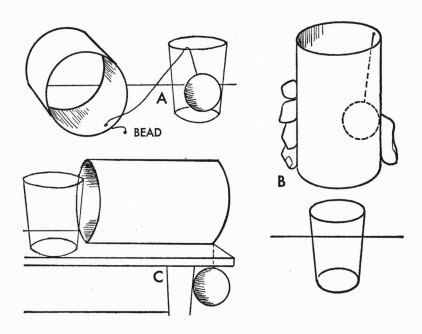

end of the thread and the knot is pulled back inside the ball. The ball then is placed on the table and covered with the tube. The end of the tube which has the tiny hole is uppermost. The end of the thread extending from the outside of the tube is pulled down and drawn taut. A very small bead is tied to the thread 1″ above the bottom of the tube. It now will be found possible to raise the tube high enough to disclose the ball and have the bottom of the tube an inch, or so, above the top of the ball. As the tube is lifted, the weight of the ball causes the thread on the outside of the tube to be drawn through the hole in the tube until stopped by the little bead. Replacing the tube over the ball will leave the thread slack on the inside of the tube. To cause the ball to rise inside the tube and be hidden, the first step is to grasp the tube with one hand so that the thumb is on the bead and the fingers are on the opposite side of the tube. Then the hand is slid down the tube using just enough pressure to pull the bead and thread to the bottom of the outside of the tube. This action will cause the thread to pull the ball up inside the tube. By increasing the pressure on the tube and retaining hold of the bead, the tube, with its hidden ball, can be raised from the table. Precisely the same actions will take the ball out of the glass and, by hiding it in the tube, make the ball "disappear."

Now that the mechanics are explained for causing a ball to vanish, a description can be given of the steps in the routine in which the equipment is used. At the start of the trick the tube is inverted and stood on the table with the end having the hole down. The ball and the full length of the thread are on the outside of the tube. The ball is inside the glass which is placed on the table next to the tube. Everything is now ready for performance but it is well to understand before reading further, that while all the moves the magician makes in this trick are natural and easy they must be memorized for they run in a set sequence. To start, the ball is taken from the glass by tipping the glass so as to allow the ball to roll out on the table. The instant the ball is on the table, it is grasped so as not to disclose that it is tied to a thread. And the glass is set back on the table. One in each hand, the ball and the tube are picked up. As the thread is six, or more, inches long the tube and ball may be held that far apart. When the tube is picked up from the table, it is grasped near the end resting on the table. The magician calls attention first to the ball and then to the tube. As the tube is mentioned, it is turned, by twisting the wrist, to permit the audience to look through it. Turning the hand still more, the tube is brought right side up. The tube is put over the glass and held about an inch above the table. The ball is dropped through the tube and into the glass. As the audience can see, the ball actually goes into the glass. At this point the bead is at the top of the outside of the tube and the thread inside the tube is slack.

Later when it is time for the ball to disappear, the magician draws the ball up inside the tube as previously described. Holding the tube straight to keep the ball from being seen, it is brought to the back edge of the table and put down. When the tube is put on the table only the front edge of the bottom of the tube touches the table. The instant the edge of the tube is on the table, the pressure on the bead is released. With the thread no longer held, the weight of the ball will cause it to drop out of the tube and hang back of the table out of sight of the audience. When the ball is behind the table, and the action is instantaneous, the tube is tipped and laid on its side so that the spectators can see through the empty tube. The ball has disappeared completely.

The confetti is changed to the ball by means of a confetti covered bottomless insert which fits the glass. This insert is made of thin sheet metal. One piece of metal is formed to have exactly the same taper of the glass but the diameter is $\frac{1}{4}''$ less than the diameter of the inside of the glass. The joint of this metal is soldered and a top is soldered in place. The outside of this top should have a very fine stiff wire soldered across it. The wire should extend beyond the edges of the glass on each side just enough so that each end can be felt. Confetti is glued all over the outside of this insert. When put in the glass the finished insert should duplicate the appearance of a glass actually filled with confetti. When under cover of the handkerchief, the insert is taken out of the glass and the ball (which had been hidden inside) falls out of the open bottom of the insert and is disclosed.

There are a few additional details to understand of the way to get the insert in and out of the glass so the audience never will suspect what is being done. The paper bag which holds the confetti is one of the kind used by grocers. A number 6 size is suitable unless a large glass is used. The bag itself is quite ordinary but has a sort of shelf inside to hold the insert until it is put into the glass. The shelf is the top of a block of light wood which is $4''$ high. The surface of the shelf is as long as the narrow side of the paper bag and a little wider than the diameter of the top of the insert. The block is glued to the inside of the paper bag so as to hold it upright and at one side of the bag. Hinged to the top of the inside surface of the block is a piece of tin which forms an easily removable cover for the insert. The purpose of the cover is to keep any of the loose confetti from going in, or on, the insert. The tin is as wide as the longer edge of the top of the block and is as long as the shorter edge of the top, plus the height of the insert, plus $\frac{1}{2}''$. The tin is hinged $\frac{1}{4}''$ from the top of the block. This is done so as to make the block act as a stop to keep the tin from touching the insert. At the upper end, the tin is bent so as to form a cover the size of the top surface of the block (see illustration). The space in the paper bag alongside the wooden block is filled with confetti almost up to the level of the shelf. Multi-colored confetti should be used as it is more attractive.

As the magician starts this section of the trick he reaches into the paper bag and takes a pinch of confetti—as much as he can grasp with his fingertips. He brings his hand out of the bag, shows the confetti and lets it flutter

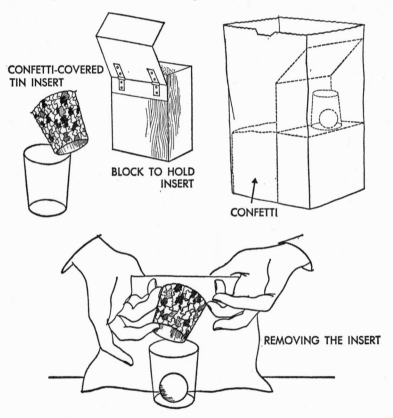

CONFETTI-COVERED
TIN INSERT

BLOCK TO HOLD
INSERT

CONFETTI

REMOVING THE INSERT

back into the bag. Then he takes the glass, puts it into the paper bag and fills it. This is done with one hand in the manner of a man filling his pipe inside his tobacco pouch. He shows the glass of confetti to the audience and empties the glass by pouring the contents back into the bag. At the start of pouring the confetti back into the bag, the magician holds the glass several inches above the mouth of the bag. As he continues pouring, the glass is lowered until it is inside the bag. Looking into the bag the magician shakes the glass as if to get all the confetti out. He looks into the bag again and moves his hand, but the movement, ostensibly to get the last couple of little pieces of paper out of the glass, actually gives him the opportunity of pushing the cover away from the insert. The magician brings the empty glass out of the bag, and again puts it in ostensibly to fill it again. The insert, with the ball inside, is upside down on its shelf. When the magican goes into the bag with the glass the second time he puts the glass right over the insert. He slides the glass to the side of the shelf so that he can get one finger under the insert and then turns the glass right side up and brings it out of the bag. Because of the confetti-covered insert, the glass apparently is again filled with confetti. The glass is placed on the table and the paper bag set aside. When the glass is put on the table the points of wires on the top of the insert should stick out of the glass so they are parallel to the front edge of the table.

Next the magician covers the glass with a small silk handkerchief. This is done in a way which makes simple the later removal of the insert. The handkerchief, so called, is an 8″ square of soft but quite heavy silk. When the magician picks up the silk he holds it by the corners of one side. After showing the silk to the audience, he lowers it, like dropping a curtain, in front of the glass. The silk goes about 3″ in front of the glass and is lowered until the magician's fingers touch the table and the glass again can be seen by the audience. Still maintaining his grip on the silk, he raises it and draws it over the top of the glass. But, and this is most important, the edge of the silk goes only about an inch beyond the top of the glass before it is released. This is done in order that the edge may later be picked up without any fumbling.

When the handkerchief is taken off the glass to disclose that the confetti has changed to a ball it is grasped, at the side made ready to take hold of, with the thumbs on top of the silk and the fingers underneath. The silk is held between the thumb and first fingers. If held correctly, and it needs a little practice to find if this is true, the second fingers are exactly in position so that the tips of these fingers press against the ends of the wire attached to the insert which extends outside the rim of the glass. In raising the silk the hands also lift the insert out of the glass. When the insert is completely out of the glass the third finger of the left hand is extended. It will be found that this finger automatically goes into the hole at the bottom of the insert. As soon as the insert hangs on this finger, the second finger of each hand releases the tips of the wire soldered to the insert. The right hand releases its hold of the silk so that the silk hangs down from the corner held by the left hand and in such a way as to hide the insert completely. The right hand points to the ball as the magician speaks of it. The right hand then grasps the silk and the insert which it covers. The handkerchief is crumpled around the insert and placed on the table.

Getting the pile of loose confetti on to the plate is very simple and depends upon the way the cup is prepared. The cup, which is inverted and used as a cover for the nothing on the plate, is made of metal and is without a handle. Cups suitable for the trick are made for a variety of purposes and usually

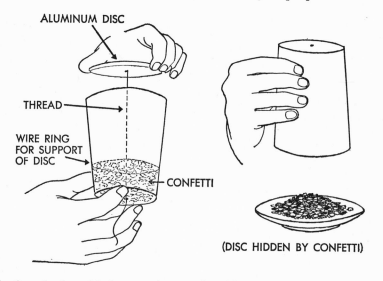

ALUMINUM DISC

THREAD

WIRE RING FOR SUPPORT OF DISC

CONFETTI

(DISC HIDDEN BY CONFETTI)

can be found where kitchen equipment is sold. The cup must be at least 4″ high and have tapered sides. A disc of thin aluminum is cut of a size to fit inside the cup about three-fourths of the way down. The way to find how far in the cup the disc should go is to put into the cup a glass and a half of confetti. The reason for the greater amount of confetti is that it takes more confetti in a loose pile to appear equal to the contents of the glass. The disc, having been made of the proper size, is put into the cup and made level. Pressing the disc in place, a pencil line is made on the walls of the cup using the disc as a guide. A length of ⅛″ wire is formed into a ring exactly the size of the disc. That is, the outside of the ring must be precisely the size of the edge of the disc. The ring is put in the cup, using the pencil line as the guide, and fastened in place with liquid solder, or a resin glue. Two very tiny holes have to be drilled at the center of the disk and one equally small hole in the exact center of the bottom of the cup. Tie one end of a very fine silk thread to the disc. The other end of the thread is run through the hole in the bottom of the cup going from the inside out. The thread is left slack so that the disc can be put on a table and the cup, right side up, beside it. The cup is filled with confetti up to the level of the ring. The disc is dropped on top of the confetti and the thread pulled taut on the outside of the cup. The thread is pressed against the surface of the bottom of the cup and, at the edge of the cup, fastened with a small piece of cellophane tape. The excess thread is cut off.

The cup can be shown, both inside and outside, to the audience and have them accept it as being merely an empty cup. No attention is called to its emptiness. The magician just shows it casually as he announces that he will use the cup as a cover to make certain the nothing does not fall off the plate. Merely scratching across the bottom of the cup will pull the thread clear of the tape and free the disc and confetti to fall on the plate. The confetti will completely cover, and thus hide, the disc. The drop is almost without sound.

Care must be taken with the thread when preparing the cup, to make certain it is taut, and doesn't inadvertently spill confetti. And, it is probably unnecessary to mention, if the disc and the inside of the cup do not match either the disc or the inside of the cup, or both, should be painted so they do look alike.

TRAVELING ON A WISH

IN this feat the magician transforms a handkerchief into a small bust of a turbaned Indian by making a knot, a couple of twists, and a few pencil marks. The magic is performed with this Little Indian Head, described in Chapter 3. The feat is based on the age old story about certain men of India who developed the power to wish themselves anywhere and to travel on these wishes instantly and invisibly. The magic is unusual, thoroughly mystifying, not difficult to perform, and will interest adults as well as children.

The performer begins this magic by giving two envelopes to a spectator for examination. One envelope is small enough to fit easily inside the other.

ESPECIALLY FOR CHILDREN

The magician asks the spectator to seal the smaller envelope, put it inside the larger envelope, and to seal it also. The nested envelopes are stood on edge, leaning against a glass, on a table, where they always are in sight of the audience. The magician picks up a second glass in which there is a handkerchief and also picks up a small square of wrapping paper and goes over to another table upon which he places the glass. He forms a cornucopia with the paper. After removing the handkerchief from the glass, he puts the point of the paper cone into the glass so that the paper is held upright. The magician then makes the Indian head out of the handkerchief and as he does so he tells the story of the Indian who could travel on a wish. After the knotted, twisted handkerchief has had the pencil marks put on to make the face, the small replica of a turbaned Indian is exhibited to the audience. The head then is dropped into the cornucopia. The magician announces that the little Indian is going to wish himself from the cornucopia to the inside of the sealed, smaller envelope which is inside the larger, sealed envelope that constantly has been in full sight. The cornucopia is unwrapped and the paper is shown on both sides, crumpled up and put aside. It is most apparent that the Indian has disappeared. Going over to the other table, the magician picks up the large envelope. After opening the envelope by tearing off one end, the magician reaches inside and withdraws the smaller envelope. That envelope is opened to disclose the Indian, which proves, of course, that it is possible to travel invisibly on a wish.

There are three parts to this routine: 1. Causing the Indian head to disappear from the cornucopia; 2. Causing the head to appear in the smaller envelope of a nest of two; 3. Making the turbaned Indian out of a handkerchief.

After making the Indian head a few dozen times it will be found that each head looks like another. This is a fortunate fact for the Indian in the envelope is a duplicate of the one made in sight of the audience.

When the magician introduces this feat he takes from his prop table a tray upon which are two tumblers, one holding a white cotton handkerchief, a square of wrapping paper and two envelopes of different sizes. The tray is put on one of the performance tables. The glass with the handkerchief and the square of paper are taken off the tray and placed at the back of the table. After the nested envelopes are leaned against a tumbler on the tray (as will be described later) the magician takes the tumbler holding the handkerchief and the piece of wrapping paper over to the other performance table.

The wrapping paper is used to form the cornucopia from which, and by means of which, the little Indian disappears. While the paper seems to be merely a square foot of brown paper, it has a hidden pocket. This pocket is made of another piece of the same paper. The extra paper is cut in the shape of a right angle triangle, one arm of which is 12″ long and the other arm 8″ long. Paste is put along the edge of the longer arm and along the edge of the hypotenuse and the triangle of paper is stuck to the paper square. The triangle is placed on the square so that its right angle is at one corner of the square and its arms go along the edges of the square. The hypotenuse will run at an angle from one corner of the paper. When completed the

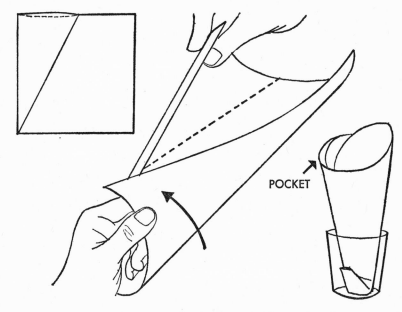

POCKET

paper square will be given a pocket having an 8″ opening from one corner of the paper and running along one edge. If ordinary brown wrapping paper is used the pocket will be invisible because of the surface and color of such paper. The pocket goes on the inside of the cornucopia when it is made and with the opening of the pocket at the mouth of the cone.

It is extremely easy to make a square of paper into a cornucopia provided the paper is correctly held. When the paper is wrongly held, the task is a series of fumbles and, very likely, a floppy cone. For the trick it also is essential that the cornucopia be made so as to have the pocket in the proper position. This is the way the paper should be held. At the start the right hand takes hold of the corner of the square having the opening of the pocket. The pocket side of the paper is towards the performer. The thumb of the right hand is on the outside of the paper (the side of the paper away from the performer and towards the spectators). The paper is grasped between the thumb and the side of the first finger. The left hand takes the diagonally opposite corner between the tips of the thumb and first finger. The thumb is on the outside of the paper. Bringing the two hands together will automatically form a cornucopia. The hands continue moving to overlap the edges of the paper. The right hand will go inside the cone and the left hand will go around the outside. When the cornucopia has the proper appearance the fingers of the left hand go right around the cone so as to keep it from unrolling. The right hand releases its corner of the paper and turns so that the thumb can press on the corner which the left hand holds. The right thumb presses the papers against the fingers which still remain in the tube. This is done so as to release the left hand and still keep the paper from unrolling. The left hand bends up about 2″ of the point of the cornucopia and holds the upturned point against the cone. The right hand releases its grip on the outside of the paper. The fingers of the right hand still inside the cone, are brought up to the mouth of the pocket and slipped into the pocket. The fingers are pushed down into the pocket and the hand turned back and forth until the pocket is wide open. To the audience this action seems merely to be the finishing touches in making the cornucopia. The paper cone is then pushed down into a tumbler which will hold it upright as well as keeping the paper from unrolling.

After the Indian head has been made, and shown to the audience, it is dropped into the cornucopia and into the open pocket. Then with the tips of the fingers the head is pushed further down in the cone so that it is all the way inside the pocket. To show that the Indian has disappeared, the fingers of the right hand go inside the cornucopia and squeeze the pocket closed. The thumb goes against the paper at the outside of the pocket. The right hand lifts the cornucopia out of the glass. The left hand first straightens out the upturned point and then, taking hold of the now free upper corner of the paper, unwraps the cornucopia. This unwrapping should be done quite slowly. With the paper straightened out it is turned between the two hands so that the audience can see both sides. With the right hand continuing to hold the pocket closed, the left hand crumples the paper into a ball. The right hand aids in crumpling the paper. When the paper is made into a ball, it is dropped on the table.

The climax of the feat is to get the Indian, just disappeared from the cornucopia inside the nest of envelopes. As already noted, it is not the same head. The smaller envelope, too, is a duplicate. There are two parts to the substitution of envelopes. The first part is to get the duplicate small envelope having the duplicate head hidden back of the large envelope. The second part is to know how to take the duplicate envelope from behind the large envelope while appearing to take it from inside the envelope. This is simple manipulation and depends upon an optical illusion. To get the duplicate envelope secretly back of the large envelope is mechanical and the simple mechanism is in the tray.

Because of the flanges around the edges of a tray it is possible to add thickness to the bottom without being visible when the extra bottom has been properly painted. A tray with deep flanges is preferable for this trick. A piece of ⅜″ plywood is cut the exact size of the bottom of the tray. Because the flanges of the tray curve on the inside where they join the bottom, the under edges of the board have also to be rounded so that it will lie flat on the bottom. A rectangular hole has to be cut on one corner of the board. The edges of the hole are 1½″ from the side of the tray and the same distance from the end. The hole must be a little larger than the smaller envelope used in the trick. The hole in the tray I use is 3½″ x 4¾″. The longer side of the hole goes along the end of the tray. A piece of metal is used as a cover for this hole and also as the device for holding the duplicate envelope. The metal not only holds the envelope but puts it in position back of the larger envelope. Any kind of sheet metal can be used provided it is both stiff and thin. I used brass 1/32″ thick. The piece of brass is hinged to the board. The hinges are at the long side of the hole near the end of the tray. At the side where it is hinged the brass has a flange ⅛″ high all along the edge, except at the very end the flange is ½″ high. The best way to make this flange, or lip, is to bend the metal at right angles ½″ all along that edge and then to cut away all but ¼″ at the end so that a ⅛″ lip remains. The lip is uppermost when hinged to the board. The wide part of the flange is the lever by which the metal is raised. The narrow lip acts as a guide for the edge of the larger envelope. The metal plate should be just enough larger than the hole in the board so that the edges of the plate will rest on the board. The hinges should be small and are put on upside down so that the hinges bend backwards when the metal is raised upright. One flange of the hinge is sunk in the top of the wood so it is flush and the other flange goes on the underside of the metal and is soldered in place. Also on the underside of the metal are soldered two strips of metal—one near each end. These strips are clamps to hold the duplicate envelope to the metal plate and only need to be long enough to go halfway up the envelope.

Before the performance the duplicate envelope, containing the duplicate Indian head, is put in the clips of the metal plate and the plate closed. The various objects required in the magic are put on the tray and the tray put on the prop table.

At that part of the performance where the spectator has examined the two envelopes, has the smaller sealed envelope inside the larger which also is sealed, that envelope is taken by the magician. It is held at the end by the fingers of the right hand. The magician goes to the table and stands the envelope on its lower edge on the tray. The edge of the envelope is put against the flange of the metal cover. As this is done, the little finger, at the lower edge of the envelope, presses the lever which causes the metal plate to stand behind the envelope. Standing the envelope on edge and pressing on the lever will be found to be a single action. As this is done, the left hand moves the tumbler on the tray so that the envelope can be leaned against it. The tumbler also holds the metal plate with its duplicate envelope of which the audience is unaware. Everything is left in that way until after the magician has made the tubaned Indian out of a handkerchief and then caused that head to disappear.

When the magician returns to the envelopes he takes hold of them with his right hand. The fingers go on the face of the envelope and the thumb goes on the hidden duplicate envelope. The envelopes are gripped fairly tightly but no real strength is used. The left hand takes hold of the tumbler. As the tumbler is moved away the right hand is brought back carefully, so as to keep the lower edge of the envelope on the tray. The right hand tilts the envelopes towards the performer as if he were sweeping something off the tray. This action will permit the metal plate to return to position flat on the tray. The action also will deliver the duplicate envelope in back of and hidden by the large one.

Pressing the palm of the right hand, as well as the thumb, against the back of the envelopes and with the fingers still on the front, the pressure is in creased. No difficulty will now be found in tearing off the end of the large envelope. The left hand takes hold of the top of the envelope, very near the end, and tears back and down. When the end of the envelope has been torn off the piece is dropped. The fingers of the left hand then open the end and go inside as if to feel for the inner envelope. The fingers actually go in back of the inner envelope or push it out of the way inside the large

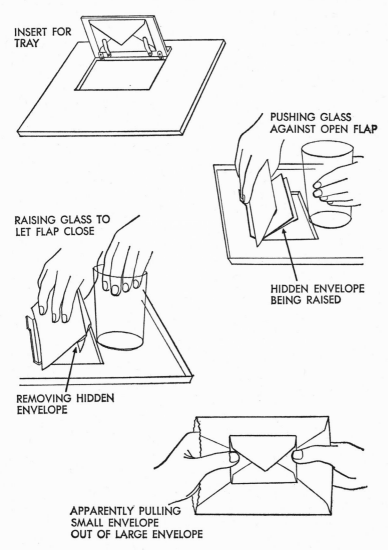

INSERT FOR TRAY

PUSHING GLASS AGAINST OPEN FLAP

HIDDEN ENVELOPE BEING RAISED

RAISING GLASS TO LET FLAP CLOSE

REMOVING HIDDEN ENVELOPE

APPARENTLY PULLING SMALL ENVELOPE OUT OF LARGE ENVELOPE

envelope. The left thumb goes on the back of the envelope until the duplicate envelope can be gripped. The left hand is withdrawn from the larger envelope and as it moves pulls the duplicate envelope from the back. The illusion of having taken the smaller envelope out of the larger one is perfect (see illustration).

All that remains to be done is for the magician, or a member of the audience, to open the smaller envelope to find that the little Indian made his trip successfully.

COIN AND CORD

THERE are standard feats of magic as there are standard pieces of music; ones which year after year continue to be popular with the public. This is magic which has been liked for many generations and is known among magicians as "The Coin in the Ball of Wool." While my procedure is almost identical with the original method, it is altered so as to make the performer's task easier and the trick even more effective.

At the beginning of this feat the magician borrows a coin from a spectator. The coin may be either a quarter or a half dollar. The coin is marked by the spectator before it leaves his hands. The magician asks the spectator to drop the coin in a small envelope. The magician seals the envelope and stands it on end on a table and uses a glass to hold it upright. The performer picks up a cloth bag and shows it. The bag is held closed with draw strings which not only are pulled tightly but also are knotted. The magician also shows a clear plastic, or glass, bowl. He puts the bag into the bowl and places the bowl on another table. He then goes back, picks up the envelope, and walks towards a spectator. The magician takes a package of matches from his pocket and gives them to the spectator with instructions to light a match and set fire to the envelope. The magician carries the burning envelope and holds it until only a small corner is left and that he drops into an ash tray. The coin has been consumed in the flames.

The magician asks a spectator to come forward. The spectator is asked to untie the knots in the draw strings of the bag and to pull open the mouth of the bag, while the magician holds the bowl, in which was placed the bag. He then hands the bowl to the spectator and takes the bottom of the bag and turns the bag upside down. A ball of cord, about 4" in diameter, falls from the bag into the bowl. The bag is set aside. The spectator is asked to find the loose end of the cord and to hand it to the magician. He also is instructed to take great care that the ball of cord does not fall out of the bowl. The magician pulls the cord slowly so that the ball will unwind but will not be jerked out of the bowl. As the cord is pulled off the ball, the magician coils it in large loops.

When he has almost all the cord (the cord is 12 yards long) he calls the spectator's attention to the fact that there is something in the center of the ball of cord. When all the cord is withdrawn that something is seen to be a small box securely bound with rubber bands. The spectator is asked to pick up the box and the magician takes the bowl, drops the cord into it and sets it aside. The spectator is asked to remove the rubber bands, to open the box and to state what he sees inside. He says he sees a coin. He is asked to take the box to the coin's owner and let him take it from the box and to see if it is marked, as he marked it. He identifies the coin and he and the assistant are thanked for their aid.

The method used in seemingly burning the coin is that previously described in "The Flight of a Coin," in Chapter Six. It not only is an excellent way of causing a coin to disappear but it puts the coin in the magician's possession prior to the time the audience believes it disappears. Secretly having the coin is essential. The coin may be marked in any way the spectator wishes, that will permit him later to identify the coin as the one he lent.

The reappearance of the coin is very mystifying because it is found inside a box bound with several rubber bands which had been in the center of a ball of cord which had been in a tightly tied bag. During his show, the magician has no more difficulty in getting the coin inside these various coverings than he would in dropping a coin in the slot of a vending machine. In fact that is what he does: he drops the coin in a slot. The slot is at the end of a rectangular metal slide which runs from the outside of the bag to the inside of the box.

The slide is made of $\frac{1}{32}''$ brass and is $2\frac{3}{4}''$ long. The inside measurements of the opening which runs the length of the slide is $1\frac{1}{4}'' \times \frac{1}{8}''$. It is essential that the coin readily will go through the slide and to insure this each corner should be a sharp rectangle. The easiest way to make a good slide is to start with two pieces of metal each $2\frac{3}{4}'' \times 1\frac{1}{2}''$. On each piece one side is bent at right angles. The bend is made the long way of the metal and is $\frac{1}{8}''$ from the edge. One piece is then put upon the other and both joints soldered. Hard solder is preferable for the job but soft solder can be used if all surplus solder is cleared out of the inside of the slide. Finally, very small holes are drilled $\frac{1}{16}''$ from one end of the slide. The holes need only be big enough for carpet thread to go through. Four holes have to be drilled in each wide side. Actually, it is easier to drill each hole through one wide side and continue through the other. The centers of the holes

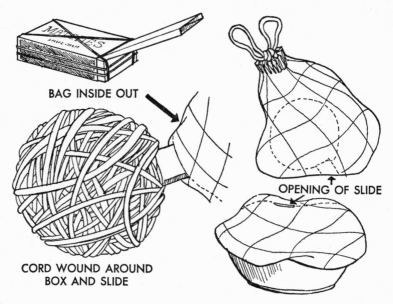

BAG INSIDE OUT

OPENING OF SLIDE

CORD WOUND AROUND
BOX AND SLIDE

are $\frac{3}{32}''$ of an inch from the end of the tube. Two holes are drilled $\frac{1}{8}''$ apart close to one narrow side of the slide and the other two are drilled the same distance apart near the other narrow side. The purpose of these holes is for the thread by which the slide is sewed into the bag.

The bag is 9″ wide and 11″ deep. The bag cannot be made any smaller and be easy to use. While it may be made larger, there is no advantage in doing so. The bag I use is made of heavy tie silk. Any silk, or rayon, having body can be used. The silk of my bag is a subdued plaid of dark green and black with thin lines of yellow. The idea is that the bag is merely a bag and shouldn't be too colorful or fancy so that it will not attract undue attention. The bag is made of two pieces of cloth so that there is a seam at the bottom of the bag as well as the two sides. The bottom seam is necessary.

In sewing the bag one corner is left open 1¼″ at the bottom and the same distance on the adjacent side. The front and back silk of this corner are tucked inside the bag. The end of the slide having the holes is sewed into this open corner at the center of the diagonal opening which is 1¾″ wide. The slide is sewed not quite to the outside edge of the material so that the silk will hide both slide and opening. Care must be taken that the end of the slide is not so far in the bag that the silk will cover the opening. When sewed in place, and the bag laid flat on a table, the slide should point diagonally across the inside of the bag. The bottom corner of the bag opposite to the one with the slide should be folded in and sewed so that both corners have the same appearance. Using silken cords, a double draw string is run through a hem at the mouth of the bag.

To prepare the trick, the bag is turned wrong side out. This will bring the slide outside the bag. First the slide is inserted in the open box. (The various kinds of boxes which can be used will be described later.) Two or three rubber bands are wound around the box. The bands are put around the box for the primary purpose of closing the box after the slide has been withdrawn. The second purpose of the bands is to make it seem to be impossible to get anything into the box because they hold it closed so tightly. Once the rubber bands are on the box, the cord is wrapped around the box until the box becomes the core of a ball of cord. The cord should be soft and very pliable, and ¼″ in diameter. It may be of silk, cotton or any other material. Suitable cord is used by upholsterers. Twelve yards of cord is required. After the cord is wound around the top, bottom, and sides of the box until it is covered, the cord is wound one way and another so as to form a ball. It will be found possible to wind the ball in such a way that when the slide is withdrawn during the performance, the cord will cover the opening where the slide had been. As the cord never is wound exactly the same way twice, nor need be, exact instructions cannot be given for winding. However, no trouble should be found in doing so. Once the ball of cord is completed, the bag is turned right side out so as to cover the ball. This must be done carefully so as not to pull the slide out of position. The draw strings of the bag are pulled so the bag is tightly closed and the strings are tied with a bowknot. The bag then is put mouth down in the bowl. It is put in the bowl so that the open corner, having the slide, is uppermost.

With the coin in his hand, where it had dropped from the bottom of the envelope, the magician goes to his prop table. With the one hand he drops the coin into the slot. With the other he picks up the bowl. The hand which deposits the coin should then rest on the bag as if it were holding it in the bowl. When he gets to his performance table, the magician places the bowl on the table and takes out the bag, turns it right side up and puts it back into the bowl. All he seems to have done is show the bag and to set it correctly in the bowl. In doing this he also pulled the slide out of the ball. As the magician carries the bowl and bag to place both on the table, he has ample time without fumbling to take, through the cloth, a firm grip of the very end of the metal slide. When the bowl is on the table, the hand which held it is freed. That hand, on the outside of the cloth, then takes hold of the ball. While that hand is held motionless, the other hand pulls the slide which raises the bag. The instant it is felt that the ball is freed from the slide, the hand holding the ball is released. The other hand continues to lift the bag. When the bag is raised enough so that the mouth is out of the bowl, the cords are taken and by them the bag is turned right side up, and left in the bowl.

After the envelope, with its "coin" is burned, the magician chooses a spectator to assist him. The magician picks up the bowl and holds it so that the assistant can untie the drawstrings and pull open the mouth of the bag. The bowl is handed to the assistant. The magician takes hold of the bottom corners of the bag and, by shaking gently, gets the ball out of the bag and lets it drop into the bowl. The bag is put on the table. The trick actually is completed as far as the magician is concerned. All he need do further is to pull the cord the assistant gives him and thereby unroll the ball. It is more effective if, when the magician first pulls on the cord, he does so by stepping back and only begins to loop it after he is a couple of yards away. The fact that the magician is at a distance from his assistant at the time the box holding the coin is found makes the magic more impressive.

At the beginning of the description of what the audience sees, it was stated that either a quarter dollar or a half dollar could be used. Either will go into the slide described and it improves the magic a little by giving that choice. But it must be remembered to have the slit at the bottom of the envelope long enough so that the larger coin will slide through easily. Before letting the half dollar slide into the hand after the envelope is sealed, it aids the magic to permit someone to feel "the half dollar inside the envelope."

All sorts of boxes can be used in which the coin will be found. The simplest is an ordinary safety match box, having a drawer. The slide will go in such a box nicely. Another box with a drawer is the kind druggists use and is made of cardboard. The pocket-size metal boxes for aspirin have a hinged cover and, when painted, can be quite attractive. A special box can be made of brass. Such a box can be made with a drawer or with a hinged cover. Nesting boxes can be made so that the coin is found in the innermost box. I use nesting boxes. Both boxes have hinged covers. The larger is closed by the rubber bands and the smaller is closed by the pressure of the cover of the outer box. The smaller box has a lock which closes by pressure but only can be opened with a key. These boxes were a present of my teacher, the late John William Sargent, who had performed the feat for many years. He had the boxes made some twenty-five years before I was born and it was not a new trick even then.

My addition to the trick is having the slide sewed into the bag. This eliminates having to get rid of the slide upon its removal from the ball of cord. It also allows the slide to be taken out of the ball or cord right in front of the audience without a suspicious move.

By the way, the original name for the feat was due to the fact that the ball invariably was made of wool yarn used for knitting. Such yarn, being very much smaller than the cord recommended here, needed to be so long to make a ball of the proper size that it took far too long to unwind and is quite unsuitable for this age of speed.

FLYING SILK

MAGICIANS frequently are asked by people who have seen their performances, "How can I learn just one or two magic tricks?" My answer always is, "You can't for in that respect magic is very much like music. If you learn to play one composition on the piano, well enough for anyone to enjoy hearing you, you will have automatically gained enough knowledge and skill to play other melodies. The same is true with magic. When a person learns to perform one feat well enough to interest and entertain his spectator, or spectators, he will find he knows enough to perform other mysteries." Here is an excellent example of that fact.

The magician shows a silk handkerchief. He rolls the silk into a ball and, to keep it from unrolling, fastens it with a pin. He drops the ball into a glass which he covers with a cardboard tube. This glass stands on one of his performance tables. On another table he has a piece of wrapping paper and a second glass. He forms the paper into a cornucopia and puts it in the glass so it will be held upright. Returning to the tube-covered glass, the magician raises the tube and shows the silk handkerchief still is in the glass. Replacing the tube, the magician explains that he is going to cause the handkerchief to leave the glass and fly inside the cornucopia. He states that the flight will be so rapid that the eye cannot follow. The tube is taken from the glass and both tube and glass are seen to be empty. He goes to the cornucopia, reaches inside, and pulls out the silk handkerchief.

Except for a very few minor details the reader has all the knowledge he needs for this feat, for it is a combination of parts of two tricks described earlier in this chapter.

The disappearance of the ball made out of the silk handkerchief is exactly like the disappearance of the ball in "Ball, Paper and Nothing." The appearance of the handkerchief in the cornucopia makes use of the same secret as described in "Traveling on a Wish" except that it is done in reverse. In that feat the packet in the paper from which the cornucopia was made was used to cause a handkerchief to disappear. The little Indian bust made out of the handkerchief was in the pocket at the end of the feat. In this new trick, the pocket contains the handkerchief prior to performance and is empty at the end. Naturally, this handkerchief is a duplicate of the one caused to disappear. This reversal does not alter the paper, nor the way it is handled, but the effect to the audience is totally different.

Now about the minor details. Unless a simple secret is known, it is rather difficult to make a silk handkerchief into a ball which will look, and can be handled, like a ball and not a floppy piece of cloth. The secret is that the ball must have a hard core around which the silk is rolled. Various methods have been tried such as sewing a tiny ball of hard rubber in the hem of one corner of the silk and rolling the handkerchief about the ball. While this works well, it is not necessary and requires using a prepared handkerchief. This is the way an unprepared silk handkerchief is rolled into a hard ball. The silk is put over the back of the left hand and one corner is brought to the palm. The hand is held with thumb pointing up and the fingers straight but held together. The handkerchief goes from the back to the palm of the hand at the crotch of the thumb and is held tightly by the thumb pressing against the side of the hand. The corner of the silk is at the center of the palm of the left hand. The right hand, also held flat, is pressed against the palm of the left hand and with the corner of the silk between the two palms. Holding the left hand still but pushing the right hand forward will cause the corner of the silk to twist tightly. When this has been done, still pressing the palms together tightly, the right hand begins a rotary rubbing action. This will cause the twisted corner to wind upon itself and to form a small hard ball. Continuing the rotary motion, the left thumb releases its pressure just enough so that little by little the handkerchief is permitted to be wound upon itself until it becomes a ball of silk. Holding the handkerchief so that it doesn't unroll, the magician pushes a pin into the silk so that it can't unwind. The pin, a needle may be used, is tied to the thread which runs through the hole in the cardboard tube. The pin, or needle, used should not be over 1″ long so it doesn't protrude from the ball. And so it will go in easily, it should not be thick. The ball of silk then may be treated exactly as was the rubber ball in the "Ball, Paper and Nothing" feat and the handkerchief will disappear just as readily and as easily as did the rubber ball.

Another small detail is to have the duplicate handkerchief folded flat when it is put into the pocket of the wrapping paper. This is done to avoid having any bulge in the paper when, prior to making the cornucopia, the paper lies open on the table. While the silk should be folded, it has to be rumpled prior to folding so it will have the appearance of the silk which had been rolled into a ball. Care always must be taken, when using duplicates, that they be in the same condition. The audience is quite willing to believe that the magician has the power to cause a silk handkerchief to make an invisible journey but people will not accept that he can iron the handkerchief while it is on its instantaneous flight.

STRAWBERRY MILK

CHILDREN always derive double enjoyment from witnessing a performance of magic. They have the pleasure of seeing impossible things occur during the show. For days afterward they find delight in imagining all the things they could do to their advantage were they magicians. Think of how delightful it would be to be able to spend each week's allowance at least twice, as surely a magician can do. Then the social advantage to be able, upon saying a magic word, to be transported to school instantly on those mornings of late arising. Who could fail to select occasions when life would be made easier by personal invisibility? All these things are so nice to dream about. Unfortunately one discovers upon reaching adulthood that magic has so little practical value.

This feat is in line with the idea that life might be more pleasurable were one a magician. It is a magical way of making strawberry milk. The magician pours a glass of milk—quite ordinary white milk. He shows a piece of cloth decorated with a pattern of strawberries. By his magic the performer causes the strawberries to leave the cloth and go to color the milk. That is the whimsical plot of the magic.

This is what the audience sees the magician do. He shows an empty glass tumbler. He places the glass on a table and covers it with a white paper tube the height of the glass and just large enough to slip over it. From a glass pitcher the magician pours milk into the glass. He then goes to another table upon which there is another tumbler. This glass holds a paper cornucopia. The magician removes the cornucopia, turns it upside down, and shakes it. Then the paper cone is replaced in the glass so that it is held upright. The magician picks up a piece of cloth and holds it so that the audience can see that the cloth is decorated with a design of strawberries. He not only shows the strawberries pictured on the cloth but he calls particular attention to them. The cloth is pushed into the cornucopia. The magician picks up a glass, or colorless plastic, rod. He sticks the rod into the cornucopia and stirs it around several times. He then takes the rod, goes back to the first table, and stirs the milk exactly as he had done with the silk in the cornucopia. The paper tube is taken off the glass, crumpled and put aside. The milk is seen to be a deep strawberry color. The magician picks up the glass and drinks some of the milk with obvious relish. He even mentions that he loves strawberry milk. Returning to the cornucopia, the magician takes it from the glass and opens it to show the cloth. The cloth now is plain, for all the strawberries have disappeared.

Coloring the milk is quite simple for all that is required is a few drops of food coloring sold by grocers. These drops are put in the bottom of the glass prior to the performance. When the glass is on the table the small amount of color in the bottom cannot be seen. When the magician shows the glass he holds it with his hand at the base and merely remembers to hold the glass upright and not to tilt it so the audience can look into it. The white paper tube is used to keep the audience from being able to see the milk starting to change color the instant it goes into the glass. The milk originally is in, and is poured from, a glass pitcher. A glass pitcher is used in order that the audience can see the milk prior to being poured into the glass. The rod is used to stir the milk in order to color the milk evenly. The reason a clear glass, or plastic, rod is used is so the audience will not suspect that the rod really plays any part in the feat. The magician can drink the milk with safety for food coloring is made to be edible. There will be no flavor of strawberries and the milk will taste as milk always does. As what he drinks looks like strawberry milk and the magician acts as if it were and claims it to be strawberry milk, there never is any doubt that is just what it is. A pre-performance test will have to be made to discover just how many drops of food coloring are needed properly to color the quantity of milk used.

Changing the cloth from the one decorated with strawberries to a plain one is done by means of a cornucopia made of wrapping paper and having a secret pocket identical to the ones used in two feats previously described in this chapter. In one of those feats the cornucopia was used to cause a handkerchief to disappear and in the other a handkerchief was made to disappear. This time the cornucopia is used for both purposes. While the effect of the magic is that the cloth has been altered, actually one piece was made to disappear and the other produced. There is a difference, too, in the way the cornucopia is handled. The second piece of cloth, the plain one which appears, is wrapped in the folds of the paper as the cornucopia is made prior to performance. It is put as near the tip as can be done without showing. The reason for this is that the cornucopia may be grasped naturally at the tip and the handkerchief will be held in place when the cone is turned upside down. Turning over the cornucopia, seemingly, demonstrates its emptiness without needing to mention the subject. The cloth decorated with strawberries is pushed into the secret pocket of the paper. When the cornucopia is unrolled the pocket is held shut to hide the printed cloth and the plain cloth is disclosed as the paper is opened. The only reason for stirring inside the cornucopia with the glass rod is that the stirring has to be done inside the glass. The stated reason for using the rod is that by it the strawberries are picked up by the rod, even though they can't be seen, and carried over to flavor the milk. The audience will accept both action and statement as most reasonable—at least in magic.

While it does not have anything to do with the performance, there is one quite unusual task in this feat. That is to find a piece of cloth decorated with a design of strawberries. The cloth must be of material which takes little space when crushed. Thin silk is excellent for the purpose although other materials can be used. There should be little or no green, or any other color, in the pattern. Dress fabrics or printed handkerchiefs are admirable. (If strawberry-printed fabrics cannot be found in your locality, those printed with cherries or raspberries are just as suitable and the milk can be called cherry or raspberry milk.) If fruit-printed material cannot be found, it is possible to use cloth having red dots on a white background by explaining that the dots symbolize strawberry juice. The second piece of cloth is of the same size and quality and is pure white. Material having dots of other colors may also be used. As example, brown dots may be called chocolate and chocolate milk made—using a different food color. Other examples could be offered but would seem unnecessary, for the idea is plain that prior to doing anything else in regard to this feat, it is necessary to purchase the cloth to be used. The story accompaniment used in performance depends upon the cloth which the magician is able to obtain.

THE ELUSIVE BLOCK

THIS is a sequence of feats of magic which will amuse, as well as mystify, both children and adults. The magic requires the assistance of two members of the audience and, if possible, these two assistants should be children. The reaction of children, as the magic occurs, is a show in itself. Children show their excitement and amazement for they have not yet learned to be calm when seeing the impossible performed.

The magician begins by taking a large block of wood and a length of ribbon from a cardboard box. The box then is shown to be empty. The block of wood is a solid cube which has a hole drilled through it. The magician threads the ribbon through the hole in the block. Each assistant is asked to hold one end of the ribbon. The block hangs in the center of the ribbon the assistants hold. The magician takes hold of the block and pulls. In full view of the audience the ribbon seems to melt right through the wood so that block and ribbon are separated. The magician then covers the block with a silk handkerchief and puts the block on a skeleton stand which is on a table on the opposite side of the platform from the table with the cardboard box. Whisking the handkerchief away the block has disappeared. It reappears inside the cardboard box. After the block is taken from the box the magician finds the box also contains many yards of silk. That is what the audience sees and what it will remember. As will be disclosed in the description of how the magic works there are several other details which the audience can see but which seem so inconsequential that they hardly will be noticed and never remembered.

This consequence is made of three separate tricks: 1. Magically removing a solid block of wood from the ribbon upon which it was hung; 2. Causing the block to disappear on one side of the platform and reappear on the other; 3. Making a quantity of silk appear in the cardboard box which had been shown to be empty. While what the magician does in one trick has, in several instances, to do with one of the other tricks the details of such actions will be described after the method of each trick is described.

The block and the ribbon are both exactly as the magician claims and as they seem to be. The block is a $4\frac{1}{2}''$ cube of wood. It should be a hardwood which will not dent easily and when stained and varnished will be more attractive than soft wood would be. I was able to get a piece of walnut of suitable size from a cabinet maker. Few lumber yards stock hard wood of such size and if they do usually will not cut off a piece to sell. It is possible to make the block by gluing several pieces of board together. Each edge of the block should be sanded just enough to keep it from being sharp but not enough so that it appears to be rounded. A hole is drilled at the exact center of one side of the block and completely through the block so as to come out at the exact center of the opposite side. The hole should be $\frac{7}{8}''$ in diameter. The edges of the hole on both sides of the block should be rounded. The size of the hole is decided by the size of the fingers of the magician. The hole must be big enough so that the first finger of either hand will go easily into the hole but should not be any bigger. If the block is solid the hole is drilled through the face of the wood not the end grain. If the block has been made of several pieces of wood the hole is drilled so as to go through all the boards. The block is then stained and varnished with a good grade of clear spar varnish. The block has to have golden edges painted on all six surfaces. How this is done and the reason which makes it necessary will be discussed in the description of the second part of the effect.

The ribbon, as was stated, is a heavy silk ribbon 1¼″ wide and 5′ long. It should be a silk which does not wrinkle as do some ribbons. While the ribbon itself is exactly as it appears to be and in itself quite innocent, something, as the ads say, has been added. This addition is a circle of very strong thread attached about 3″ from one end of the ribbon. This heavy thread is black and, according to where it is purchased, is called carpet thread, or shoe thread. A length of this thread is made into a loop which, when stretched, is 1″ long. The ends are tied with a square knot which, after tying, should be tested to see that the thread does not slip through the knot. After the knot has been securely tied the threads are cut off close to the knot. This loop is put over one end of the ribbon and slid down 3″ from the end. There it is held in place by sewing it with a single strand of the finest silk thread—ooo, if possible, and at least oo thread. When completed, the open loop of thread around the ribbon should stick out at a point 3″ from one end of the ribbon.

The magician threads the block on the ribbon. The ribbon, as the audience plainly can see, not only goes through the block but is put through twice so as to make a loop around the block and so tying it to the ribbon. While that is what the magician seems to do, and the audience is convinced having seen done, it is not quite what he does.

This is the way in which the ribbon goes through the block. At the beginning the magician holds the ribbon in the left hand by one end. The ribbon is grasped by the thumb and first finger so that the loop of thread is hidden by the second, third, and little fingers. The ribbon hangs down so that the other end is just above the floor. In his right hand he holds the block of wood. It is at this point in the presentation that the magician selects two children to assist him. The sex of these children is immaterial but they should be at least eight years old. The children are handed the block of wood to examine. Then one child is told to hold the block while the other is asked to look at the ribbon and to hand the magician the lower end. The magician, of course, never releases the end of the ribbon he holds. Taking the end of the ribbon the child gives him, the magician threads the ribbon through the hole in the block. He pulls the ribbon through the block, taking a step back as he does so, and brings the two ends of the ribbon together. While seemingly only putting the ends of the ribbon together so that both may be held with the left hand, the magician puts the one end through the loop of thread which is fastened to the other end. There is no difficulty in doing this because the loop of thread is hidden from the sight of the audience and is large enough to slip the ribbon through easily. The magician makes certain that, with his left hand, he has a firm grip on the two ends of ribbon

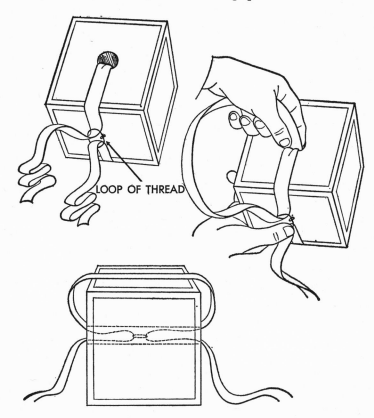

LOOP OF THREAD

and then asks the boy to let go of the block. The magician is holding the ribbon high enough in the air so that the block does not strike the floor when the boy releases it.

As the magician is exhibiting the block hanging from the ribbon he takes hold of the double ribbon with his right hand. He grasps the ribbon as near the ends as the left hand permits. As with his right hand, the magician takes hold of the two thicknesses of ribbon, he sticks the end of his first finger through the loop of thread. Pulling his hand down the double strands of ribbon he breaks the fine silk thread which has held the loop of carpet thread to the ribbon. Because the silk thread is so fine it breaks very easily. The magician continues running his right hand along the ribbons until the block is reached. He then releases the ribbon, as well as the loop of thread, with his right hand and takes hold of the block of wood. The instant the right hand holds the block the left hand releases the ends of the ribbon which are permitted to flutter down towards the floor. At this point the magician is holding the block so that the loop of thread is against the side of the block away from the audience. Putting the block on his left hand the magician changes the position of his right hand so that the thumb holds the loop of thread against the block and the fingers go against the face of the block. Having again taken hold of the block with his right hand the magician removes his left hand from under the block.

As the magician holds the block the center of the length of ribbon is inside the hole in the block. At each side of the hole the ribbon goes around to the back of the block through the loop of thread, and hangs down. It will now be plain, and the illustration will make it more obvious, that were one end of the ribbon to be pushed back through the hole on the same side of the block from which it came out, the ribbon would be free of the block except for the loop of thread. The magician does this and after the ribbon is through the hole he continues pulling the ribbon until the loop of thread is brought inside the hole. In order to do this he relaxes the pressure of his thumb on the thread. As the loop of the thread is pulled from the back of the block into the hole, the block is turned so the audience never can see the thread. At this point the ribbon goes into the block through the loop, back out of the hole, around the outside of the block into the other end of the hole, through the loop of thread and back out of the hole. To the audience it appears as if the block was tied onto the ribbon and the magician explains that what he has done is to fasten the block onto the ribbon.

The magician asks each of his assistants to take one end of the ribbon and to wind the ends around their hands to ensure a firm grip. Next they are told to step back so that the ribbon is taut. The magician then lets go of the block so that everyone can see it hanging suspended by the ribbon. The block should not be released by the magician until he can feel that the ribbon is holding it. Were he to drop the block he might break the loop of thread by which the block actually is held and thereby release the block inadvertently.

As the children hold the ribbon from which the block is suspended the magician recounts what has been done. A solid block of wood has been tied on to a strong ribbon and the ends of the ribbon are held by the assistants. He then reminds the audience that if neither assistant releases the ribbon there is no way to get the block off the ribbon except by magic. Reminding the children to hold tightly to the ribbon and to keep it taut, the magician takes hold of the block and, with a jerk, lifts it in the air. Jerking the block will break the loop of thread and release the ribbon so that the block is free. The children again are given the block to examine and to assure themselves that it is quite as solid as it was when they first looked at it. The magician takes the block and puts it aside on a table and asks the children to make certain that nothing has happened to the ribbon either. The magician retrieves the ribbon, thanks the children for their help and sends them back to their seats.

The second part of the routine is the disappearance and reappearance of the block of wood. This is made possible through the use of a skeleton brass frame. As previously mentioned the edges of the block are gilded. When the brass frame is put over the block the frame is invisible for it looks exactly like the gilt edges. When the edges of the block are gilded the block already has had a coat of transparent spar varnish. This makes a non-porous surface upon which to put the gold. The gold should go along each of the four edges of each face of the cubic block. The gold edge is $\frac{3}{16}''$ wide and has to have its inner edge absolutely straight. The outer edge joins the gold on the adjacent side. The easiest way to get the gold edges straight and of the correct width is to cover with masking tape the entire surface of each side, except for the edges to be painted. Great care must be taken to have the masking tape put on to exact measurements and tightly stuck to the wood.

The skeleton brass frame is made of $\frac{1}{4}''$ angle brass, $\frac{1}{32}''$ thick, and brass strips of the same width and thickness. The top edges and the edges of the four uprights of the frame are made of the angle brass. The four bottom edges are made of the brass strips. At all connecting corners the brass should be filed to make lap joints and the joints soldered. When finished the frame should be of such a size as to fit over the cube freely but not loosely. The frame, to repeat, should look exactly like the gold edge of the block.

Having made the frame for the block, it is necessary to make a container for the frame. This is made in the same manner as was the frame. There

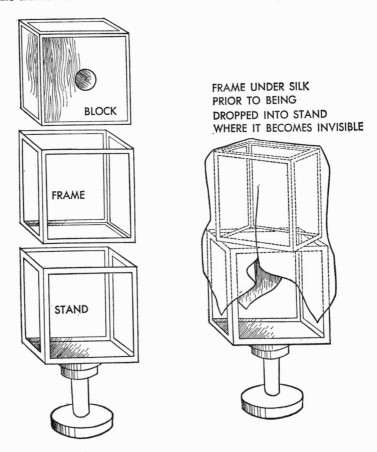

BLOCK

FRAME

STAND

FRAME UNDER SILK
PRIOR TO BEING
DROPPED INTO STAND
WHERE IT BECOMES INVISIBLE

are three differences. The angle brass, and the brass strips, are ⅜″ wide (that is ⅛″ wider than was used for the frame). A square of brass is soldered to the inside flanges of the horizontal angle brass. This brass square makes the bottom of the container—in other words, while the container is made in the same way the frame is made, it is inverted in use. To the brass square is attached some sort of pedestal. While I made a four legged support, it is less work to solder in place a short brass candlestick with a large base.

The only other requisites necessary to perform the disappearance and reappearance of the block are the cardboard box, from which both block and ribbon originally were taken, and a silk handkerchief. The handkerchief should be 18″ square and dark in color. It may be a solid color or have a pattern. The silk should be as light weight as possible without being transparent. A darker color is less likely to be transparent.

Prior to the performance the frame is placed upside down on the table behind, and hidden by, the cardboard box. The container stands on its pedestal on another table on the other side of the platform. The handkerchief is in the container.

At the conclusion of the feat of removing the block from the ribbon, the block is put aside while the children pull on the ribbon. In putting the block on the table it is put into the frame which is hidden by the cardboard box. The best way to hold the block when putting it in the frame is to put the second finger into the hole in the block and hold the block as if it were a bowling ball. Holding the block in this way makes it easy to put it in the frame quickly and quietly. When the magician retrieves the ribbon from the children he gathers it up and puts it on the table behind the cardboard box. As soon as the ribbon has been dropped, the magician picks up the block. At this point, it will be recalled, the frame is upside down. The frame covered block is picked up so that, with the palm of the hand over the block, the fingers and thumb on opposite sides of the block grip both block and frame. The frame has to be held too as, at this point, it is upside down and could drop off.

Holding the block out in front of his body, the magician walks over to the container and takes out the handkerchief. He then puts the block diagonally on top of, not into, the container. He spreads out the handkerchief and shows both sides of it to the audience. Having exhibited the handkerchief, the magician spreads it over the palm of his left hand so that the center of the silk is right over the palm. With the right hand the block is again picked up remembering to hold the frame as well. The right hand sets the block on the center of the handkerchief but does not release it. Both hands, pressing against the block, turn the block over. This will drape the handkerchief over the block and at the same time turn the frame right side up. While, under the handkerchief, the right hand continues to hold the block, the left hand makes certain that the silk covers the block completely. As soon as the handkerchief is adjusted properly, the block is picked up with the left hand and replaced on top of, not inside, the container.

The magician tells the audience that what he intends to do is to have the block leave where it is and go across and hide inside the cardboard box (and he points) all the way over there. He continues by explaining that there are two ways in which this can be done. "One way," he says, "is like this." He picks up the silk covered block and, impressively as possible, he carries the block across the stage and puts it in the cardboard box. In a rather embarrassed manner the magician says, "Of course, it isn't necessary to be a magician to do it that way but let me show you the other way." As he offers to show the audience the magical way to make the block cross, he lifts the silk covered block out of the cardboard box. At least that is what the audience believe they see him do. Actually all that he takes out of the box is the silk covered frame—the block is left in the box. The magician rapidly recrosses and puts the "block" back on top of the container. The magician announces that he will now make the block go into the cardboard box the magical way. Taking hold of the top of the "block" through the handkerchief with his right hand the magician, with his left hand, takes hold of the hem of the handkerchief nearest the audience. He then twists the "block" so that it can drop into the container. The left hand holds the silk so that it does not flutter and disclose the absence of the block. The metal frame will make the same sound as does the block of wood when it is dropped. "Seeing" the "block" dropped into the container, and hearing it drop as well, is convincing evidence that the block actually is there. As soon as the block is in the container the magician moves a short step away from the table.

The magician announces: "The block is about to make its trip. It will happen very rapidly, so I beg you to watch closely." The magical countdown —10-8-6-4-2-boom."

As "boom" is said the magician reaches over, grasps one corner of the handkerchief and jerks it away. Everyone can see that there is no block in the container and the frame cannot be seen as it matches the container. The magician crumples up the handkerchief and tosses it into the container, turns and walks across to the box. Reaching into the box the magician takes out the block and exhibits it to the audience.

As the magician starts to put the block back into the box, he acts startled. He quickly puts the block on the table and reaches into the box. From the box he pulls yard after yard of silk. He holds the silk in big loops as he takes it from the box. When all the silk has been removed from the box the magician tumbles it back into the box—or as much as he can get in, for the silk more than fills the box.

Secretly getting the silk into the box actually is the first thing the magician does in the routine. It is described last in order to keep effect and method together. The cardboard box may be almost any size if it is deep enough to hide the block completely and the side facing the audience is at least 8″ long. Provided it meets these specifications the smaller the box the greater the effect of the production. The box must have a separate cover as is usual for cardboard boxes. The only preparation required is a neat $\frac{1}{16}$″ hole in the cover. The hole is made at the exact center of one edge of the cover at the point where the cardboard is bent to make the flange which goes around the sides of the box. The hole is made by placing a large needle at the correct spot and flat on the inside surface of the cover. The needle is pressed through the cardboard far enough so that the point of the needle can be seen on the outside of the cardboard. The needle then is withdrawn and pushed into the hole from the outside. By pushing the needle little by little from first one side of the cardboard and then the other, it is possible to make a neat hole which will not be noticed as it is so small and does not have rough edges. In the following description, the side of the cover having the hole will be called the back of the cover as it always is put on the box with that side away from the audience.

If this routine is not done in the same performance as the magic of "A Boy and a Box of Candy" the same length of silk and the same holder can be used. When done together a similar length of silk is required and an identical holder. However, one alteration has to be made in the holder. A very small hole has to be drilled close to the elastic at each end of one of the bars of metal. One end of a length of thread is pushed through one hole and tied to the metal bar and the other end of the thread put through the hole at the other end of the bar and tied. By pulling on the center of the thread a triangle is formed. From the metal base of this triangle to the apex formed by the thread should be equal to half the width of the cover. The thread is pushed through the hole in the cover starting from the inside. The loop of thread on the outside of the cover is kept from being withdrawn by a pin. A short glass beaded pin such as florists use is best for the purpose. The pin is pushed into the cardboard of the top. Care must be used in inserting the pin that it goes straight into the cardboard and the point does not come out on either the outside or inner surface of the cover. The pin is pushed all the way into the cardboard. Over the head of the pin is looped the thread which is tied to the holder. It will now be obvious that when the cover is on the box the bundle of silk will hang down inside the box and that when the cover is stood on its front edge with the top towards the audience the silk will hang behind the cover. In order to keep the audience

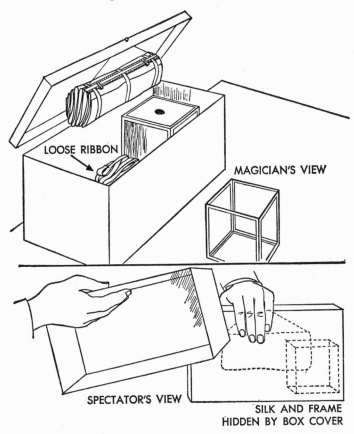

LOOSE RIBBON

MAGICIAN'S VIEW

SPECTATOR'S VIEW

SILK AND FRAME
HIDDEN BY BOX COVER

from seeing the bundle of silk and yet show both box and cover merely requires memorizing a sequence of actions. All the actions are completely normal which makes the trick both simple to do and very effective.

At the beginning the covered cardboard box is on the table. Inside the box are the wooden block, the length of ribbon, and the suspended bundle of silk. The magician takes off the cover of the box. He does this by taking hold of the cover at the back and raising it toward the front of the box until the cover is perpendicular. Actually this action pivots the cover on the front edge until it is upright before it is raised from the box. The cover is then stood on edge behind the box and held in that position with the left hand. While in removing the cover it is more natural to use both hands, the right hand actually plays no real part. The left hand takes hold of the cover in the center of the back (where the pin is) and maintains its grip while holding the cover on its edge. Having the hand in this position also hides the glass head of the pin which can be seen although it is not apt to be noticed.

Having taken the cover off the box, the magician takes the wooden block out of the box and places it on the table. He follows by taking the length of ribbon from the box and putting it beside the block. He then picks up the box and shows it to be empty. This is done by taking hold of the top edge of the back of the box and tipping it forward. The box is raised from the table and turned to the right and left so that everyone is assured of the emptiness of the box. These moves will show all the inside and bottom and the sides of the outside of the box. The box having been shown is put back in its place on the table.

The cover is put back on the box by reversing the actions used in removing it. That will put the bundle of silk, which the audience never has seen and is unaware of, back inside the box. While seeming to adjust the cover the magician withdraws the pin from the cover and drops it on the table. Because of the glass head this can be done without fumbling which keeps the action from being noticed.

The magician then makes a remark to the effect the cover will not be needed and takes it off again. The cover is removed exactly as it was the first time. Lifting it from the back first will draw the thread out of the hole. The weight of the bundle of silk is enough to do this. As soon as the cover is off the box the magician in putting it aside turns it so that the inside (which never has been seen by the audience) is exposed. No attempt should be made to show the inside of the cover, but the cover is so handled that it just happens that the inside may be seen.

The bundle of the silk is now in the box, although the audience is unaware of the fact, and will remain there unseen until the end of the routine. After the block has been taken out of the box all the magician has to do, prior to pulling out the yards of silk, is to release the holder by squeezing it.

Nine. MORE EXCEPTIONAL MAGIC

THE tricks in this Chapter are akin to those in the previous two Chapters in their appeal to audiences and in where they can be performed. Again there is apparatus to make and considerable practice required to master presentation. Nothing which has to be made will be found to be beyond the knowledge of one having completed a school shop course or one having a home workshop possessing the usual stock of tools. The person who does not want to make everything himself will find his local cabinet maker and tinsmith very cooperative and he will have no difficulty in assembling the parts. However the required equipment is made, the various feats of magic described will be found to verge on the miraculous.

HO CHANG—THE BENEVOLENT

HO CHANG, one of the seven gods of good luck, may be said to be the Chinese Santa Claus. Ho Chang—as pronounced in at least one dialect— is his Chinese name. In Japan he is known as Hotei. He also is revered in India and through much of the East. He is a god, or Saint, holding the position very similar to St. Nicholas of Christianity. While St. Nicholas and Santa Claus are different people, Ho Chang, though a single person, plays a dual role; he is a Saint and benevolently generous in his gifts at the same time. Very regularly his followers forget his Sainthood and ask only for his generosity quite as, in the minds of many, there is confusion regarding the roles of St. Nick and Santa. Statues of Ho Chang are made in great

quantity. An image of him may be found in the majority of Oriental households and, because of his genial expression, figures of him also are found as ornaments in many Occidental homes. Ho Chang has another similarity to Santa Claus in that he is fat and has a noticeably protruding and rotund abdomen. While Santa is known for "a belly which shakes like a bowl full of jelly" it plays no part in his bringing presents and must be somewhat of a bother when he climbs down chimneys. On the other hand, Ho's belly plays a major part in the request for granting a wish. The request is made directly to a statue of Ho Chang and during the solicitation, the petitioner rubs the abdomen of the figure. Tummy rubbing, of course, is far easier a task than writing a letter to the North Pole workshop of Mr. Claus, and furthermore, the pledge of superior conduct for the prior year is not required by Ho Chang.

Every artist who ever has sculptured a figure of Ho Chang has given him a kindly face embellished with two very large ears. While it pleases me to feel that my own countenance is kindly there can be no doubt that my ears are of generous size. Figures of Ho Chang always are given large ears because, it is believed, large ears are an indication of a generous nature. My regard for Ho Chang is even greater now that the years have given me a rotundity like his except, if you please, somewhat less obtrusive. It is obvious that my feeling of kinship for Ho Chang, and so enjoying the wonderful stories told about him, would make me want to bring him into my show. It is of no importance whatsoever that I was pleased with the trick I devised to perform with a statue of Ho Chang, but it is important that the trick always pleases my audiences. They are interested in the little Saint and the story told of his prowess in granting wishes even to the point of making an invisible and indetectable journey and they enjoyed witnessing the demonstration proving the validity of the story.

MORE EXCEPTIONAL MAGIC

My statue of Ho Chang is a seated figure made of cast brass. It is 3½″ high and quite heavy. I purchased it many years ago but in the intervening years, as well as recently, I have seen similar figures in department stores and Oriental shops. I even have seen them in those establishments with names as exaggerated as a magician's patter for each is called a "5¢ and 10¢ Store." While, as noted, my statue is of brass, similar figures come in a variety of other metals and different materials such as wood and ivory. All can be used in the trick. Now that you know Ho Chang, it might be well to describe the magic the audience sees.

The magician begins this feat by picking up a brass box and opening a door, which makes the face of the box, by swinging it on its hinges. Inside the box are four pony-size liqueur glasses. The glasses are removed from the box and placed on the table to form the corners of a rectangle. After the glasses are in position the door of the box is closed and fastened and the box is inverted and placed upside down on the table. The magician picks up a small and very thin board and places it on the glasses so as to make a raised platform. Next he picks up the cover of the box with one hand and with the other takes the box. In putting on the cover the box is turned right side up and the covered box is placed on the little platform which had just been made. Finally a weight is put on the cover.

While he does these things the magician talks about what he has done and what he is doing. As example, in opening the door of the box he states, "This brass box contains four glasses." After the glasses are removed it is obvious that what the magician holds is a simple brass box with a door and that it is empty. Turning the box upside down confirms the emptiness of the box. The magician describes how he is making the little platform as he puts the board on the glasses. The platform, while completely devoid of trickery, is unusual and by pointing out its innocence the magician not only satisfies his audience but focuses attention on the platform rather than the box which everyone readily accepts as just a small empty box made of brass. Once the covered box is on the platform the magician says, "This box stands in plain sight on this raised platform so everyone can watch it and see that it doesn't disappear or have anything else happen to it." Then picking up a little brass paperweight and placing it on top of the box the magician says, "And I'll weight the cover to keep it in place."

The magician then points to the figure of Ho Chang sitting on a book. As if it were a tray, the magician picks up the book with the idol and holds it so the audience better can see the brass idol. As the spectators look at the little god his name is announced and the statement made that many people believe he is capable of granting any wish. The magician goes on to express the hope that Ho Chang is willing to show his powers. When this is said the magician picks up the brass figure. To free his hand of the book the magician turns it edgewise and sticks it under the arm of the other hand. Bringing his hands together the magician squeezes the idol which causes it to disappear. As the magician takes his hands apart, and shows them open and with the fingers widely spread, it is obvious that the brass figure has disappeared completely.

As he shows his empty hands the magician explains that what he wished Ho Chang to do was to make an invisible journey. He goes on to say that he is anxious to word correctly the request to complete the trip. As this is said the magician takes the book from under his arm and holds the front cover toward the audience. The magician continues talking and states "this is a very rare book containing descriptions of many of the wonderful things Ho Chang has done." Then, turning the book so that he can read it, he opens the cover and leafs through the book until he seems to find the right page. After reading a few seconds he says, "Ho Chang, please be so kind and so gracious as to end your journey inside that solid brass box on the little platform." Closing the book and putting it back on the table, the magician walks over to the box. First, he removes the weight, then takes off the cover and puts both on the table. Next he opens the door of the box. As everyone can see Ho Chang serenely rests inside the box and almost fills it.

The magician takes the brass idol from the box. The figure is turned around so that the audience can see all sides. At the conclusion of the trick Ho Chang is placed back on his book on the table. There he sits during the remainder of the show and his bland smile may be interpreted by the audience as his showing a little personal pleasure at their amazement.

Ho Chang's invisible journey is brought about, as is true with many transportation feats in magic, by blending two tricks so as to make a single effect. In the first instance an idol is made to disappear, and second, another idol is made to appear. Of course, for the two separate tricks to be accepted as one feat the two idols must be identical or, at least, to be so nearly alike that the audience will notice no difference. It is fortunate for the magician that, because they are produced in quantity, the less expensive figures are most similar. The magician also is lucky in that most representations of

Ho Chang show him in a seated position. Even the standing figures, due to the long robe he invariably is wearing, makes a solid mass which has no extended arms or legs to interfere with the trick. Whereas the trick I do is based on the stories connected with Ho Chang and a sculptured image of him, the reader may wish to use some other figure and another story plot while utilizing the mechanics I have designed. If he does so he will have an unique effect and will have considerable personal pleasure, as he evolves his version of the trick, as well as in the finished product. I have seen a wide variety of small statues—human, animal, and bird—of a suitable size and shape which could be used for the trick. The statue I have of Ho Chang, while 3½" high, tapers up from its base, an oval 2¼ x 3", to the head with its round crown ¾" in diameter. Any figure of these general dimensions can be used unless the magician has hands much smaller than the average. The figure can be no larger than may be hidden by holding one slightly cupped hand in front of it.

As what the magician does is not one trick, but two, each will be described by itself. The magician begins the effect by actually completing the production of the second idol although the audience is unaware that this has been done. It is not disclosed that secretly an idol has been put into the box until after completing the other trick of making an identical idol disappear. The tricks will be described in the order the magician performs them.

The size of the brass box is determined by the size of the figure used. I made my box 4¾" high, 4" wide and 4" deep. These are outside measurements. On the inside the box is ¾" higher than the idol and 1" wider. The depth of the box is the same as the width so that the bottom of the box is square. Actually only to contain the idol the box would not need to be so deep but the box is made in these proportions to enhance its appearance and to facilitate getting the god into the box secretly. When completed the box should give the effect of being exactly the size properly to hold the figure. The front of the box is hinged to one side of the box with a piano hinge so that the entire front opens like a door. Opposite the hinge is a hasp which when fastened keeps the door shut. Both the brass hinge and hasp are riveted in place. Either screws or rivets are the usual means of attaching these items and in this instance rivets make the job easier. The sides and back of the box are made of one piece of brass 1/32" thick, 12" long and 4¾″ wide. By making two right angle bends in the brass 4″ apart the sides and back are completed. The bottom of the box is made of ⅛″ thick brass which is fitted into the back and sides of the box and soldered in position. The bottom is made of brass four times the thickness of the rest of the box for two reasons. One reason is that it is easier to solder into place and holds the shape of the box better. The second reason is that on the inside of the box to the brass is riveted a piece of ⅛″ steel which covers the entire bottom. The reason for riveting the steel to the brass is because it is not only very easy to do but it avoids the possibility of warping either brass or steel with the heat needed for soldering one to another. The bottom of the box has to be absolutely flat. The need for the steel plate will be explained a little further on. The top of the box is made of 1/32″ brass. The brass is cut in the form of a cross with the center part ⅛″ larger than the box itself (in my box 4⅛″) and with arms each ¾″ long. The arms are bent at right angles and the corners soldered. The cover should fit on the box easily but not be so big as to slide around.

Both the inside of my box and the inside of the cover are enameled Chinese Red. The color makes the box more attractive, shows off the brass idol to advantage, and masks the fact that the bottom of the inside of the box is steel rather than brass. The box, as it appears to the audience, is a simple brass box and, with the exception of the steel plate on the bottom, that is just what it is.

My figure of Ho Chang is of cast brass, as has been noted. Such cast images always are hollow as is mine. However, whether the figure is solid, or hollow, is a detail which merely designates the way the figure is altered for the trick. It is necessary to insert a small horseshoe magnet inside the figure so that the tips of the arms of the magnet are flush with the base of the idol. If the figure is solid a hole has to be made big enough to insert the magnet and to glue it in place. With a hollow figure the magnet is held in place with plastic wood. In either instance, once the magnet is solidly fixed, the base of the figure is covered with a piece of felt. This not only adds to the appearance of the figure but also hides the magnet and deadens the sound when the magnet is attached to the box. The magnet used should be small but powerful. The magnet I have is 1¼″ high and has the same width at its widest part. It will lift a weight of three pounds which is quite sufficient, particularly as the idol plus the magnet, plastic wood, and felt weighs

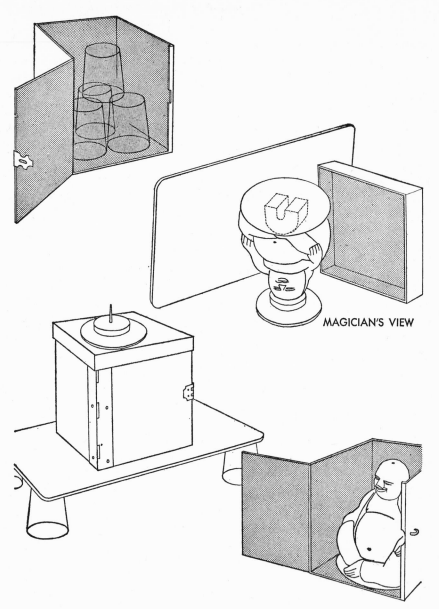

MAGICIAN'S VIEW

exactly one pound. It will be obvious that if the idol is held upside down and the inverted box with its steel bottom is put over the figure the magnet will securely attach the one to the other.

As the round pate of the idol makes it quite impossible to balance it on its head it is necessary to use a support to hold the idol upside down. This support not only has to hold the idol so that it stands firmly on its head but must raise the figure so that when the box is put over it, the magnet will reach the steel. Lastly the support must be released from the idol the instant the box is raised and without requiring the magician to do anything to detach it. To fulfill these requirements a very simple kind of a support is used. It has a thin plate as the base which has to be big enough to keep the figure from toppling over. Mine is $1/16''$ thick and $2\frac{1}{2}''$ in diameter. To this plate is soldered a block to raise the idol to the proper height. The block I use is round, $2\frac{1}{2}''$ in diameter and $7/16''$ thick. The center of the block has a hole drilled to take an $1/8''$ rod. The rod is soldered to the block and is made to protrude $\frac{1}{2}''$ above it. So as to stand the idol on its support an $1/8''$ hole is drilled directly down in the center of the crown of the head. The extended part of the rod is rubbed with a piece of emery cloth so that the rod will slide easily out of the hole in the head of the idol. The block in the support gives it enough weight to hold the support on the table when the idol is removed. Actually, the support is made to look as if it were a paperweight, and is used as a weight later in the trick. The support is made entirely of brass.

It now will be understood that the support holds the figure upside down so that the magnet will attach itself to the steel plate when the box is put over the idol. While that is how the image gets into the box, the magician also must know the routine which keeps the audience from seeing this action. It will be recalled in the description of what the audience sees that the magician starts by building a little platform. The platform is made by using the 4 liqueur glasses, taken from the box, and covered with a small board picked up from the table. While the platform does isolate the box, as the magician points out to the audience, it has two other functions which the audience does not recognize. The glasses which form the upright supports of the platform have the added purpose of demonstrating most effectively that the box is completely empty when the glasses are removed. The glasses used are of such a size as to fill the box. There is no more positive way of showing a container to be empty than by first showing it to be full and then removing the contents. The board's first use is to act as a screen to mask the idol standing on its head on the support. The board is stood on edge on the table about $2''$ in front of the idol. The board is held upright by leaning it against the cover of the box which stands on its side and at right angles to the board. The size of the board is indicated by its use as a screen. My board, made of hard wood, is 8″ long, 5″ wide and ⅛″ thick. When the board is stood in front of the idol both the figure and support are completely hidden from the spectators. When it is used as part of the platform it obviously is just a simple board.

After the glasses have been put in place and the door of the box closed, and fastened, and the box inverted, the magician puts the box on the table and over the idol. As the box is put down, the magician, with his other hand, takes hold of the board and raises it from the table. Raising the board is done the instant the box touches the table. If these actions are done properly the audience never realizes that part of the box was out of their sight even for an instant.

Once the board is put in position on the glasses the magician picks up the cover of the box with his left hand, and, as he holds it up so the audience can see it, picks up the box with the right hand. As at this point the box is upside down the magician twists the box, a quarter turn, so that the open top of the box is to his left. Bringing the top to the box, he slips it in place. The box is turned rightside up and placed on the platform. The magician picks up the support and says, "I'll place this weight on the cover to keep it in place." Thus making use of the support keeps anyone from noticing it on the table and from wondering what it is. It is helpful that the rod which holds the idol makes an excellent handle to pick up the weight. The magician has completed the work for the finale of the trick and is all ready for the disclosure of the idol at the proper moment. But the audience is quite satisfied that all the magician has done is to put an empty brass box on top of a simple little platform.

What to the audience is the beginning of the trick, that of making an idol disappear, is possible because of the fact that people assume that what should exist actually does exist. It is based on the same principle movie makers have used for years. They show a street lined on both sides with buildings. The viewer mentally gives three dimensions to each building because he knows that besides height and width a building also has depth. All the movie makers supplied were the faces of the buildings but because the viewer can see the face of the buildings he, mentally, gives depth to each building. While the figure I use originally was 2¼″ deep at its thickest part, it has had the back sawed off so that what remains of the figure actually is only ¾″ thick. When the figure is facing the audience what each spectator sees is what he would see were the idol whole. Each person will accept that he sees a complete idol because he knows that an idol has back and sides as well as a face even though they are not visible. After the back of the figure has been cut off, the edges of the sides of the front of the idol are filed so that the back is flat and can be soldered to a flat piece of brass. It is best to use brass larger than the idol and, after soldering, saw and file away the excess brass until it is even with the sides of the figure.

What happens when Ho Chang disappears is that the prepared idol is hidden in a hole in the book on which the figure rests. My book is only 1⅛″ thick (quite a thin book) and no one ever considers the possibility of a thick solid brass idol going into the thin book. After a description of how both idol and book are made an explanation will be given as to what the magician does to make the audience believe that the idol has dissolved in his hands while actually it was hidden in the book.

The simplest way to get a book to look like a book is to use a book. A cloth bound book of the proper size and thickness and with the desired appearance of being rather old may be picked up for almost nothing at a second-hand book shop. It is the contents of a book which make it valuable not its size. It may well be that such a book can be found around the house. My book is 6¼″ wide by 9″ high. My book is 1″ longer than twice the height of my idol. The first thing to be done to the book is to remove the cardboard which gives the stiffening to the cloth of the back cover. The first step is to pull off the end paper on the inside of the cover. The paper which is removed will not be used again and may, therefore, be taken off in sections. With the end paper off the cloth of the cover will be disclosed. Care should be taken in pulling the cloth from the cardboard that the cloth remains intact. The cardboard does not matter as it has no further use. However, exact measurements of the cardboard (length, width and thickness) must be made.

A piece of metal, or wood, the same thickness as the cardboard taken out of the cover, is cut to the length and width of the cardboard. I used a piece of aluminum largely because I find it easier to work in metal than in wood in this type of job. With drills and a fine saw a hole is cut in the metal of the shape and size of the idol and the idol is hinged to the metal. The bottom of the hole, i.e., the place where the base of the idol goes is at the exact center of the metal. The hole is cut to the pattern of the back which has been soldered to the idol. It will be found helpful to make a template

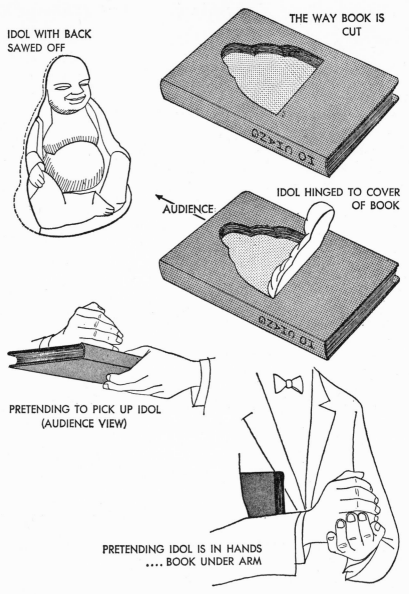

IDOL WITH BACK
SAWED OFF

THE WAY BOOK IS
CUT

IDOL HINGED TO COVER
OF BOOK

AUDIENCE

PRETENDING TO PICK UP IDOL
(AUDIENCE VIEW)

PRETENDING IDOL IS IN HANDS
.... BOOK UNDER ARM

for this and another purpose described later. When finished the hole, starting with a straight line at the center of the metal, follows the silhouette of
the idol and has the edge of the opening for the head about ½″ from one
end of the metal. A piano hinge of thin metal is used to fasten the idol to
the metal plate. One leaf of the hinge is riveted to the base of the back of

the idol and the other leaf is riveted to the metal plate. When properly hinged the figure should either seem to sit on the metal plate or fold into the hole in the plate so that the back of the idol and the plate make one continuous flat surface. The pin of the hinge is sunk into the plate.

Once the idol is hinged to the plate, pages of the book have to be cut out so as to give space for the idol when it goes into the book. Careful measurements must be made so as to place the template on the correct spot on the last page of the book. The idol fits into a hole in the lower half of the pages. Drawing around the template will show how the pages of the book have to be cut. It will not be found difficult to cut the paper with a sharp knife. A thin piece of metal is put under the last to be cut in order not to mar the 6 or 8 pages in the front which are left intact. Having made the hole in the pages of the book the plate is glued to the cloth making the back cover. What then has been done is to substitute the plate (with its idol) for the original cardboard stiffening of the back cover. After the glue has dried a sharp knife is used to cut through the cloth so as to separate the idol from the plate and permit it to swing on its hinge. There is one added thing to do so as to eliminate any chance of the white paper being seen in the hole when the idol is on top of the back cover. The bottom of the hole should be covered with black paper, or cloth, and the side edges either also covered or colored with black ink.

Because the hinge is attached to idol and plate so that the flat side is uppermost it can be swung only so far when the idol is raised from the book. Actually the hinge is being opened in the opposite way to what is intended and it is so constructed that it will open only a limited way in this direction. The hinge will go only far enough to hold the figure upright and, because of the shape of the figure, upright, in this instance, means a little past perpendicular. In other words, because of the shape of the idol and the manner in which the hinge is attached to it, the idol front, without any catch, will remain upright on the book. It will appear to be a complete idol resting on a book.

In picking up the book the left hand takes the book while the right hand seemingly holds the idol so that it does not slide off. Actually the right hand keeps the figure from falling into the book which might occur were the book accidentally tipped forward a fraction of an inch. Once the book is off the table the left hand tilts the book just enough to keep the figure upright and the fingers of the right hand are released.

The magician tells his story about Ho Chang and calls attention to the little brass figure. Then, with his right hand, he takes the idol from the book. What he actually does is to put the side of his right hand and little finger on the surface of the book directly in front of the brass image. He then cups his hand as if he were taking hold of the idol. As this is done the right thumb is bent and the tip of the thumb is brought against the side of the first finger almost at the knuckle. In this position the hand seems to be grasping the idol which is completely hidden by the hand. The right hand, remaining cupped, is moved forward. As this is done the book is tipped just enough so that the figure starts to fall forward. The idol will fall against the right hand and as the hand continues its movement the idol is allowed to go noiselessly into the book. The moves are most natural and, therefore, quite convincing. (See illustration.)

As if it were holding the idol the right hand continues slowly to move forward. The left hand, moving more rapidly, tilts the book and puts it under the right arm. Releasing the book the instant it is held by the right arm, the left hand is brought quickly under the cupped right hand as if it were helping to hold the idol. A second after the hands are brought together the magician begins squeezing the idol into nothingness. This is done slowly and, seemingly, by the use of considerable force. Still moving slowly, the hands are taken apart and the fingers extended and widely spread. There is no doubt, in the mind of any spectator, that the hands which held the god are now empty and that the idol has disappeared.

The left hand again takes the book but, this time, it is grasped so that the book is rightside up. The fingers of the left hand are held at the back of the book which is the natural way to hold a book. In this instance holding the book that way also keeps the idol from falling out of its hiding place inside the book. The magician in talking about the book holds its face toward the audience and points to the title. The title, by the way, is made by lettering on a piece of cloth which is glued on the cover of the book in the proper position. The title used need only be the name, "Ho Chang." It is well in selecting the book to be used that one be chosen having lettering which easily can be covered. As the book, even though it has been altered to hold the idol, still is a book, the front cover can be opened and the pages can be leafed through. In pretending to look in the book for the proper wording of the request to the idol the magician need not go beyond the first few pages all of which have been left intact. Checking in the book for the exact wording of the proper way to address the god adds to the story plot of the trick. It also convinces the audience that the sole purpose of the book is for reference.

Now that Ho Chang has been made to disappear and the request made for him to reappear inside the box the trick really is over. All the magician has further to do is to remove the weight from the top of the box, remove the cover from the box, and to open the door at the front of the box. All these things should be done slowly so as to give the spectators the opportunity to observe that nothing tricky is being done. When the box is opened the audience plainly can see the idol serenely resting inside the red enameled shrine. And to the spectators the story of Ho Chang's powers is as good an explanation as they can imagine to account for the idol being in the box.

Even though the feat has been completed the magician does a couple of more things in order to make the trick even more impressive. First he takes the idol from the box. Because of the magnet this has to be done in a certain way. First, with his left hand, the magician grasps the box from behind and raises it off its little platform. Then, with his right hand, he takes hold of the head of the idol and presses it forward and, simultaneously, pulls the box backward. These actions produce a leverage so great that the magnet is separated easily from the steel and the idol is taken out of the box. The box is then put down and the idol is turned so that the audience can see all sides. The idol is dropped back on the book and appears to the audience to be exactly as it was prior to making its invisible trip. Of course, as the spectators do not know, this is another idol and this time the book is laying face up on the table. The reason for dropping the idol onto the book is so, by sound, everyone may know the figure is solid and heavy. The idol is released only a couple of inches above the surface of the book which is high enough to make a thud and not so high that there is a chance of having the idol topple over.

While it would seem to be so obvious as to be unnecessary to mention, the idol must go into the box correctly if it is to be found facing the audience when, at the finale, the front of the box is opened. However, it is the point of the trick where an error is most apt to be made. I find having the idol in its upside down position on its stand facing me, as I stand at the side of the table, to be best. Then I hold the box, also upside down, with the door toward my body. In these positions of box and idol, I find it easiest to get the idol into the box quickly and correctly. This detail is mentioned last to stress its great importance.

THE ASTRONAUT CARDS

MAGIC which invariably intrigues and delights an audience is where an inanimate object, or objects, responds to the performer's command and shows the power to act as well. Such a feat is the rising cards, which often is given a topical title on the printed programs. Audiences like this demonstration of the magician's power so much that literally dozens of methods have been devised for its performance. Several of the means used are suitable only for exhibiting on a stage and require the aid of a hidden assistant. Others are mechanical and can be constructed only by the most skilled chronometrical maker, and cost a hundred, and more, dollars. The following method is not costly, may be shown within a few feet of the spectators, and is utterly deceptive. This method also eliminates various of the other difficulties and makes the performance quite easy.

This is what happens from the viewpoint of the audience. The magician takes a deck of cards from its cardboard case. The case is put aside and the cards shuffled. Three spectators each chose one card from the deck. A fourth spectator is given the deck of cards with instructions to so hold the pack that the three selected cards may be returned to the deck, wherever the spectators holding those cards desire. The spectator is then asked to shuffle the cards thoroughly and give the deck to the magician. He then returns the deck to its case, leaving the top open, and puts the case with its cards into a little holder on his table so that the case stands, and is held, on end. The magician requests that, one after another, the selected cards rise from the deck and fall out of the case. Slowly each of the cards chosen by the spectators rises from the deck and tumbles from the case to the table. The deliberate and spooky way in which the cards come out of the deck greatly enhances the effect. Except as director of proceedings the magician seems to play no part in the action of the cards.

There are two parts to the trick. The first is the way in which the three spectators are each induced to take a particular card and yet made to believe that in all instances free choices had been made. The second part of the feat is the secret motivation for the cards and the way in which it is controlled.

The control of the choice of three cards can be done in a number of ways. One was described in Chapter 6 for the feat called "By the Sense of Touch." While that method is both certain and excellent, it is a trifle slow when used in combination with this rising card feat. Forcing three cards by sleight of hand is a superb method but requires an inordinate amount of practice which only a professional is apt to bother with. A special deck of cards is used in still another method. The deck is made up of duplicates of each of the three cards—17 of one card at the top of the deck; 17 of another forming the middle of the deck; and 17 of the third at the bottom. By offering each spectator only one section of the deck to choose from each will have to take a particular card. Besides being expensive, this method has the disadvantages of not being able to show the deck or shuffle the cards, nor of using the deck in another feat. The method I suggest using has none of the handicaps mentioned. An ordinary deck of cards is used and, if desired, another card trick may be done prior to the performance of this feat. The deck secretly is prepared by shortening the three cards which are to be "chosen." Each of the three cards has $\frac{1}{16}$" taken off of one end. This may be done with a photo-trimmer, scissors, or a sharp knife. The cutting must be most accurate so that each card is exactly the same length. Because trimming the cards will flatten the curve at the rounded corners, it is necessary to reround the corners. This can be done with manicure scissors and is quite easy if another card is used as a pattern to follow.

At the start of the trick, the deck is half out of the card case which will eliminate fumbling at the time as well as not disturbing a later part of the trick. When the cards are taken from the case, the three short cards are on top of the deck. Holding the face of the cards toward the audience, the magician shuffles the deck. Using an ordinary overhand shuffle it will not be found difficult to keep the three cards on top of the deck. It previously has been noted that cards may be kept on the bottom of the deck during what appears to be a very thorough shuffle. By turning the face of the deck rather than the back to the audience, the top cards can be held in place quite as easily. When the shuffle has been completed the magician cuts the deck and, thereby, brings the three cards together near the center of the deck. After completing the cut, one end of the deck is tapped on the table. While this seems to be only for the purpose of squaring the deck, it really is done so that the short cards are driven down to the end of the deck which strikes the table.

The magician takes the deck in his left hand with the face of the cards towards the audience and the end of the deck which had been tapped on the table pointing toward the floor. The left hand holds the deck at its lower end with the fingers on the face and the thumb on the back. The deck is squeezed tightly. The fingers of the right hand are put on the table edge of the deck and the thumb on the bottom edge. Bending the cards, by pulling back the fingers of the right hand and then raising them gradually, the cards are permitted, one at a time, to snap back in position (see illustration). This is called riffling the deck. When this is done with a short card, or cards, in the deck a louder snap will be heard when the short card, or cards, fall.

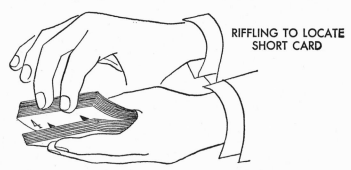

RIFFLING TO LOCATE
SHORT CARD

This is because the short card, or cards, being short, will fall with the long card preceding them. The difference in sound will not be noticed by the audience but will be very apparent to the magician. The magician should stop the riffle the instant he hears the snap made by the short cards and lift those cards he still holds with his right hand from the lower part of the deck. He lifts his left thumb to make this possible. The top three cards of the part of the deck he holds in his left hand are the short cards he wants the spectators to take. He may offer that part of the deck to three spectators, one after another, for each to pick up one card. Or, he may offer the deck to but one spectator to pick up a card. In this case the riffling process is repeated twice more in order for the second and third spectators to think their cards came from different locations in the deck.

In order for the spectators to think that they are choosing cards, the magician leads the spectators to believe he is following their commands. He does this by riffling the deck and as he does so he says, "I am going to run through the deck like this and as I do so I want someone to say stop. Will you, sir, be the one to tell me to stop." One person must understand that he, or she, is the one person to say the word. When the performer knows the person he naturally would say Mr. Jones, or Miss Smith, or Bill or Mary, rather than sir or madame, but he has to make it definite that only one person is to speak. The magician begins to riffle the deck so the cards are released slowly. He watches the face of the one who is to tell him to stop. As the person's lips begin to move, he releases the cards more rapidly so as to reach the short cards as the word is spoken. It is amazing how little practice is required to learn the proper timing so as to seem to stop the instant the person speaks and yet to have let the short cards fall.

Once three spectators have been induced to take particular cards, and without being aware that their selection has been less than free, the magician takes pains to convince the audience he does nothing with, or to, the cards. He designates a fourth spectator to take the deck. He is asked to hold it so the three cards may be returned and, after the cards are back in the deck, to give the deck a thorough shuffle. After the cards have been well mixed the magician takes the deck and puts it back in the case. The case is put in a little holder on his table. The purpose of the holder is to support the case so that it stands on one end. At the magician's command, the three cards the spectators "selected" rise out of the case and fall to the table.

The cards which rise are duplicates of the cards the spectators took from, and returned to, the deck. This necessitates purchasing two identical bridge-size decks in order to do the trick. The narrow, or bridge-size, cards have to be used in this trick. It is also necessary to purchase a standard-size deck in a cardboard case which opens at one end. The standard-size cards are wider than the bridge-size. This deck is purchased only to obtain the case. A wider case is required because it has to hold, besides the deck, a metal container from which the cards will rise. This container is made of metal $\frac{1}{32}$" thick. It has a front, back and two sides. It needs no bottom, and the top has to be open. The inside measurements are $2\frac{5}{16}$" x $\frac{1}{8}$" and must be exact. Such a container will permit a bridge-size card to go into it easily and will not allow the card to wobble when being raised by the thread which is the motive power. Two inserts have to be made for the container. While these inserts may be playing cards, it is just a little better to make them of metal $\frac{1}{64}$" thick and the size of playing cards. Metal inserts do not require having the corners rounded. At the center of one end of the container and $\frac{1}{4}$" from the open end a $\frac{1}{16}$" hole is drilled. This hole not only goes through both back and front of the container, but through the two inserts as well. The hole has to be in exactly the same position in all four pieces of metal. In order to be able to tie one end of the thread to the container a second hole is drilled in the front of the container just beneath the first hole. It is necessary to round the edges of all the holes so as to avoid having sharp metal cut the thread. The container is glued inside the card case. The lower back of the container is glued to the inside of the back of the card case. The card case is made with a crease near the top of the back to permit the flap to bend away from the top of the case. This part of the back of the case is not glued to the container.

With a needle a hole is made in the cardboard of the back of the card case to correspond with the hole in the back of the container. A black silk thread, of triple O thickness, is run through the hole in the case and the back of the container, through the holes in the two inserts, and through the hole in the front of the container where it is tied securely. The three cards which are to rise are put into the container in the following manner. One card is pushed between the front of the container and the first insert. The thread is pushed down by the card so that it goes from the hole in the front of the container, down the face of the card, under the card, up the back of the card and through the hole in the insert. The second card is pushed between the two inserts so that the thread goes under the card. The third card is pushed between the second insert and the back of the container. It will now be found, upon pulling the thread which extends from the card case, that one card after another will rise and topple from the card case. It will be noticed that the cards rise in reverse order to the way they went into the container.

The holder for the card case has a double purpose. As is obvious, it holds the case so it stands on end. What the spectators do not realize is that it also adds enough weight to that of the deck and the case with its container so the case will not move on the table when the thread is pulled. The holder should weigh a minimum of 6 ounces. A simple design for such a holder is a bar of metal of the proper weight having two upright strips of metal soldered in the front and two more strips at the back. These uprights need extend no more than 2" above the top of the base to hold the card case. The front uprights should be $\frac{3}{4}$" from those at the back. If having the uprights separated this much permits too free movement of the card case, it

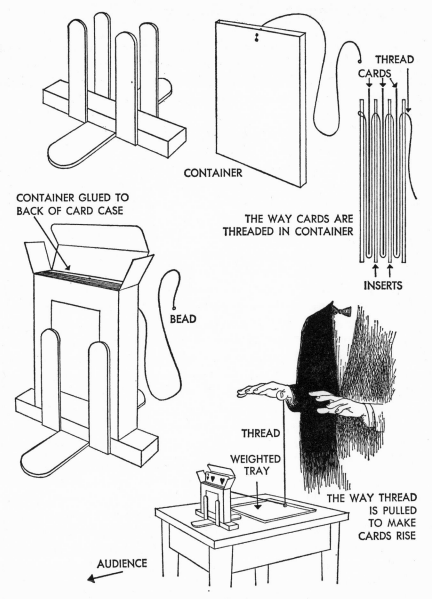

CONTAINER

CONTAINER GLUED TO
BACK OF CARD CASE

THREAD
CARDS

THE WAY CARDS ARE
THREADED IN CONTAINER

INSERTS

BEAD

THREAD

WEIGHTED
TRAY

THE WAY THREAD
IS PULLED
TO MAKE
CARDS RISE

AUDIENCE

is advisable to have cloth, or felt, glued to the inside surfaces of the uprights. The uprights on one side of the holder should be separated 1¾″ and those on the other side should be directly opposite them. In order to have the audience give no consideration to the holder, I always introduce it by saying, "I have discovered a new use for a menu holder, such as restaurants use.

It will hold a deck of cards upright." The holder, with its cards, is placed on the front edge of the table.

One other piece of equipment is required—a small tray. The tray should be no smaller than 4″ x 6″ and may be as large as 6″ x 8″. The tray has to be weighted so that the over all weight will be at least 8 ounces. The weight can be a sheet of metal fitted to the inside of the tray and glued in place. In the center of the rim of one of the short edges of the tray is drilled a hole for the thread to run through. On the tray at the beginning of the trick is the card case containing a deck of cards and the menu holder. These things the audience can see but the length of thread running out of the card case, which the audience can't see, also is on the tray. The tray is placed on the back of the table, the side furthest from the audience, with the end having the hole for the thread towards the back of the table.

When that part of the feat has been reached where it is time for the cards to rise, the magician, standing back of the table, picks up the end of the thread. More about how the thread is picked up and held will be described later. The thread runs from the case at the front of the table, through the hole in the tray at the back of the table, and to the hand of the magician. By moving his hand either forward or upward, he will pull the thread and, thereby, cause the cards to rise. Because the pull of the thread is reversed in direction by going through the hole in the tray, the magician seems to have no part in the rising of the cards. First he raises the thread diagonally above and back of the tray until all the slack is out of the thread. Then to make the first card rise he moves his hand forward and up. While to cause one card to rise 6″ of thread must be pulled from the container in the card case, the magician seems not to move his hand except to wiggle his fingers. This is due to his hand being so far away from the cards and because a forward movement will not be noticed. Because the thread holes are so near the top of the container, each card will fall out of the card case at the conclusion of rising. When a card falls the magician raises his hand and pulls it back so that he is ready to pull the thread for the next card by moving his hand forward.

Secretly picking up the end of the thread and holding it so as to be able to pull the thread and motivate the cards should not cause trouble. However, there are different ways in which it may be done and a person will find one method easier than another for him. The method I use, because for me it is the easiest, requires having a small flesh-color bead, about ⅛″ in diameter, tied to the end of the thread. I pick up the bead with the first finger and thumb of my left hand as, with my right hand, I lean forward over the table and straighten the card holder at the front edge of the table. Straightening up I bring my hands together and, looking directly at him, ask the first spectator to announce the name of the card he had selected. As the question is asked, and answered, I have ample time to stick the bead into the crotch of the thumb of the right hand and to grip the bead with the thumb. This is done with the backs of the hands towards the audience and the hands cover the action. For the person afraid of dropping the bead, a loop on the end of the thread is excellent. The loop is waxed so that it stays open. Like the bead it, too, is picked up by the left hand and put in place on the right. The loop may go over the thumb or one of the fingers whichever is found more comfortable in action. For a performer who does not wear a ring, or wears none on his right hand, he may prefer to have the thread to a ring which will go easily on one finger. It doesn't seem as if it could be true but the ring will not be noticed.

The second and third spectators, in succession, also are asked to name their cards, and these cards, too, rise and fall on the table.

After all the cards have fallen on the table, the magician drops the thread with its bead, loop, or ring, back on the tray and at the same time picks up the holder with its case and cards, and replaces it on the tray. Finally he picks up the three cards, shows them again to the audience, and drops them on the tray to conclude a very impressive demonstration of magic.

THE SHEIKH'S RING

Entertaining as are the Egyptian conjurers, and charming as is their magic, they all depend upon their own skill and knowledge for their mystification. At least that is true with all I met in the land of the Sphinx. None had a personal genie to assist him. They also traveled by the mechanical means of the present rather than gliding through the air while seated on a carpet. The delightful Arab stories of magic and sorcery are, regretfully, only stories. It seemed to me that a story about "The Sheikh's Ring" would be the basis for an interesting feat of magic. The details of the story are rather hazy in my mind for it was read to me many years ago, when I was a young boy. However, the principal points I recall, and the magic, are built around them. First, an outline of the story.

There was a wise and kindly Sheikh whose most valued possession was a gold ring which had been given him by the King. A thief stole the ring and, so that no one would know he had it, he tied the ring to a string and hung it around his neck under his robes. When the Sheikh discovered his loss he thought of the magic fishline a wizard had given him. The wizard had said this remarkable cord would go anywhere and would bring back whatever was desired. The Sheikh directed the fishline to bring back the ring and the line disappeared. The next morning the fishline reappeared and the ring was tied on it.

The story is told not at the beginning but near the climax of the trick. This is done for two reasons. The first is that a magician should never tell what he is about to do. The second is that in telling the story the magician is able to remind the audience what has been done and to give reasons for each step.

This is the magic to go with the story. The magician takes the cover off a small cardboard box and shows it to be empty. Replacing the cover, he gives the box to a spectator to hold. Showing a flat reel upon which is wound a length of fishline, the magician asks a second spectator to wrap the line and reel in a handkerchief and to hold it tightly. Next a ring tied to a loop of string is exhibited. A third spectator is asked to hold the loop of string and to cover his hand and the string and ring with a handkerchief.

As all that the magician has secretly to do has been accomplished when this stage of the magic has been reached, he tells his story. As the story is told, the magician explains that the magic fishline was packed away in a chest and hidden by clothes. The handkerchief covering the reel is to hide the fishline. The handkerchief covering the ring represents the robe under which the thief hid the ring.

When the reel is unwrapped the assistant finds the fishline has disappeared. When the handkerchief is taken off the string loop, that assistant discovers the ring no longer tied on it. When the first assistant opens the small cardboard box, he sees the ring tied securely to the center of the fishline.

There are three parts to this trick. First, the way to get the fishline and ring into the box after it has been shown empty. Second, to get the fishline off the reel without the knowledge of the assistant. Third, to get the ring off the loop of string without the person holding the string being aware that it was done. Each part will be described separately.

First, there is the small cardboard box in which, after it has been opened and shown to be empty, the string with its ring appears. The box is just a cardboard box which, for the purposes of the magic, has had certain improvements. The box I use was sent me by my competent and friendly druggist. It contained powders prescribed by my equally competent and friendly physician. The acquisition of the box is mentioned only to point out that even an illness can be of advantage to a magician. The box I got, and use, is 3½″ long, 2⅜″ wide, and 1½″ deep. The cover, which comes halfway down on the box, is separate from the box. It would seem to be, and appears to be, a most common box. Actually it is until certain alterations are made. These changes in the box are threefold. First, at the bottom of the box, there is added a strip of cardboard which goes around all four sides of the box. This cardboard is ¼″ high and 1/16″ thick. It is covered with white paper to match the rest of the inside of the box. Upon this cardboard rests a piece of tin 1/16″ smaller than the inside measurements of the box. On both sides, this tin is covered with white paper. The cardboard acts as a support for the piece of white paper covered tin. In the ¼″ of space between the bottom of the box and the tin, there is hidden 5′ of fishline to which, at the center, is tied the ring. This ring, as the reader has surmised, is a duplicate of the one which later disappears. The ring should be large enough for a man's finger. A plain band oddly marked is most suitable for both story and trick. The odd markings fit the story and a wide plain band appears to be larger than a signet ring, or one with a setting, and yet takes less space. My rings are very inexpensive and seem quite authentically Arabic, which I am quite certain they are not.

In the center of the cover of the box is a small magnet. The magnet I use is ⅛″ thick, ⅞″ long and 3/16″ wide. A hole, the size of the magnet, is cut out of the center of the cover. As the cardboard is less thick than is the magnet, another piece of cardboard, with a matching hole, is cut to fit the inside of the cover and is glued in place. Paper is pasted on both the inside and the outside of the cover to conceal the existence of the magnet. When the prepared cover is put on the box and the box is turned upside down the tin will fall into the cover where it is held by the magnet. Upon turning the box right side up and removing the cover, the ring and string will be disclosed. Because of the paper covering the magnet there is very little sound when the tin falls into the cover, but to use the magician's term, the trick will "talk." This sound can be hidden if the magician will thump the box with his finger as he turns the box upside down. The sequence of moves the

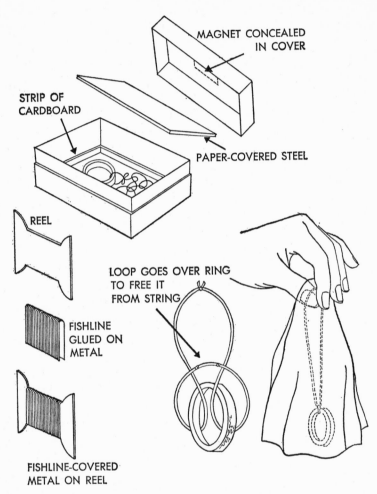

MAGNET CONCEALED IN COVER

STRIP OF CARDBOARD

PAPER-COVERED STEEL

REEL

LOOP GOES OVER RING TO FREE IT FROM STRING

FISHLINE GLUED ON METAL

FISHLINE-COVERED METAL ON REEL

magician makes, prior to giving the box to the assistant, seemingly are made merely to show an ordinary small cardboard box to be empty. The moves also remove the false bottom. These are the moves. The magician picks up the box by gripping the lower part between the thumb and second finger of the left hand. He takes hold of the cover with the thumb and second finger of the right hand, and takes it off the box. He turns the inside of both box and cover toward the spectators as he says, "An empty little cardboard box." In turning the box to show it, the first finger goes inside and presses against the tin. The inside of the box is shown with a slow sweeping move which ends with the box being upside down. The way the box is held appears to be the natural way to hold it and showing the inside of the box as well as turning it upside down satisfactorily proves it to be empty. At the same time the inside of the box is shown with the left hand, the inside of the cover is shown with the right. The same slow sweeping move is used and the only difference is the first finger goes on the outside of the cover. After the cover has been replaced on the box the right hand is released. The left hand quickly turns the box upside down. This is when the right hand thumps the box to hide the sound of the falling fake bottom. The box is slowly turned back so as to be right side up. Turning the box slowly will permit the ring to slide back into position without making any noise. When the assistant is given the box he is instructed to hold it with both hands. While the stated purpose of holding the box in this way is to protect it, the actual reason is to keep the assistant from shaking the box and hearing the ring move inside it.

The flat reel upon which the fishline is wound, or, rather, appears to be wound, is without trickery. While my reel is of white plastic it may be made of wood, or metal, if preferred. The design of the reel is like the silhouette of a dumbbell. It should be about 2¾" long, 2" wide and ⅛" thick. The center bar is 1¾" long and 1⅛" wide. From the center bar nubs project at the ends. These nubs are to keep the line from sliding off the bar. A thin piece of metal, about which the audience never knows, is made to cover the bar of the reel. The width of the metal is 1/64" less than the length of the bar. The metal is formed into a U so that it will cover the front, the back and the top of the bar. Each arm of the U is 1/16" longer than the width of the bar. This metal is put on the reel and the fishline wound around it. About 6' of line are required. The fishline is glued to the metal as it is wound. The gluing has to be very carefully done so as to be certain all the line is stuck to the metal, and that the glue does not show nor get under the metal so as to glue it to the reel. After the glue has dried completely the fishline is cut at the center of the open end of the metal. Metal and line can then be taken off the reel. After the metal is removed from the reel the cut ends of the line are trimmed in a straight line almost, but not quite, even with the edges of the metal. These line ends are touched with glue to keep them from raveling and becoming fuzzy.

When finished, the fishline covered metal easily will go on, or off, the reel. On the reel the appearance is exactly that of fishline wound around a flat reel. The magician exhibits the reel by holding it between the first finger and thumb near the open ends of the metal with the opening pointing towards the crotch of the thumb. A firm grip is taken so as to squeeze the metal to the reel. The reel is turned back and forth as it is shown and the effect of the line going around and around the reel is perfect. The magician hands the assistant a handkerchief and requests him to cover the reel. As the assistant drapes the handkerchief over the reel, the magician, under cover of the cloth, reverses the reel in his fingers so the open part of the metal is uppermost. As this action is covered the magician has ample time to make it and the turning is easy to do. When the assistant has the handkerchief in place, he is asked to take hold of the reel by gripping it through the cloth. He is asked to take hold of one end of the reel in each hand. When the assistant has the reel firmly held, the magician takes his hand away and, clenched in his fist, he has the line covered metal.

The magician then puts his hand in his pocket and pulls out a loop of string with a ring tied on it. Naturally, he also does something the audience knows nothing about—he leaves the fishline covered fake. At this point two-thirds of the feat has been accomplished. He has caused the fishline to leave the reel and he has put into the empty box a ring tied to a fishline. And the audience is unaware of either action.

The magician exhibits the loop of string with the ring tied on it. He may, if he wishes, give the string and ring to someone for examination. The ends of the string are tied together with a very secure hard knot. The knot may even be dipped in sealing wax so everyone is certain it cannot be untied. This knot, by the way, plays no part in the trick except to make it more convincing. Everyone knows that a solid ring cannot be taken off a loop of string without untying the string or breaking it. While the ring seems to be tied to the string in a way which would prohibit it from being removed and leave ring and string intact, this is not true.

Prior to tying the ends of the string together to form the loop, a single knot is tied $\frac{1}{2}$" on either side of the center of the string. This is the only way in which the string is prepared. The ring is tied on the loop of string in this way. The center of the bottom of the loop, i.e., opposite the knotted ends, is pushed through the ring. The double string is opened and brought over the outside of the ring. When the strings of the big loop are pulled the ring becomes tied on the loop. Because of the two single knots, which had been tied in the string prior to making the loop, the ring seems to be tied on the string in a complicated knot. To take the ring off the string is the work of an instant. All that needs be done is to take hold of a small loop at the top of the ring, which goes around the strands of the string, and pull that loop down over the ring. The ring is held by one hand as the other pulls the loop over the ring. As soon as the loop goes over the ring, it is free to pull off the string. (See illustration.)

Removing the ring from the string is done while the assistant is holding the string and under cover of a handkerchief. There is quite enough time to do this while the assistant is making certain he is holding the string through the handkerchief. A very convincing bit is for the magician, after he has removed the ring from the string, to pinch both together and bring them out from under the handkerchief. The other hand raises one side of the handkerchief to make this possible. As these moves are made he tells the assistant, "You have to hold tightly to the string for you do not want to lose this ring." The one hand goes back under the handkerchief with the ring while the other hand drops the side of the handkerchief back in place. The hand with the ring releases the string, holds the ring hidden in its loosely closed fingers, and drops to the magician's side.

Everything now is completed except for the magician to tell his story, to have one assistant find the ring is missing, the second assistant to find the fishline is gone from the reel, and the third assistant to discover that in the box he holds is the ring tied on to the fishline.

The amazement the face of each assistant shows as he discovers he is not holding what he believed he held attests to the effectiveness of this feat. While nothing the magician has to do is at all difficult, each action requires practice in order that it may be done smoothly.

FLOWERS—WITH THANKS

THERE are only a few examples of magic which have an especial appeal to ladies and yet also interest men. This is an outstanding example of such a feat for it is attractive and as impressive as it is impossible. The magic has added value from the performer's point of view because it is not at all difficult to perform.

This is what the audience sees and hears. The magician asks that some lady in the audience be so gracious and so trusting as to permit him to borrow a ring for a few minutes. The magician goes to the lady offering to lend her ring and hands her a small purse. He asks her to examine the purse, to put the ring into it and to close the purse. He asks her to do this, he tells her, because he wants to safeguard the ring as well as to make certain that no one touches the ring while it is out of her possession. Then, as if it just occurred to him, he suggests that perhaps if someone other than himself were to hold the ring the lady would have less worries. He takes a colorful handkerchief from his pocket and makes a bag out of it by bringing the four corners together. He asks a gentleman to hold the corners of the handkerchief in one hand. Taking the purse from the lady he puts it inside the handkerchief the man is holding. Once the purse is in the handkerchief the magician asks the man to take hold of the purse, with his free hand, by gripping it through the cloth. Then in order for the lady to see how well her ring is protected the man is asked to stand and face her.

The magician, returning to his prop table, picks up a paper bag of the fancy printed variety, such as are used by gift and candy stores. As he places the bag, which obviously is filled with something, on one of his performance tables, he remarks that today he purchased a small souvenir for the lady who would be so charming as to trust him with her ring. Looking toward the man holding the handkerchief wrapped ring, the magician appears to be worried. He hurries over to the man and tells him that he is holding the ring too tightly and that it would be better were he to release it. As the man takes his hand away from the ring the magician reaches over, takes hold of the handkerchief just below the man's hand, and jerks it out of his grip. The magician acts as if it were the man's fault that he no longer holds the handkerchief and tells him, "But you weren't holding the handkerchief tightly as I told you to do." Holding the handkerchief with one hand, the magician feels for the purse with its ring with the other. The magician, as he feels the outside of the cloth, brings his hands together. Taking two corners of the handkerchief, one in each hand, the performer allows the cloth to fall open—obviously the purse and ring are gone. Turning once more to the man, the magician, in a sad voice, says, "And I trusted you to guard the ring."

Turning to the owner of the ring the magician says, "The gentleman seems to have lost your ring. While he hunts for it I'll get your souvenir." While those sentences are said very seriously, the accusation that the man was responsible for the ring's disappearance is so outrageous that everyone realizes it is part of the show.

The magician picks up the bag from his table and points out that the top of the bag has been folded over and held closed with cellophane tape. He rips open the bag and takes out a parcel wrapped in gift paper and tied with a ribbon having a fancy bow. With scissors, the ribbon is cut and the paper torn to disclose an attractive metal box of Chinese design. The magician holds the box and turns it so it may be seen from all sides. The box is held shut with a hasp through which is a metal pin. The pin is withdrawn, the hasp is opened and the top raised. As the top is opened, the box is held so the spectators can see its contents. Inside the box is the purse and a small corsage. As he, too, looks in the box, the magician smiles and in a pleased voice says, "Well, we don't have to worry any more about the safety of the ring."

The magician goes to the lady so she may take the purse from the box and take back her ring. As she takes her ring from the purse, he takes the flowers from the box. He closes the box and puts it in his pocket, or under his arm, so as to have both hands free. He takes back the purse with one hand as he hands her the corsage with the other. Immediately after the lady has the flowers the magician reaches into the air and finds a glass headed florists pin. He offers the pin to the lady with the remark that she may wish to pin on the flowers.

As what the magician does and what he says usually occur simultaneously, a description of a feat of magic seems more lengthy than does the actual performance. Furthermore the description must mention the appearance of various items which can be seen in the performance and then do not have to be described.

There are two secret parts to this feat. The first is the method used to cause the purse with its ring to disappear from the handkerchief. The other is how the purse and ring was put inside the double wrapped, secured metal box. Both depend upon the type of purse used to hold the ring. I have found a soft leather purse is admirable for the purpose. At various times I have used purses held closed with a snap fastener, with a zipper, and with a prong stuck through a loop. All are satisfactory. The purse should be no bigger than 2½″ x 3″. It does not have to be exactly that size. It must not be larger and may well be smaller as long as a ring will go in it. Actually there have to be two purses but they do not have to look alike as one is never seen. They do have to feel alike.

The handkerchief should be of as heavy material as can be obtained for it must be opaque. The handkerchief must be at least 18″ square. The material should have an overall pattern of small design. The handkerchief may have a border of solid color but there has to be a design at the center. Two handkerchiefs, identical in color and pattern, are needed. A piece of cloth from the second is needed to make a pocket to hold the second purse at the center of the handkerchief used in the trick. The pocket is closed on all sides so that the purse cannot fall out or be seen. Perhaps the most satisfactory way of making the pocket is to glue the one piece of cloth to the other. Naturally it is necessary to use the type of adhesive made for use on cloth. Using glue avoids needing to hem the extra piece of cloth for the adhesive keeps the edges of the cloth from raveling. The purse in the pocket should contain a ring. The ring is without a set and should be fairly thick. It can be of the cheapest metal for it is never seen. In making the pocket the purse should be placed on the handkerchief so that one edge is exactly at the center of the material. The rest of the purse extends upwards above the center line but should be equi-distant from the two sides of the handkerchief. The piece of cloth is glued so that the purse will stay in that position. After the adhesive on the pocket has dried, the four corners of the handkerchief should be picked up and held together. Holding the cloth in this way will make a bag out of the handkerchief. The hidden purse should be inside the handkerchief and at the bottom of the pocket. Taking hold of the outside of the handkerchief the purse with its ring can be felt.

In the performance at the point where the woman has closed the purse in which she has put her ring, the magician takes the handkerchief from his pocket. When it comes from his pocket it is nicely folded. Holding the handkerchief with one hand he takes hold of one corner of the cloth with the other. Without saying a word, it is amazing how convincingly the magician proves that the handkerchief is quite ordinary—by bringing it out folded and then opening it with a shake. Because of the pattern of the material and the way the bag is made, the handkerchief can be handled most casually without the audience suspecting that it is not as innocent as it appears. As a matter of fact the more casual the magician is in handling it the less he will excite suspicion. However, the magician must be certain when he gathers the four corners of the handkerchief to form a bag, that the pocket with its purse is inside the bag. The magician can make this requirement easy to follow by the way he folds the handkerchief before the show. He folds it so that when it is shaken out the pocket side of the handkerchief is towards him.

Having made a bag out of the handkerchief the magician gives the gathered corners to a man and asks him to hold them firmly in one hand. The magician then takes the purse from the lady and, going back to the man, he opens the handkerchief and sticks the purse into the bag. The magician puts his hand into the bag with the purse. He puts his hand in as far as it will go easily. As soon as the hand and purse are inside the bag, the magician asks the man to take hold of the purse with his free hand. The magician asks the man if he also can feel the ring inside the purse. During these questions the magician withdraws his hand from the handkerchief bag and with it the original purse. When the magician takes his hand out of the bag he has the purse in his clenched fist. As the man is satisfied he has hold of the purse and its ring, and the audience accept his word for it, there is no reason for them to pay any attention to the magician as he withdraws his hand. And as the purse is hidden inside his hand there is nothing for anyone to see were they to notice. Once the magician gets his hand out of the bag he drops it to his side, or sticks it in his pocket, as he continues to give instructions to the man about never letting go of either purse or handkerchief.

The magician goes to his prop table and picks up the paper bag. This he does with his back toward the audience. While in general a performer does not turn his back to the audience, he does do so when it would be awkward to do otherwise. When returning from the spectators to go to his prop table, it would be ridiculous to back up. It is the natural thing to do when leaving the spectators to turn around and walk away. That this is the natural and permissible thing to do is fortunate in this instance for it makes the trick so easy. In walking to his table the magician gets the hand, in which he holds the purse, in front of his body. When he reaches for the bag, he does so with both hands. The one hand grasps the bag and the other sticks the purse into the parcel. As the opening is quite large, this action is instantaneous. While it is permissible for the magician to turn his back to the audience as he walks to his table, he must pick up the bag and turn around at once. It rarely is permissible for a performer to stand with back toward the audience. He can turn immediately, for picking up the bag and inserting the purse are done simultaneously. He holds up the bag for the audience to see, mentions that he purchased a souvenir, and puts the bag down on one of his performance tables.

The magician has accomplished three things after he has left the spectators. He has put the purse with the borrowed ring into the package, he has introduced the package to the audience, and he has taken his eyes off the man holding the handkerchief. This last fact makes it possible to look at the man with surprise and to state that the man is squeezing the ring too tightly. Questioning the man's actions makes it reasonable for the magician to return to him. And that is when the magician makes ring and purse disappear from the handkerchief.

It was not carelessly written that the magician instantly sticks the purse into the package. Not only does the purse go inside the sealed bag, but it also goes inside the ribbon tied gift paper and inside the metal box. And remember the bag is shown to the audience, as is the gift wrapped box, and finally the metal box itself. Getting the purse through barriers is so unbelievable that no one ever has suspected that it could be the solution to the trick. But it can be done and here is how.

As there has to be a box to wrap and put into the bag, the box will be the first item described. My box was made of two different metals and that fact in addition to the design of the box gives it the appearance of an old Chinese box. The inside measurements of the box are 6" long, 3¾" wide, and 1" deep. The inside dimensions are noted because it is more simple, in making the box, to work from those measurements. My box is made of aluminum. That metal was not used in the Chinese boxes of old but they did use metals having the same appearance. The box is trimmed with brass. There are brass corners, fancy brass hinges and hasp, and the box is held closed by a brass rod which goes through the loop of the hasp. While the brass corners add to the attractiveness of the box, they are not put on the box solely for the sake of appearance. Their other purpose will be given in the details of construction of the box. The cover of the box is just a flat piece of aluminum.

The secret of the box is that one side of the box can be opened. This side is made to push into the box and, because of spring hinges, snap back into position. The brass corners on the end of the box having the movable part act in a dual role. They serve as stops so that the springs in the hinges can push the metal only so far and also cover the cracks between the movable side and the rest of the box as well as covering the rivets which hold the spring hinges.

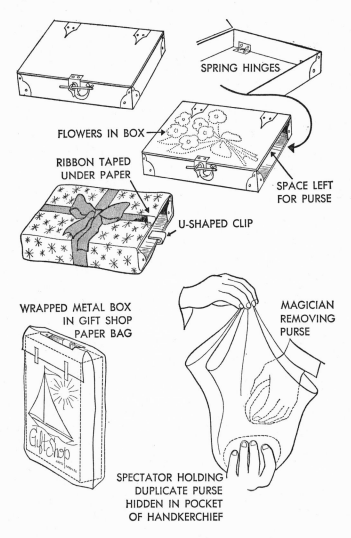

SPRING HINGES

FLOWERS IN BOX

RIBBON TAPED
UNDER PAPER

SPACE LEFT
FOR PURSE

U-SHAPED CLIP

WRAPPED METAL BOX
IN GIFT SHOP
PAPER BAG

MAGICIAN
REMOVING
PURSE

SPECTATOR HOLDING
DUPLICATE PURSE
HIDDEN IN POCKET
OF HANDKERCHIEF

The box is made of one piece of sheet metal ³⁄₆₄″ thick. Metal of this thickness will make a substantial box and yet have it light enough so it may be handled easily. The metal is cut so as to give it the appearance of a three armed cross. The center of this cross is $3\frac{3}{4}'' \times 6''$. Each of the three arms is $1''$ long. Two of the arms extend from the long sides and one from the short side. When the metal has been cut the arms are bent up at right angles. When the arms are bent the metal forms three sides and the bottom of the box. Another piece of the same metal is cut for the open side of the box. This metal is attached to the box with the spring hinges. As it has to move freely, it is cut so as to give $\frac{1}{64}''$ clearance at each end. The dimensions of this piece are $1''$ high and $3\frac{23}{32}''$ wide. The spring hinges are of brass and are $\frac{1}{2}''$ wide. As it is difficult to find the proper hinges commercially, they must be made. This is a fiddlesome task though not difficult. First the pin of the hinge has to be removed. This is easier to do if when purchasing the hinges ones are selected which have very free action. After the pin is removed the two sides of the hinge are pulled apart. Then the center loop of one side is removed either by filing or with a jeweler's saw. Removing this loop gives the space for the spring. Eight turns of $\frac{1}{64}''$ spring steel wire are made around a rod of the same diameter as the pin of the hinge. Each end of the wire should protrude $\frac{3}{16}''$ from the coil. The hinge is then reassembled with the addition of the coil spring. Care must be taken in assembly that the spring is put in so that the ends of the wire are on the inside of the hinge and the spring's action is to force the hinge open. Two such spring hinges are required. (See illustration.)

The spring hinges are riveted to the extreme ends of the bottom of the loose piece of metal. After the hinges are attached to that metal it is put in place in the box and the other arms of the hinges are riveted to the bottom of the box. The ornamental brass corners are then attached to the outside of the box. Each of these corners is made to go across the corner of the bottom of the box and come up each side to a point at the top of the box. The corners are made of brass and may be purchased although they are easy to make. Each corner is cut from one piece of brass which when flat is square, with the diagonal measurements of $2''$ which must be exact. The sides measure approximately $1\frac{3}{8}''$. One quarter of the square is cut out. The part cut out is triangular in shape and runs from the exact center of the square to the two corners of one side. Each of two sides of this triangle are exactly $1''$ long. After the brass for each of the four corners has been cut the pieces are put together and filed as one. These pieces are filed so that the outside edges are attractively curved. Upon finishing filing, each piece is bent so that the metal forms a three sided corner piece and the edges where the side pieces meet the metal is soldered from the inside. The corner pieces are then riveted to the box. Each corner is held by two rivets going through the bottom of the box. In my box, I also put a fake rivet into one side of each of the corner pieces. This was only for appearance and is not necessary.

Finally a piece of metal is cut for the top of the box. This metal should be a hair line larger than the box itself. The top is hinged to the box by having small but fancy brass hinges riveted on the outside of the box. On the opposite side of the cover a hasp is riveted. The loop for the hasp is on the front of the box. Finally a brass rod 1½" long is made to fit tightly through the loop when the hasp is in place. I have made a hole in one end of the rod I use. Through this hole I have tied a narrow ribbon. The other end of the ribbon I have tied to the hasp. This was done in order never to separate the rod from the box.

Before wrapping the box the corsage is put in it. There is room inside the box for a very attractive small corsage. It should be made of tiny roses, or a variety of other flowers which do not easily crush. Orchids, among several other flowers, should not be used as they bruise so easily. Artificial flowers, also, are attractive and may be used. The flowers should be tied with a ribbon. The corsage should be no more than 5" long and is put in the box so that the flowers are opposite the end which opens. This is done so as to leave room for the purse at the open end of the box. By arranging the flowers so that they are flat rather than high, it will be surprising to see how large a corsage the box will hold.

The box is wrapped in a colorful and attractive gift paper. A piece of such paper is cut to 9" x 11". The box is placed on the paper so that the side of the box which opens is in the center and almost to one of the 9" long edges. The paper is tightly wrapped around the box the long way and sealed with cellophane tape. The end of the paper is folded in the manner normally used in wrapping and it too is held with cellophane tape. The ribbon then is tied around the paper. The ribbon goes both ways around the box and is drawn as tightly as possible and tied. The ends of the ribbon are made into a fancy bow. In tying the box in this way the ribbon will have gone across the side of the box which opens. The ribbon has to be cut at the center of this side. Each end is folded back, pushed under the paper and stuck in place with cellophane tape.

When the box has been wrapped in this manner the movable side of the box is pushed open. It is held open by a U-shaped piece of spring metal 1″ wide. The metal spring goes inside the box and on top of the paper on the outside of the box. (See illustration.)

The box next is put into the paper bag. The bag is the kind stores use for gifts and undoubtedly a friendly store will give bags for use in this magic. As the stores have their names on such bags they usually are glad to give away a few for the advertising. These bags have flat edges as do envelopes. They do not open out wide as do grocery bags. The bag should be about 10″ long and wide enough so the box will go inside. The box, open side uppermost, is put in the bag and the top of the bag folded over so that it goes on the face of the bag to which it is stuck by several pieces of cellophane tape. Once the box is in the bag and the tape is holding the bag closed, it will be found possible to feel the open end of the box through the paper of the bag. With a sharp knife an oblong hole is cut in the paper at, and the size of, the hole in the box. Because of the way the bag folds, this hole will be at the back and almost at the top of the bag.

When the magician goes to his prop table to pick up the bag, he does so with one hand. At the same time the purse, with the other hand, is pushed through the hole in the bag and into the box. When the bag is put on the table it is placed back down so that the hole in the bag is hidden.

Later when the bag is picked up attention is called to the fact that the bag is sealed with tape. The bag then is torn off the package. The package is held with the palm of the hand covering the open end and with the fingers and thumb on top and bottom of the box. Held in this way the box can be shown quite freely.

Scissors are used to cut the ribbon around the gift paper. This seems to be done in order to open the box more rapidly. Using scissors also permits the magician to cut the ribbon at the open end of the box where it has been stuck to the paper. In taking the ribbon off the box, the magician has the opportunity without being noticed to remove the spring which holds open the side of the box. Once the spring is taken away the spring hinges will close this side. The gift paper next is torn off the box. The box is exhibited on all six sides as it can be for all the sides are now closed.

The magician pushes the bar free of the hasp, lifts the hasp and opens the box. As the lid of the box is raised the box is tipped toward the audience so that everyone can see the contents. This part of the routine must be done slowly, and so very carefully that it is obvious that nothing tricky is being done. As nothing is, this presents no difficulty.

All that remains to be done is to take the box to the lady, let her take her ring and present the corsage to her. The florist's pin is behind the coat lapel where it easily can be found. Pretending to pluck the pin from the air adds a tiny fillip to the climax of most attractive magic.

A CARD AND CIGARETTES

THE following example of magic is a perfect illustration of a feat depending upon the use of apparatus and in which the spectators would swear none was used. Everything looks so fair, so open and above board, that it seems impossible trickery could play a part. The simplicity of the plot adds to the effectiveness of the magic.

What the audience will remember having seen is that the magician took his cigarette case from his pocket, opened it and showed it to be full of cigarettes, closed it and gave it to a spectator with instructions to put it in his pocket. Another spectator was given a deck of cards and requested to shuffle it thoroughly. He then chose one card, looked at it and replaced it among the other cards. At the magician's demand the chosen card disappeared and was found inside the cigarette case by the spectator who was holding it.

That is what the audience will recall having seen. There are several other points about the feat that will not be remembered as they seem to be such unimportant details. However, as the reader is well aware, in magic all details are important and particularly those which appear to be inconsequential.

The card which appears in the cigarette case is a duplicate of the one the spectator is induced to take. The cigarette case is an ordinary cigarette case which has been altered so that when the magician opens it no card is seen but it contains a card when opened by the spectator. I use a plain, flat silver case. Such cases are not expensive and being the kind of case a person would normally carry adds proof, or what is accepted as proof, that the case itself has nothing to do with the magic. The case, made for the standard size, not king size, cigarettes is $3\frac{3}{4}''$ long, $3\frac{1}{16}''$ wide and $\frac{3}{16}''$ thick. Along one short end is a hinge. On the end opposite the hinge there is a nub which, when pressed, permits the case to open. The nub extends from the end of the lower side of the case. The cigarettes lie on this lower side and are held in place by a spring hinged flat bar. This is a description of the case when it is purchased.

This is the way the case was altered. First, the pin of the hinge was carefully removed. The pin also went through a loop which held the bar so that when the two parts of the case were separated the bar also was taken out. The spring was cut off the loop of the bar. Then a second bar was made and was soldered to the loop. Each of the bars was bent away from the loop so that the bars were parallel and separated only enough for a cigarette to go between them. The case was then reassembled and the pin put back in place. Cigarettes were then put between the two bars. When the case was opened in the normal way the cigarettes covered the bottom of the case and were held in the case apparently by the one bar. However, were the case opened upside down, due to the movable double bar, the cigarettes would seem to be in the same position and held there by a bar. Actually this is the second bar and the cigarettes are now in the top of the case, which, due to the case having been turned over, is in the bottom position. When opened either way the inside of the case and the cigarettes have the same appearance for, because of the double bar, the cigarettes can flop either way. If a playing card is put in the top of the case, the cigarettes will hide the card when the case is opened with the bottom of the case uppermost. The magician opens the case in this way and shows the inside of the case with its cigarettes. He then closes the case and gives it to a spectator. The spectator naturally will open the case right side up and thereby disclose the card. So much for making the card "reappear."

The spectator whom the magician has selected to choose the card is asked to stand at one side of a table. He is given a deck of cards and is requested to shuffle them thoroughly. The magician stands back of the table as if he merely wished to watch what his assistant does. When the shuffling is finished the magician asks the assistant if he is satisfied that the cards have been so thoroughly mixed that neither he, nor anyone else, could have any idea of the order of the cards. When the assistant acknowledges that to be true the magician gives him further directions.

"Now I would like you to do two more things for me. First I want you to think of a number—a number say between 10 and 25. You, of course, realize that there has been no prearrangement between us, but I wish you would tell everyone that is fact. Thank you. Now you have a number in mind. Fine. Will you take the cards you so thoroughly shuffled and count down to the number in your mind. As you take off each card will you please drop it in a pile on the table? The reason I ask you to drop each card as you take it from the deck is so you, and all the rest of us, can see that you take but one card at a time. This is to avoid your accidentally counting wrongly. Please count the cards off the deck until you have the number of cards on the table equal to the number you mentally selected."

While the cards are being counted the magician takes from his pockets a pencil and a blank white card. When the assistant has completed counting the cards the magician, as he drops the card and the pencil on the table, says, "I'll take the remainder of the deck and put it aside. What I want you

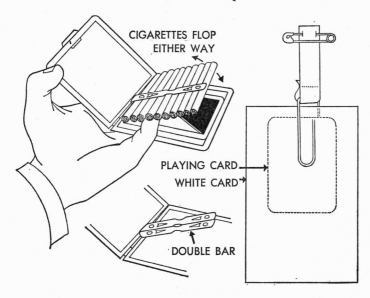

to do is to write on the paper, the name of the card you last put down— the one at the number you selected." While what the assistant is given to write on actually is a card, it is called paper so as not to confuse it with a playing card. The magician asks the assistant to turn around when he looks at his card and writes down which it is so that the assistant alone will know the card.

While the assistant is writing the name of the card, the magician picks up from the table the cards put there by the assistant. The magician asks the assistant when he has completed his writing to put the paper in his pocket and to place the card on those the magician holds. When this is done, the magician cuts the cards and places them on the table. The assistant is thanked for what he has done and asked to return to his seat.

MORE EXCEPTIONAL MAGIC

The magician says that he would like to remind everyone just what has been done so far. That a case holding cigarettes was shown and given to a spectator, in whose possession it has been ever since. That a second member of the audience thoroughly shuffled a deck of cards and freely selected one card. That he wrote the name of the card on a paper which he holds. And finally, the chosen card is somewhere among the cards on the table. The magician then states that he, without being told which card had been selected, will cause that card to leave the table and go inside the cigarette case. Turning to the person holding the cigarette case, the magician says, "Be sure to hold the case tightly closed."

The magician explains that he is going to show that the card has left the table. "But," he says, turning to the spectator who chose the card, "It might be a good idea for you to show to some of your neighbors the paper on which you wrote the name of your card." He then picks up all the cards from the table, slowly shows each card and after showing it drops it face up on the table. When all the cards have been shown the magician says, "You didn't see your card, did you? Of course not, for it has gone inside the cigarette case. Before the case is opened, will you please call out the name of the card you chose. Now will you, please, open the case and take out that card. It is inside the case, isn't it? Thank you both for your help."

The way the cards are handled by the assistant and by the magician is accurately stated but not completely so. Two unnoticed but crucial details were omitted. Up to the point where the assistant has dropped cards on the table to the number he had in his mind, everything is as described. The first detail not mentioned has to do with the magician's dropping the white card and pencil on the table. Under the white card, the magician has a playing card and both it and the white card are dropped on top of the cards counted. It is this card which the assistant looks at and writes the name of —and believes he chose so freely. The magician drops the white card in order, or so it appears, to have a hand free to take the remainder of the deck the assistant is holding. The reason for using a card for the assistant to write on is that a card will fall to the table and so hide the playing card under it. A paper flutters down and may well separate from the playing card and so disclose the trick.

No skill whatsoever is needed to drop the white card and playing card as one. Naturally the cards have to be aimed so that the playing card will land on top of the pile of cards, but as the cards are dropped an inch or so, that presents no difficulty, particularly as the assistant was instructed to drop his cards, as he counted them, into a pile on the table. As his pile will be quite irregular the extra card never will be noticed.

In order to have the playing card under the white card and be able easily to get hold of both together a little holder is used. The holder is an ordinary wire paper clip. Through this clip is run a piece of ribbon, or tape, about 2″ long. The tape is folded back so that the clip hangs from it and the tape is pinned, with a small safety pin, on the inside of the jacket just under the left sleeve. The two cards are slid into this clip. The playing card faces toward the coat lining and on top of it is the white card. Reaching under the coat with the right hand both cards are squeezed together and taken from the clip. In bringing the hand away from the jacket it is turned so that the playing card is hidden under the white card. (See illustration.)

The second unmentioned detail is also one never noticed. It will be recalled that while the assistant is writing the name of the playing card upon the white card, the magician picks up the cards on the table. When he has these cards squared he holds them in his hand with the backs uppermost. He casually brings the cards in front of his mouth and licks the top card exactly as if he were moistening an envelope. The magician asks the assistant to put his card on the rest. The magician immediately squares the cards and cuts them so that the assistant's card will go about the middle of the small packet of cards. The magician must make these actions so slowly and so fairly that it is obvious no trickery has been done. Once the cards have been cut they are pressed together firmly. This will cause the selected card to adhere to the moistened card below it. When the cards are shown one at a time, the selected card is not seen as it is stuck to another card. As these cards are stuck together there is no difficulty in handling the two cards as one.

The reason the card is caused to disappear from among only those cards which had been counted on the table rather than the complete deck is that it expedites that part of the trick.

If the reader is worried that someone will notice the action of moistening the card, he can pretend to cough as he brings the cards to his mouth. If he will make the action several times in front of a mirror, he will find it can be covered so that it will not be seen and that the trick does not require a case of incipient bronchitis.

Ten. BEYOND THE FIVE SENSES

This Chapter contains feats which seem to audiences to be the result of the magician's super mental powers. Magic of the mind, being part of magicians' programs for only a couple of centuries, is a very new field in the most ancient art of magic. These tricks, for greatest effect, should be presented in a serious vein as if the performer really were possessed of the mental powers he seems to demonstrate. But actually claiming these powers to be genuine takes the magician out of the category of entertainers and puts him among the charlatans. In presenting this type of magic, the magician should take every precaution to have his audiences remember his magic as being not fraud but delightful entertainment.

THE CLEVER POLTERGEIST

The reader very probably does not believe in ghostly occurrences such as transparent wraiths, disembodied voices, and spirit raps. My own disbelief is complete. However, ghost stories supply excellent plots for feats of magic when told with a straight face. The chief actor in the story used for this trick is a poltergeist—the term for a mischievous ghost. The poltergeist in the story was very clever and liked to show off. His tendencies to exhibitionism gives the plot for the magic. The feat is unusual, amusing, and quite astounding.

According to the story the poltergeist enjoyed jiggling a teaspoon in a glass. This inclination was discovered one evening when the mistress of the house inadvertently left a spoon in a glass. After all the house lights had been extinguished the poltergeist began dancing the spoon up and down in the glass. On subsequent nights the poltergeist would find a spoon and put it in a glass so he could play his game. The noise was quite annoying to the family. One night in desperation the man of the house called out, "Will you please stop that ghastly racket!" After a moment of silence the spoon was heard to strike the glass twice. As is common knowledge when a ghost raps two times that means "no." The man then called out, "If you won't stop the noise, will you answer questions?" The spoon hit the glass three times which, of course, meant "yes." The family spent many sleepless nights asking all sorts of questions and invariably the poltergeist knew the answers.

In the performance the magician tells the story, puts a spoon in a glass on a table and covers them so the poltergeist can have darkness. The magician then states that he has borrowed the ghost for the evening. He goes on to say he believes that it will interest the audience to know that the name of the ghost is "Willie," and that he was born in 1821 and died from injuries received in the war with Mexico. The spoon is heard to strike the glass and correctly answers questions to which only the spectators know the answers. That is what the audience believes happens, but, as invariably is the case with magic, the facts are somewhat different.

The trick depends upon two points. 1. The magician also knows the answers to the spectators' questions although it does not seem possible that he could have such knowledge. 2. The ear is a most unreliable organ when it comes to locating the source of sound and, even, differentiating between similar noises.

There is nothing at all tricky about the glass, the spoon, the tube, or the small square of cardboard used to make a top for the tube. The expressed purpose of using the tube and its cover is to put the glass and spoon in darkness. The actual purpose is to keep the audience from being able to see that the spoon never moves in the glass. The sound, which the audience accepts as being caused by the movement of the spoon in the tumbler comes from within a box placed on the same table. That sound is under the control of the magician. The box with its mechanism for creating the sound of a spoon striking a glass will be described after instructions are given for the magician to discover what three spectators believe they alone know.

The spectators have no selection of subjects regarding the questions they will ask the poltergeist to answer. But as each spectator is given a choice within the subject given him he will be satisfied. The three subjects are: the name of a selected card, the date on one coin selected from a number of coins the spectator has taken from his pocket, and the name of the brand of one cigarette chosen from ten cigarettes, each of a different brand.

The spectator actually is given a free choice of one card from an entire deck. When the card is selected the spectator is asked to put it in his pocket without even looking at it or letting anyone else see the card. The magician knows which card is selected because the cards are in the memorized order described in "The Hungry Jackass" chapter (Chapter 5). All he has to do is to cut the deck at the place where the card was selected by the spectator and place the cards which had been above the selected card on the bottom of the deck. The entire pack then is placed, face up, on the performance table the magician is using for the trick. When it comes time for the disclosure of the name of the card the spectator has chosen, all the magician has to do is to look at the face of the card showing on the deck which is upside down on the table. The selected card will be the next one in the sequence memorized. These are the questions asked the poltergeist about the card and the way the answers are given by the jumping spoon.

"Willie, do you know the name of the card selected, which even the gentleman does not know?"

(The spoon jumps 3 times.) "Three times—that means yes. Willie, tell me how many spots are on the card." (The spoon jumps as many times as there are pips on the card. If the card chosen was a court card there is no sound. Then the magician states that the card chosen must be a picture card and he names the picture cards until he gets a "yes" answer.)

"Thank you, Willie, now we know the value of the card. Was it a red card? (The magician correctly names the color of the card and gets a "yes" answer.) Was it a diamond? (The magician names the wrong suit and gets a "no" answer.) Oh, then it must have been a heart. Willie, you say the card is the six of hearts. Now we'll ask the gentleman to take the card out of his pocket to see if you, Willie, knew what no one else did. Willie, you are wonderful."

Naturally the card chosen may be any other card in the deck. The illustration given was to show how the questions were given and the answers made. The manner of disclosing what each of the three spectators choose will be given, as above, after explaining how the magician ascertains the choice. In actual performance all three selections are completed before Willie is even mentioned. The description is given in this way in order to make each part of the trick more easily understood.

The second "choice" is one coin from among many. This is so bold that one's first reaction is that the method wouldn't work. The reader has my assurances that not only is the method practical but easy to do. In the many years I have performed this trick I never have had anyone even mildly suspicious.

The magician states that he needs the assistance of a gentleman who knows he has a number of coins loose in his pocket. He steps up to the man who acknowledges his solvency, at least in the matter of coins, and asks him to take all the coins from his pocket and hold them in his closed hand. The magician then asks the man to open his hand. As soon as the hand is opened, the magician touches the coins and pushes them just a little. As he does so he says, "I hope you will be kind enough to permit me to borrow this dime." As this is said he takes his hand away and turning his hand over he exhibits a dime held by the tips of his fingers. The magician goes right on talking, "But so that neither you nor I will have to worry about the loan, will you hold your dime in your other hand." As the man takes the small coin the magician instructs him to hold tightly to his dime but to put the other coins back in his pocket.

The reason this trick is bold is that the dime actually belongs to the magician who, prior to beginning his show, learned the date on the coin. As he asks for the aid of a spectator, the magician puts his hand into his pocket and takes hold of the dime. The coin is taken so that it is held on the fleshy middle part of the first joint of the first and second fingers and covered by the pad of the thumb. The third and little fingers are curled in towards the palm. Held in this manner it will be found that the dime is completely hidden. When the magician reaches towards the coins in the spectator's hand, he extends his first finger to push the coins slightly—naturally, he retains hold of the coin with his second finger and thumb. After the little push on the pile of coins, which seems to be an essential part of taking one coin from many, the magician pushes the dime to the tips of his fingers, the first finger going back in position, and simultaneously he turns his hand palm up. In talking to the spectator about the coin, after it has been "picked up" the magician always is careful to say "your" dime, or "your" coin. That sounds right to the spectator for everything done by the magician is so natural that the spectator believes the coin to be his. In answer to the reader's question at this point: Yes, the trick does cost you ten cents every time you perform it but you will find the effect well worth the expense.

When the magician asks Willie to give the date on the coin the spoon jumps once and stops. The magician goes on talking.

"One, Willie? Oh, you were starting to give the complete date. I think we may assume, Willie, that the first two figures are a one and a nine. Just give the last two numbers. (The spoon jumps 6 times, stops and then jumps once.) The date on the coin is 1961. Will the gentleman please look at the date on the coin and tell Willie if he is right."

It will be noticed that when the spectator selected the card it actually was a completely free choice and the magician later learned which card had been chosen. The magician knew the date on the coin because actually it was no choice. The third item used is a cigarette and the spectator has an entirely free choice of one cigarette from the ten cigarettes offered—each of a different brand. While the choice is free, it is meaningless because of an additional factor in the trick which has not been mentioned and which the audience will forget because it does not seem to have any connection with the way the trick works.

First a detailed description of what the audience sees in the cigarette part of the magic. The magician takes a small tray upon which there are ten cigarettes and holds the tray so as to permit a spectator to make a selection of one cigarette. The spectator is told to hold that cigarette concealed in his hand. The tray is given to another spectator who is told to pass out the remaining nine cigarettes to smokers in the audience. As the cigarette is being selected by one spectator, the magician gives a neighboring spectator a card which he takes from his pocket. Written, or printed, on the card are the names of the ten different brands of cigarettes which had been on the tray. These names are written in a column and alongside of each name is a number. When Willie is asked to tell which cigarette was chosen he jumps the spoon a number of times. Having the spectator refer to the number on the card he is holding, it will be found that the name following that number is the name of the cigarette selected.

The spectator actually has a free choice, as has been noted, of the cigarette. What he does not know is that the magician has the cigarettes in a certain order on the tray but not the same order as are listed on the card. The order is one to make it easy for the magician to notice which cigarette is taken from the tray and for him instantly to know the number on the card. The reason it is easy is that he never has to count above five.

At the time this book is written the ten cigarettes most widely sold in the United States have brands which were not among the ten most popular brands when I first thought of using cigarettes in this trick. By the time the reader does the trick, the top ten cigarette list may again be different. Besides, the reader would be wise to use a list of the most popular cigarettes sold in his locality for, even in cigarettes, there are geographical preferences. The first task is to make up a list of ten different brands of cigarettes. In making up the list filter and plain, king size and regular should be mixed so there is no noticeable order. The list of names is written on a card in a vertical column. In front of each name is written a number. The numbers are written in sequence with "1" in front of the name at the top of the list and "10" in front of the last name in the column. This is the card which is given to the spectator.

For his own convenience the magician makes up a second list which will designate the order of the cigarettes when placed on the tray. This list should not have the cigarettes in the same order as are the names on the list given the spectator. This is to avoid the possibility of the spectator's remembering that he, as example, chose the first cigarette in the row and found it also to be the first name on the list and so become suspicious. Exchanging the first five numbers with the second five will make all but the third cigarette in a different position. The tray list would be made with the numbers in this sequence 6-7-8-9-10-1-2-3-4-5 and after each number would be written the name of the cigarette found at the corresponding number on the spectator's list. The cigarettes are put on the tray in a row with each cigarette parallel to the others so they look like ten ties in a railroad track. The cigarettes are put on the tray from left (the performer's left) to right. When the performer picks up the tray he must be certain he is holding the tray in the way to have the cigarette in the proper order. Reversing the tray would be disastrous for it would put the cigarettes in a different order. It will make the magician's task more simple if at the center of the bottom of the tray there is a mark noticeable to the magician. If this is done, and five cigarettes are placed on either side of the mark, the magician can know the number of the cigarette chosen by just half a glance. The magician knows that the numbers to the right of center, and reading from left to right are 1,2,3,4,5. The numbers from the left of the row, reading again from left to right, run 6,7,8,9,10. It will be found after a few minutes practice the magician will instantly know the number of the cigarette selected, and as shown on the card.

As the selection is being made the magician is busy taking the card with the list of cigarettes from his pocket and giving it to another spectator. This action will seem to show the magician's total disinterest in which cigarette is chosen. At the same time he is not so occupied as to be kept from glancing at the tray. Immediately after the cigarette has been chosen, the magician tips the tray just enough so all the cigarettes will roll to one end. They then are passed out to various spectators each of whom will find he has a cigarette unlike the chosen one.

After Willie has hit the glass with the spoon to indicate the number of the cigarette the magician announces the number and asks the spectator holding the card to call out the name written by that number. When the name is stated the spectator holding the cigarette is told to open his hand and verify that Willie again is right.

So much for what Willie knows and how he gets his knowledge. All else that has to be noted is how Willie causes the spoon to jump in the glass. Earlier it was stated that the sound of the spoon striking the glass came from another location. This can be done because in certain instances it is impossible to locate the source of a sound. If at the front of his performance table the magician has the glass and spoon and at the back of that same table he has a box containing a sound-making mechanism, no one's ear can distinguish the location of the origin of the sound. This is because the sound from either location will reach both ears of a spectator at the same time. It is possible only to know the direction from which a sound comes when it reaches one ear before reaching the other.

The obvious reason for having a box on the table is that various of the objects used in the magic were brought to the table in the box. And, at the conclusion of the mystery these objects are returned to the box. The box therefore will not cause suspicion, particularly as it is a simple cardboard box. The box used should be as small as possible so as to seem to be completely filled when first brought to the table. The box has only to hold the tumbler, the tube (which can be over the glass), the cardboard square for the top of the tube, a spoon, and a deck of cards. The tube should be 2″ higher than the glass in order to give the teaspoon space to do its jumping. Perhaps it would be better to say the tube should be 2″ higher than the end of the spoon when it stands in the glass. The tube should be of lightweight paper so it is ob-

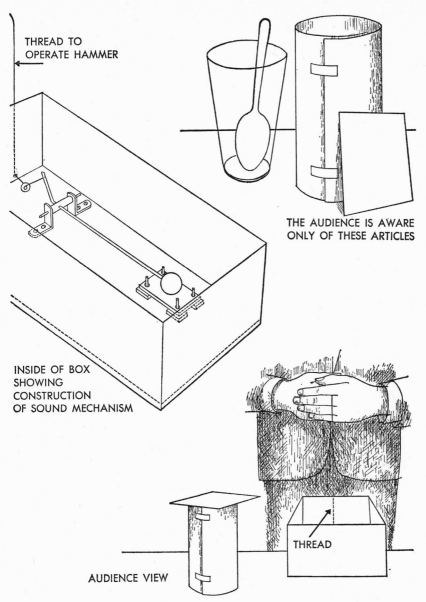

THREAD TO
OPERATE HAMMER

THE AUDIENCE IS AWARE
ONLY OF THESE ARTICLES

INSIDE OF BOX
SHOWING
CONSTRUCTION
OF SOUND MECHANISM

THREAD

AUDIENCE VIEW

vious it has no other function than to act as a cover. The box I use is 9″ long, 4″ wide, and 4″ high. This box holds a tube 8″ long and 3″ in diameter; the tumbler which has a diameter of 2½″ and is 4¼″ high; the teaspoon which is 6″ long; the cardboard square and the deck of cards. While items of the size noted (plus the secret mechanism) will go into a box of the dimensions given it will be well to get the contents together before looking for a box. If a suitable cardboard box of the proper size and nice appearance is not easily obtained, it is suggested that a box be made and that is no great chore.

At the bottom of the box is a metal plate. This plate serves a double purpose. It gives weight to the box and the mechanism is attached to it. The plate should weigh a pound, preferably more. It should be the length and width of the inside of the bottom of the box. This weight is needed to hold the box in position on the table. Gluing a piece of sheet rubber on the bottom of the box will aid in keeping the box from sliding on the table. The mechanism inside the box is a hammer which is activated by a thread which goes through the box and is pulled by the magician. The hammer hits on a loose thin steel plate. The ear cannot distinguish any difference in the sound of metal striking glass or striking metal which can vibrate. This steel plate is put at one end of the box. The plate is 3″ x 2″ and $\frac{1}{16}$″ thick. In the plate near each corner is drilled a hole $\frac{3}{16}$″ in diameter. These holes go over four $\frac{1}{8}$″ rods which are pressed into properly spaced holes in the metal weight at the bottom of the box. On top of the metal weight a small piece of leather, like a washer, is put over each corner rod. The metal plate is put on top of the leather washers. When the top of the plate is struck, the plate will vibrate and because of the rods the plate will stay in position. Because of the leather washers the plate makes no noise when it falls back into position. A specially made hammer strikes the plate. The head of the hammer should weigh an ounce. I used a short piece of $\frac{1}{2}$″ brass rod. The striking surface of the hammer should be rounded. A hole is drilled in the side of the hammer head. Into this hole is pushed a stiff, thin metal rod. I used a $\frac{3}{32}$″ steel rod and soldered it to the head. The steel rod was cut off $8\frac{1}{2}$″ from the edge of the head. Under a torch the end of the wire opposite the head is bent up at right angles and $1\frac{1}{2}$″ from the tip. $\frac{1}{8}$″ from the end of the tip is drilled a $\frac{1}{32}$″ hole. On the inside of the bend is soldered a piece of the same wire. This wire $\frac{3}{4}$″ long extends equally on either side of the long wire so that it forms the arms of a cross. The ends of this short wire are rounded. These ends go into $\frac{1}{8}$″ holes drilled part way into two small metal blocks. These blocks are $\frac{1}{2}$″ square and 1″ long. The holes are drilled into one end of each block. The ends of the cross bar of the wire having the hammer head are put into the holes of the metal block which are screwed to the metal weight at the bottom of the box and near the end opposite to the small metal plate. The blocks are so placed that the hammer head will go directly over the center of the metal plate. At the end of the metal weight, at the end opposite the plate, is soldered a screw eye. In the end of the cardboard box and in line with the screw eye, a small hole is made. After passing a thread through the hole at the tip of the turned up end of the metal rod the thread is brought down, put through the screw eye, and then pushed through the hole in the cardboard box. A pull of two ounces on this thread will raise the hammer. Giving slack to the thread will permit the hammer to fall and strike the metal plate. This will make a sound identical with that of a spoon striking the sides of a glass standing on a table.

When performing the trick the magician should stand about two feet away from, and directly back of, the table. The thread should be long enough so the magician can hold it when he stands back of the table. On the end of the thread on the outside of the box is tied a ring. The ring should be of such a size as to fit snugly around the second joint of the second finger of the right hand. One of the rings for a small-size curtain rod is suitable for the purpose and will fit the average finger.

When the filled box is brought to the table all the thread should be inside the box except the end having the ring. In putting the thread in the box, it must be laid from side to side in the box so it can be pulled out without snarling. The thread should not be looped inside the box. As the magician tells his story about the poltergeist named Willie, he slips his finger into the ring at the back end of the box—the front end of the box faces the audience. When the ring is on his finger the magician closes his hand and holds it against his body at waist height. With the hand so held the ring is hidden. He then steps back slowly until the thread almost is taut. He then places the tips of the fingers of his left hand on the knuckles of his closed right hand. In putting the hands together the thread is allowed to go between the first and second fingers of the left hand. The fingers of the right hand are opened so that the fingernails touch the palm of the left hand. With the hands in this position it will be found that the second finger of the right hand can be moved back and forth without the movement being seen by anyone in front of the performer. The magician then moves back another inch or so until the thread is quite taut but not so far that the thread raises the hammer in the box. The hammer is operated entirely by the movement of the one finger.

The magician knows the answers and can operate the hammer mechanism so as to divulge them. Because the audience does not realize either fact the feat is quite puzzling. However, how entertaining the magic is made depends upon the thought, and practice, the magician has given to the presentation.

When prior to the beginning of this feat the magician brings the box to the performance table, the box is resting crosswise on top of the tray upon which are the cigarettes. At the end of the trick everything is returned to the box except the tray which is put, upside down, on top of the box as a cover.

CHROMATIC VIBRATIONS

MANY people believe that each color of the spectrum gives off vibrations which are unlike the vibrations of any other color. This trick is a combination of thought transference and a sensitivity to color vibrations. The thoughts are sent by one spectator to another spectator who has been chosen because of a susceptibility to chromatic vibrations. Because more than one extra-sensory ability is demonstrated, the effect is particularly impressive.

The colors used for the vibration test are those used in the designs of the flags of the more than 100 countries belonging to the United Nations. While these flags are most varied in design and combination of colors, there are only a total of nine major colors used . . . red, white, green, yellow, black, orange, light blue, dark blue and brown. Future changes may occur.

Nine cards are shown, each of which is of a different one of these colors. The performer announces that it is necessary to test sufficient of the spectators until he finds one who responds strongly to color vibrations. To select the right person, the performer shows the colored cards to and feels the pulse of two spectators, one after another. These two spectators are eliminated with the remark: "Not quite as sensitive as I wish." Unless the performance is before an all male audience, the person finally chosen should be a woman. Her pulse is felt and the performer states that by the beat of her pulse he can tell that she has great sensitivity to colors. Whereas under certain mental stress, a person's pulse beat will change, this has nothing whatsoever to do with the trick. However it sounds very plausible and later in the trick makes the spectator and the audience believe that she had something to do with the choice of colors.

The selected spectator is then given the 9 color cards and 9 envelopes and taken to a performance table, and told to examine the envelopes. She is left there and told to put one of the color cards in each envelope and seal it.

While this is being done, the performer goes to another spectator who is asked to choose by chance the name of one of the countries belonging to the United Nations. When the choice has been made, if the spectator does not know the colors of the flag of that nation, he is given a chart showing the flags of each country and told to identify the flag of the country he chose and to concentrate strongly on the colors of that flag.

Returning to the spectator who has the color cards sealed in the envelopes, the performer requests her to mix the envelopes and to lay them in rows on the table. The performer asks the spectator to make her mind receptive and at the same time takes hold of her wrist so that the pulse may be felt. The performer then points to one envelope at a time and because of the pulse variation, the performer is able to know the spectator's choice of envelopes, and these he pushes aside. When the spectator opens the envelopes, it is found that the choice of colors are those upon which the other spectator had been concentrating.

While this is what the audience sees and believes occurs, there are, as this is magic, several details the audience does not know about.

A bit of chicanery is perpetrated on each of the spectators who help in the trick. The spectator whose task is to send his thoughts to the other, actually does not have the choice of thoughts he seems to have. This is what the audience believe happens.

Before approaching this spectator, the performer picks up a small cloth bag and tells the audience that the bag contains cards and on each card is written the name of one of the countries belonging to the United Nations. He reaches in the bag and pulls out several cards, and one at a time drops these cards back in the bag. As each card is dropped into the bag, the performer reads off the name of a country. The performer then steps up to the spectator and asks him to put his hand in the bag and stir the cards around until they are thoroughly mixed. He is then instructed to take one card, and one only, from the bag without looking at it, or permitting anyone else to see it. He is told to hold the card in his clenched fist. The performer, looking directly at the spectator, asks the question: "You are satisfied that you mixed the cards thoroughly?" As the performer says this, he reaches in the bag and takes out a couple of the cards and, showing the names written on these cards to the spectators, says: "They certainly seem to be well mixed.

You couldn't find countries further apart alphabetically or geographically than Denmark and Paraguay." Dropping these cards back in the bag, the performer asks the spectator to step up to one of the performance tables.

Seemingly the spectator at this point has made a free selection of the name of one country out of a choice of more than 100.

What actually happens is that every card in the bag had the name of the same country written on it. When the performer, at the very start, takes out cards and reads off the names as he drops them back in the bag, he actually is merely reciting the names of a number of countries he has memorized and he is far enough away from the spectators so they cannot see the writing on the cards. While the spectator is mixing the cards in the bag, which, as they are all the same, he can do most freely, the performer is holding the bag with one hand. He puts his other hand in his pocket where there are two cards, one with the name of Denmark written on it, and the name of Paraguay on the other. He takes hold of these cards by pressing them between his thumb and second joints of his fingers. He withdraws his hand from his pocket keeping the back of his hand toward the audience so as to conceal the cards. He then puts that hand in the bag and bringing it out shows the two cards that he was holding when he put his hand in the bag. He shows the names on these cards to the spectators and drops the cards back in the bag.

When the spectator has been brought to the performance table, he is asked to look at the name on the card he has "chosen," but to let no one else see what country he has selected. He alone is to know his choice. He is asked if he knows the major colors in the flag of the country he has chosen, and in case he is not absolutely certain, he is shown the color chart depicting in alphabetical order all the flags of the countries belonging to the United Nations, and told that the chart is the official one put out by the United Nations. (The reader may purchase such a chart by writing to Sales Section, United Nations, New York. The current cost is 40¢.)

He is told just to look at the chart but not to touch it, so as possibly to indicate the name of the country he has in mind. He then is told to concentrate on the colors of the flag.

The name of the country I have used in this feat is Bolivia. The major colors in the Bolivian flag are red, yellow and green. I chose Bolivia for several reasons. First, as the name begins with a "B," it is quickly found in the alphabetical list. Second, the colors are unexpected to the audience, because few people know that there are eleven countries using these colors. Third, it is not the combination of red, white and blue which so many nations use.

At this point, one assistant has made a choice of three envelopes which still are sealed and she and the audience do not know the colors of the cards in these envelopes. The other assistant has selected a country and knows the colors of the flag of that country, and has been concentrating on the colors and he alone knows what he is thinking. That assistant is now asked to announce the country that he chose and the colors of the flag of that country. He calls out that the country he chose was Bolivia and the major colors of the Bolivian flag are red, yellow and green.

The first assistant then is requested to open the envelopes that she chose and to remove the cards. The cards are found to be the same three colors— red, yellow and green.

This, of course, "proves" that the one assistant was able to concentrate and send thought waves and that the other assistant not only was receptive to these thoughts, but also was sensitive to the vibrations of colors.

The second bit of chicanery is the "choice" of three of the nine colors by the assistant, which also is simple to perform and it too is most convincing. Needed for this "choice" are nine cards and nine envelopes. What generally are called "pay envelopes" are excellent for the purpose. The cards, plain thin white cardboard, are made of such a size as to fit the envelopes used. On one surface of each card is pasted a piece of paper of the proper color. Glossy paper comes with the required colors. Between the cardboard and the colored paper of three of the cards are put small pieces of shim steel, or pieces of a safety razor blade. Each piece of steel is put at the exact center of the card. The pieces of steel are put under the red, yellow and green papers. It will be obvious that, even when the cards are in the envelopes, by use of a magnet, it will be possible to find the red, yellow and green cards. (In order to avoid any telltale bumps caused by the metal, white paper of the same thickness as the steel, with a hole cut out the exact size of the metal, should cover all the rest of the surface of the card. The colored paper is pasted on top of the steel with its mat.) The magnet used is one of the round rod variety. It should be ¼" in diameter and ¾" long. The magnet is painted brown, or a deep red, and is substituted for the eraser in the end of a lead pencil. When, point side up, the pencil is held loosely and passed over the envelopes, but not quite touching them, the magnet will be drawn to the steel inside a card. To find each of the three wanted colors, the pencil is passed across the center of the envelopes. As a card is located, it is pushed out of line until all three cards are separated.

After the assistant knows the colors of the flag of the country he chose and is concentrating on those colors, and the performer has returned to the assistant with the color cards in the envelopes, he instructs her to mix the envelopes so that neither she nor anyone else could know the color in any particular envelope. After the envelopes have been shuffled he asks that they be put in rows on the table. The performer apologizes for asking his assistant

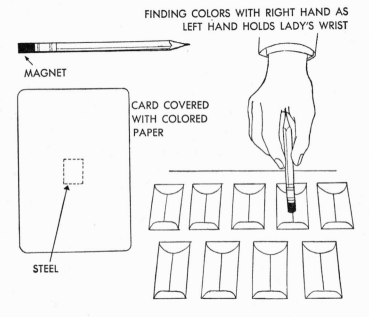

FINDING COLORS WITH RIGHT HAND AS
LEFT HAND HOLDS LADY'S WRIST

MAGNET

CARD COVERED
WITH COLORED
PAPER

STEEL

to do all of the work, but he wants her to remember that he never has touched cards or envelopes, after she sealed them. He says that now he will merely point to the envelopes as he feels her pulse and that by the change of pulse beat, she will indicate the colors to which she now is sensitive. With his left hand, the performer takes hold of the wrist of the assistant. Taking a pencil from his pocket he explains that he will use the pencil as a pointer. He passes the eraser end of the pencil over the centers of the envelopes.

Putting the pencil down on one envelope the magician says, "Your pulse speeded so much this must be your first choice." He then pushes that envelope out of line. The same actions are repeated twice and a second and third envelope are found and pushed out of line. In finding the second envelope, the performer says, "Well, your pulse certainly jumped then—there is no doubt about this choice." As the third envelope is found the magician states, "This one, fine. It certainly is easy to follow the thoughts of one with a trip-hammer pulse. Three colors so far—that eliminates Sweden and Greece and several other countries having but two colors in their flags." The performer keeps on pointing to envelopes to find if the assistant is going to vibrate to a fourth color. Finally he tells her, "You don't seem to be interested in another color. That means the country is not one with four colors in its flag as has Libya."

Unbelievable as it might seem, not only is the audience convinced that the choices of envelopes are made by the spectator but the assistant believes so too.

An additional detail is important to remember and it is written last in order to make it impressive. In order to lift the pencil when it is stuck to an envelope the magnet has to be disconnected from the steel in the card. This is done, after the envelope has been pushed out of line, by twisting the pencil so the round tip of the magnet rolls off the steel. While the spectators can see that the pencil is being twisted the action is meaningless and of no importance to them for the twisting always is done after an envelope has been chosen. If the action even is noticed it will be considered as just a flourish having no significance.

10,000 TO 1

THERE is an expression, which comes from betting circles, that the possibility of some particular event happening is a "ten thousand to one chance." It is meant to infer that while the occurrence of the event is not utterly impossible it would be wise to consider it most exceedingly unlikely. This mystery seemingly has 9,999 chances of failure and but 1 of success and yet invariably it comes out correctly. Parenthetically, it must be remembered that a magician's feat has to work, for the one thing an audience never will forgive, nor forget, is a magician who fails in anything he attempts.

While the trick is not a mathematical one, and there is no adding, subtracting, multiplying, or dividing, it is based on the use of numbers. These numbers, all single digits, are written on small pieces of cardboard with holes at their tops. I use metal-bound key tags in my performance. There are forty of these cards, or tags, and one numeral is printed on each. Four of the tags have a zero printed on them. On four more is printed the figure 1. Each of the other digits also is printed on four separate tags.

Now were someone, at random, to choose 4 of these forty figures and still, by chance, arrange them in a four digit number, the result might be anything from 0000 to 9,999. In short, there are ten thousand possible combinations.

This is what the audience believes happens. The magician shows the forty numbered tags and puts them into a small bag which is handed to a spectator. After the spectator mixes the tags by stirring them in the bag, with his hand, he takes four tags from the bag without looking at the numbers on them. The magician takes these tags and hangs them on hooks on a simple window display stand with the backs of the tags facing the audience so the numbers cannot be seen. A second spectator is given a local telephone directory and is told to open it at random. The spectator then is asked to make a choice between the left hand page and the right hand page of the book. Next to select one column of the chosen page and to pick one telephone number in that column. That is, he is to pick out the number of four figures which indicates the subscriber's particular telephone and is to ignore the exchange number. When the spectator has selected the number he is asked to read it aloud. The magician repeats the number and as he calls out each figure he turns one tag on the stand. The number made by the four tags is identical to the number found in the telephone book. Two spectators have by hazard each chosen a number of four figures and the numbers are identical—a 10,000 to 1 chance.

This is particularly impressive magic because it seems so open and above board. And so much of it is just as fair as it appears. The number tags are just what they seem to be—tags with numbers on them. There is no trickery about the simple cloth bag, nor the little display stand, nor the telephone directory.

The trick is possible because of two items not yet mentioned. They were not mentioned in the description of what the audience sees because, I have found, people so seldom recall these items when recounting what happened. This is true because neither item apparently has any real part in what is done.

The first object is a small cardboard box in which the magician has the numbered tags. The box I use is 2½" x 3" and is 2" high. It has a separate cover. On the cover I have pasted the label taken from one of the boxes containing the tags when I purchased them. The box has been tricked but before explaining how it is well to know the way the box is used. At the start of the trick the magician picks up the box and removes the cover which he places on the table. Putting his fingers in the box he takes out several tags and reads aloud the number of each tag as he drops it back into the box. He takes pains to have the spectators see each number as he calls it out. The box is put back on the table and the magician picks up the little cloth bag which is inside out. In showing the bag the magician turns the cloth to make the bag right side out. Without specifically mentioning the bag to be quite ordinary, the magician demonstrates its innocence by turning it inside out. Then holding the bag in the left hand, with the fingers inside so that the mouth of the bag is held open, the magician with his right hand starts taking tags from the box and dropping them in the bag. The tags are dropped into the bag rather slowly so that there is an opportunity for everyone to see the numbers. When nearly all of the tags have been put in the bag the magician picks up the box and pours the remaining tags into the bag. This leaves him with a bag full of numbers in his left hand and an empty box in his right. Holding both bag and box he goes to a spectator and asks him, or her, to take the bag. (If it is not an all male audience by all means use a lady's aid in this part of the trick.) The spectator is asked to hold the bag in one hand and to put the other into the bag and stir the numbers until they are well mixed. The next request is to select one tag and, without looking at the number, to drop it into the box. The spectator is requested to do this three more times so that altogether four tags have been dropped into the box. The magician then retrieves the bag with his left hand and in his right hand holds the box in the air where everyone can see it as he returns to his table.

At the table the magician drops the bag of numbers and picks up the little stand. The magician introduces the stand by saying: "This little window display rack will be very useful in keeping the tags in the plain sight of everyone." The stand is merely a bottom holding an upright to which is a cross bar. On the cross bar are four hooks. While the stand is especially made for the trick it does have the appearance of stands used by jewelers, and others, in window displays the better to show the items offered for sale, and it will be accepted as such a stand. As was said previously, there is nothing tricky about the stand. (See illustration.)

As soon as the magician has called attention to the stand he replaces it on the table. Immediately the magician pours the four tags into his left hand from the box in his right. The box is then put aside. It is at the point of pouring the numbers from the box, an action which seems so fair, that the first half of the trick is accomplished.

What really happens is that the box, because of its construction, substitutes for the chosen tags the four tags needed to make the trick work. This substitution is made through the means of a hinged flap at one end of the box. The flap is made of metal and is covered with the same sort of paper which covers the box. The top of the flap has an ⅛" flange. The hinge, a ¾" brass hinge, holds the flap away from the box so that when the flap is against the end of the box there is a compartment the width and height of the box ⅛" deep. Into this compartment are put the four tags the audience never suspect exists. The hinge is so placed that when the flap is pushed to the bottom of the box it is ⅛" away from the bottom. Putting the flap in this position makes a compartment to hold the four tags which the spectator took from the bag. The flap is hinged so that it will stay firmly in either position but can be pushed easily with one finger. The magician will find that he has several opportunities to move the flap without anyone seeing the action. I do it just prior to sliding the tags into my hand. It will be recalled, when the display stand is replaced upon the table after showing it, that the box still is in the magician's right hand. He tilts the box so as to make the 4 tags slide to one end. As this is done the open top of the box is towards him and away from the audience. Now, exactly as if one of the discs hadn't moved, I stick the forefinger of my left hand into the box. In doing so I put the tip of my finger against the flange at the top of the flap and push it to the bottom of the box. At once I withdraw my finger, cup the left hand and pour the tags out of the box and into my hand. At this point the box is upside down with the four tags safely in the compartment along the bottom. Still upside down the box is placed on the table.

While everything the magician has done seems so honest and natural he has exchanged the four tags. If at the start of the trick the four tags hidden in the end compartment are put so that their numbered sides face towards the inside of the box they will slide out into the left hand face up. This will permit the magician, without fumbling, to pick up the tags in the right

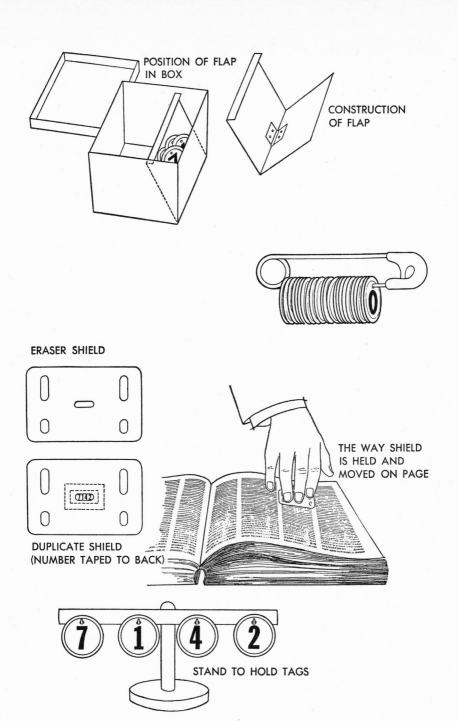

POSITION OF FLAP
IN BOX

CONSTRUCTION
OF FLAP

ERASER SHIELD

DUPLICATE SHIELD
(NUMBER TAPED TO BACK)

THE WAY SHIELD
IS HELD AND
MOVED ON PAGE

STAND TO HOLD TAGS

order as he hangs them on the hooks on the stand. While the flap, being covered with the same kind of paper as is used on the box, is practically unnoticeable, it is well, while near the spectator, always to hold the box by that end with the fingers inside the box and the thumb on the outside. Afterwards it is held with the fingers and thumb on opposite ends.

The article which makes possible the second part of the trick is an "eraser shield." This is what typists use to make neat erasures at such times as the typewriter fails to spell correctly. Such shields have little holes of various sizes and shapes and sometimes are made of thin metal and sometimes of plastic. The typist selects the hole of the appropriate size and so places the shield over the paper that the hole is at the letter or word to be erased. The solid part of the shield keeps the eraser from rubbing out, or smudging, any letter wished kept. Even to those persons who never had seen such an article, its use immediately is obvious when shown the shield and told its purpose. The shield the magician uses may be one purchased, provided it is made of opaque material, or it may be made. I made mine of very thin stainless steel and probably went to the bother merely because, as a rather fussy individual, I wanted the center hole to be of a certain size exactly. The hole is just large enough to show one telephone number. The way the shield is used in the trick is that it is placed at the top of the column chosen by the spectator so that the center hole is right over the first number. The magician keeps the tips of his first and second fingers over the hole so that the spectator cannot see the number exposed. The magician announces that he will slide the shield slowly down the column until the spectator instructs him to stop. He calls attention to the fact that until his fingers are lifted no one can possibly know which number has been chosen. When the magician raises his fingers from over the hole, the spectator is asked to read aloud, and to memorize, the one number he has chosen from all the numbers in the telephone book. As soon as the number is read, the magician picks up the shield with one hand and simultaneously closes and picks up the telephone book with the other. Walking back to the table the magician drops the book and picks up the display stand. He then asks the spectator to repeat aloud the telephone number he had found by chance in the book. The numbers spoken and those on the tags are identical much to the amazement of everyone— except the magician.

The expressed purpose of using the shield is to have the numbers covered until one actually is chosen. This insures that the number actually is selected by chance and not picked because it happens to appeal to the spectator. As the reader will be aware, the stated purpose of using the shield, while so reasonable as invariably to be accepted by the audience, is not the true reason. The real reason is that the number the spectator reads is attached to the under side of the shield so that it is directly under the center hole. He never has the chance to read any other number but is convinced he had an infinitely large choice. That there is a number stuck to the shield does not occur to the spectator because he has handled the shield and is assured that it is only what it is supposed to be. This is possible because the magician has two identical shields—one devoid of trickery and one tricked. The one the spectator handles is the innocent one.

Usually there is a degree of difficulty in substituting one object for another right in front of an audience. In this instance it is very easy. This is because of the sequence of what the magician does as well as what he says. At the point in the trick when the magician has just finished hanging the "selected" tags on the hooks of the display stand he picks up a telephone book from the table. On the book lays the eraser shield. The magician explains to the audience that to continue in his magic he will use two objects—one which he has purchased and one he has borrowed. Picking up the shield from the book he announces, "This eraser shield used by typists I bought and (holding up the directory) this telephone book I borrowed." Going to the spectator he later will ask to "choose" a number in the book he hands him the shield. As the spectator takes the shield, the magician tells him, "You probably have seen these shields used." He then goes on to describe just how they are used. The magician merely describes the use of the shield. He is careful not to say anything about its being unprepared or devoid of trickery, or anything else which might create suspicion in the minds of the spectators. To them the shield obviously is merely a plate with holes in it and, as this is what it actually is, they will be satisfied it can have no part in the trickery provided the magician does not make such a suggestion. Taking back the shield seemingly only to free the hands of the spectator the magician gives the telephone directory to him. As the spectator receives the book the magician instructs him to look through the book and to make certain that it is the local telephone directory. Putting it this way, the magician makes certain that everyone knows that what the spectator has is merely one copy of the directory put out by the local telephone company and is devoid of trickery, without putting in the minds of the spectators that it might be possible to make a telephone book tricky.

At this point the spectator is examining the telephone directory and the magician is standing with the eraser shield in his hand, waiting for the spectator to insure, and so to state, that he holds the local telephone directory. When the spectator is satisfied with the book, the magician requests him to open the book, quite at random, and to hold it open on his lap. As this is being done the magician steps back a step and, as if to keep his hands even from making a gesture, puts both hands in the side pockets of his jacket. Were he to put but one hand in his pocket, the action might be noticed but putting both hands in his two coatpockets never is noticed. The hand holding the eraser shield leaves it in the pocket and picks up the prepared shield. In getting ready for the trick, prior to the show, the magician must make certain that in his pocket the prepared shield is right side up and face forward. It would not do for the numbers to appear upside down on the page or for the shield to have the paper stuck to the wrong side. The magician asks the spectator to choose the left or the right hand page. Then, as he asks the spectator to select one column on that page, he steps towards the spectator and at the same time takes his hands from his pockets. The shield, unbeknownst to everyone, has been changed. The magician places the shield at the top of the column selected so that the center hole is directly over the first number. His fingers are on the shield. The thumb is at the left side of the shield (his left), the tip of the first and second fingers over the center hole and the third and little fingers at the right of the shield. (See illustration.)

Announcing that he will slide the shield slowly down the column, and doing so very slowly, the magician asks the spectator to say "stop" whenever he wishes. The instant the spectator says "stop" the magician holds the shield still. After making inquires as to whether the spectator's choice was free, and being told it was, the magician tilts his hand so that the first and second fingers are raised in order that the center hole is open to him but still not visible to the spectator. The magician says, "You have stopped me just between two numbers. Shall I go up or down?" Whichever is said the magician moves the shield a very small fraction of an inch. This is a very subtle and convincing piece of chicanery which accounts for the number pasted on the back of the shield being squarely in the center of the center opening of the shield. Another most convincing point is that the text of the directory can be seen through the other openings in the shield as it is moved, therefore it must change under the center hole. The magician raises, actually pulls back, the fingers covering the center hole. He keeps the thumb and other fingers pressing the shield to the book. This seems to be so as to insure that the shield does not move away from the number selected but actually so that it will not be seen that the number moves with the movement of the shield.

After the number has been read aloud the magician picks up both shield and book. This apparently is done only to relieve the spectator of the burden of holding them which is kind to the spectator but it also conceals the magician's secret which is kind to him.

Everything now has been done except to convince the audience that even at a chance of 10,000 to 1 the magician will win. This best can be done by reminding them what has happened (or what they have seen happen and been told about) and then slowly and most fairly bring the trick to its climax.

This is an extraordinarily impressive feat of magic which, manipulatively, is easy to do. However, its effectiveness depends upon how well the performer has memorized the details of everything he has to do and how forthright and simple he can make what he does seem to the audience.

Not too incidentally, the number the magician attaches to the back of the second shield (the one the audience knows not of) is cut slightly larger than the hole in the shield, then is stuck to a piece of cellophane tape and the tape stuck to the shield. The number is cut from a page of another local telephone directory. I hope that no one connected with the Bell organization criticizes anyone at Scribners because I suggest such a depredatory act.

In recent performances of this feat I have added a detail which, while having nothing to do with the method of deception, seems to make the trick even more impressive. At the beginning of the trick all the numbered tags are shown to be impaled on a giant-size safety pin. On the pin the tags all face one way and are in numerical order from 0000 to 9,999. The safety pin, with its tags, is in the cardboard box. When the tags are introduced, the pin is opened and the 40 numbers are shown to the audience as the tags are taken off the pin and dropped back into the box. From this point on, the trick is performed as previously described. The pin I use is brass, 4″ long, and was purchased at a "notions counter."

ESP

EXTRA-SENSORY Perception, usually shortened in conversation to ESP, is the psychologist's term for those abilities some people are supposed to have which do not depend upon utilizing the five senses. For years brilliant and dedicated psychologists have been making tests to attempt to discover if some people have the power of telepathy, precognoscence, clairvoyance or some other extra sense. By their tests many psychologists are convinced they have proven the existence of such abilities, many others feel the tests are not conclusive, still others feel the tests have done nothing to shake their skepticism. I fall in the latter group. Even those who accept the hypothesis that some people possess ESP abilities have to admit that either the people, or their unusual powers, cannot be depended upon for any regularity of success. It is the uncertainty of the completion of any one test which makes ESP such a superb subject for magic. The very idea of ESP puts it in the realm of the unusual and in the magician's demonstration he always is successful.

This is a demonstration apparently proving the performer's powers of precognition. He shows that he is aware of what is going to occur even prior to the start of what finally happens. He shows the same success whether the choice of action is left to the decision of a person or left solely to chance. Used for the performance are cards devised by psychologists for their tests. The cards are called ESP cards and a pack consists of twenty-five cards. The faces of the cards have simple designs printed on them. There are five designs and each is printed on five cards. Pictured are: a square, a circle, a star, a cross or plus sign, and three parallel wavy lines termed waves. Such decks of cards can be purchased in book shops and where adult games are sold.

What the audience accept as occurring in this feat is that the performer takes a card from a deck of ESP cards and places that card where it will remain in plain sight. Only after that has been done does a spectator choose one of the five designs found on ESP cards. It is found that the performer had, in advance, selected the same design. Again the performer selects one design, this time without looking, and sets the card aside—again where it constantly can be seen. He then places five cards, each of a different design, upon a simple, small easel, or stand, with the backs of the cards towards the audience. A spectator has mixed the cards prior to their being put on the stand. A die is given to a spectator to roll. He is told that the number on the die which is on top at the end of the roll will indicate which card, counting from the left, will be the card chance selected. He also is told that if he rolls a six he must roll again as there are but five cards to choose from. The card at the number selected by chance is turned face towards the audience and proves to have the same design as the performer previously had chosen and also by chance. No one credited with extra-sensory perception can be certain of the results he may have. The performer invariably has success and everything he does seems so very simple and fair.

As so much has been written about ESP in newspapers and magazines as well as books, it may be assumed that the audience will have some general knowledge of the subject. It will be unnecessary for the performer to say much about extra-sensory abilities but he should mention that he will demonstrate the power of precognition—of being able to know in advance what is going to happen. He picks up a deck of ESP cards, takes them out of the case and shows them to the audience. He states that he will use the cards in his demonstration. In order for the spectators to keep the designs in mind he tells them that he will place one of each of the five designs where everyone can see them. He puts five of the cards, faces towards the audience, on the easel as he makes his remarks.

The performer takes five more cards, one of each design, and shows them to have exactly the same designs as the cards on the easel. The backs of the cards are turned to the audience and the performer makes a selection of one card. This card he pushes into a tumbler. As the back of the card still is towards the audience no one, except the performer, is aware of which design is on the card in the glass.

The performer picks up a small plate upon which in a pile are five metal bound key tags $1\frac{1}{4}''$ in diameter. The performer states that upon each tag is drawn one of the five designs. He goes to a spectator and requests that the tags be mixed around on the plate but the designs are to be kept face down in order to eliminate any possibility that the performer, by thought transference, could influence the mind of the spectator. When the spectator has finished mixing the tags he is told to choose one tag, to take it from the plate, and to hold it hidden in his hand so that no one, including himself, can know which design was chosen. The performer, pushing the tags together on the plate, asks the spectator if he is satisfied his choice was entirely his own and that in no way was he influenced. "In that case," says the performer as he tilts the plate and dumps the remaining tags in his hand, "Will you please hold in your other hand the four designs you discarded."

The performer steps back from the audience and asks the one spectator to see which design he had selected and to announce its name. When the name is spoken, the performer steps to the easel and picks up the card of the selected design. "This," he says, "is the design you chose. That is right, isn't it?" Holding that card in the air by the tips of the fingers of one hand, he turns the glass, with the fingers of the other hand so that the card in the glass will face the audience. "The designs are identical as you can see and remember I made my choice some time prior to the gentleman's making his choice."

With one exception, what the performer seems to do is what he actually does. The exception has to do with the plate and tags. Neither plate nor tags are quite what they seem. When the performer offers the spectator the five tags to choose from the choice is without meaning for each tag carries the same design. Under the rim of the plate is glued a small container which is open at the side towards the edge of the plate. In the container are four tags having the four designs not found on the tags on top of the plate. After the spectator has picked up one of the five tags on the plate the performer asks if the choice was completely free and uncontrolled. As the question is asked the performer with the fingers of his free hand pushes the remaining four tags in a pile. The tags are pushed to a spot on the plate where the pile of tags can be held on the plate by the thumb of the hand holding the plate. The plate is held in the natural manner with the fingers underneath the plate and the thumb on the top. The fingers have the added purpose of covering the tag container so it will not be seen at the time the plate is tipped, bottom towards the spectators. The plate seemingly is tipped in order to slide the tags on the plate into the performer's hand. Actually those four tags are held by the thumb and the tags which go into the hand slide out of the container under the plate. This substitution is completely deceptive and almost completely mechanical. The plate I use is small enough to go into the side pocket of my jacket and is put into the pocket as the four tags are given to the spectator.

The little container is a box having bottom, top, one end and two sides. The container is made of very thin metal $\frac{1}{64}''$ or less. I made mine of shim brass. The complete little box is made of one piece. The outside dimensions are $1\frac{3}{8}''$ square by $\frac{3}{16}''$ thick. The box is made of one piece of metal. Enough

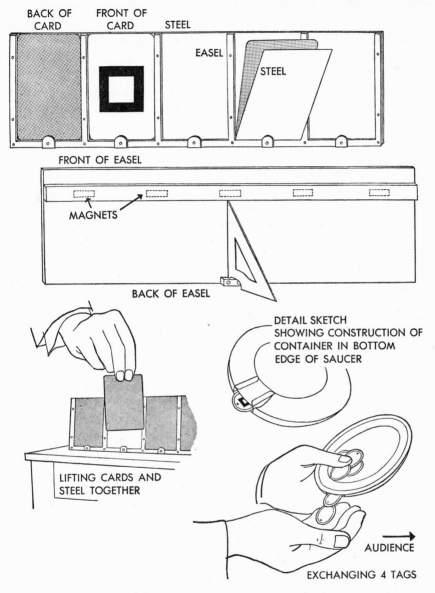

BACK OF CARD FRONT OF CARD STEEL

EASEL

STEEL

FRONT OF EASEL

MAGNETS

BACK OF EASEL

DETAIL SKETCH
SHOWING CONSTRUCTION OF
CONTAINER IN BOTTOM
EDGE OF SAUCER

LIFTING CARDS AND
STEEL TOGETHER

AUDIENCE

EXCHANGING 4 TAGS

metal is left on each side of the bottom (⅜" per side) to bend up to make the sides and bend again over the side edges of the top. The metal is cut away on the sides of the end and top so that when they are bent in place they are exactly the right dimensions. The flanges of the sides which come over the edges of the top are kept in place with solder.

The plate may be a china one, or plastic, or a brass ash tray of the form of a plate. The container should be glued under the rim of the plate. If the plate is carefully selected one will be found which will sit on the table, even with the container in place.

So much for the first test. In this test the easel was used for displaying the cards and its purpose was most innocent. Its use was so obviously unconnected with the first mystery that when the easel is used as part of the second test it excites no suspicion. Its part seems just as fair in the second test as it had in the first. Appearances aside, the easel accounts for the success of the second test.

At the end of the first test all five cards are taken off the easel and given to a spectator. He is instructed to keep the cards and to mix them until he is certain no one can know the order. The magician holds the easel flat, as if it were a tray, and as one at a time, the spectator hands the performer the cards he puts them along the easel. The easel is again turned edgewise and returned to the table. A spectator rolls a die. The spots on the top of the die indicate by number which card is to be used. Due to the construction of the easel, any card turned face forward will have the right design. In other words, were all five cards turned over all would have the same design. But also due to the construction of the easel, after the selected card is turned over—face forward, another card or two may be turned over to show the spectator the different designs he would have had were a different number to have come up on the die.

It will be recalled that in the second test, as in the first, the performer picks one of the five designs and puts a card with that design in a glass. Naturally he has to remember to put in the glass the design which the tray is set to bring forth. The methods used permit preparing either test to have a different design for each successive performance.

The easel is made of brass and aluminum. The body of the easel is of hard polished aluminum 12⅞" long, 3½" wide and 1/16" thick. A suitable piece of aluminum can be purchased in stores where kitchenware is sold. Flat aluminum with one turned up edge is used for baking cookies. On the face of the aluminum are ¼" strips of brass 3/32" thick. One strip runs the length of the aluminum plate at the bottom. At right angles to the bottom strip and touching it are six strips made from brass of the same dimensions. Two of these strips are at the right and left edges of the aluminum. Four other strips, acting as dividers between the cards, also are used. These strips are attached to the aluminum with small aluminum rivets. The easel now will have five sections each the exact size of an ESP card. Riveted to the bottom strip at the center of each section is a small brass guard. These guards, little tongues of brass extending $\frac{1}{8}$″ over the face of the card, are necessary to keep the cards from falling off the easel. On the back of the easel a brass strip runs the entire length of the aluminum and $\frac{1}{4}$″ from the top. There are two apparent reasons for this strip. The strip keeps the aluminum from bending and the standard of the easel swings from it. This brass strip is $\frac{3}{8}$″ wide and $\frac{3}{16}$″ thick. What is not apparent is that the strip is hollow. I made mine by sawing hollow square brass lengthwise and cutting it so as to have the proper thickness. Brass plugs were made for each end of this U shaped strip of brass and were soldered in place. Attaching the back strip to the aluminum also may be done with rivets, although I used machine screws and tapped the vertical brass strips on the face of the easel. Before the back strip is fastened in place small flat oblong magnets are put in the open side of the strip. These magnets are spaced so as to be at the center of the back of each card section. Shims of paper are put back of each magnet so that its surface will touch the aluminum. Small pieces of wood of the proper size are put between the magnets so they will be held in place and kept from sideways movement. The back strip is then fastened in place and the standard of the easel attached to it. The standard should be made so that when the easel is standing it leans back at an angle of 20 degrees.

The magnets are used to hold very thin flat pieces of shim steel. Prior to the show five identical ESP cards are put face towards the easel, one card in each section. On top of these cards are put the pieces of steel. The steel is cut the same size as a card but the corners of the steel are not rounded. The pieces of steel are very close in appearance to the sheet of aluminum and the way the trick is done the audience never have the chance to compare the two metals. (See illustration.)

Needed for this double feat are two decks of ESP cards in order to have sufficient number of any given design. The cards should be available before the easel is made so as to be certain in each step of construction that the easel is exactly right for the cards. After the easel is finished the top edge should be lowered, with a very fine file, until it is found that rubbing the pad of the thumb at the top from back to front will push forward a card. As the steel is the same size as a card it will be pushed forward as well as a card in front of the steel. Taking hold of the top of such a sandwich of cards and steel with the thumb away from the audience and the fingers towards them, the performer lifts all three as one until they are above the tongue at the bottom. Still tightly squeezing the cards and steel, the wrist is turned so as to invert all three. The other hand then takes a tight grip at the (now) top and replaces all three in the section from which it was taken. This is the way one card is exchanged for another. The movement might be thought to appear awkward and thereby suspicious. With very little practice it will be found to be a most natural move which excites no suspicion.

When the performer wishes to take the visible card from the easel, as in the first effect, all that he has to do is to press very lightly on the exposed surface of the card and pull up. As soon as the card has been raised high enough for the thumb to take hold the card is removed from the easel. The action in taking hold of a card to remove it appears identical to the way it is gripped when the exchange of cards is made.

SIGHT UNSEEN

THIS is a particularly effective feat with the ESP cards which convinces the spectators that the magician has power beyond the sense of sight. The trick depends upon using envelopes which have been marked by trimming them with scissors in a way which never will be noticed. The method is described in Arches, Loops and Whorls in Chapter 4.

It will be recalled that five envelopes were used in the trick described. It also will be remembered that there are only five different designs used in an ESP deck. At the beginning of this trick, the magician takes one card of each design from the deck and hands a card apiece to five spectators. He also gives each spectator an envelope just large enough to hold a card. The spectators are instructed to put the cards into the envelopes and to seal them.

While the five spectators are doing their work, the magician asks to be blindfolded by another spectator. The blindfold consists of two foam rubber powder puffs which are placed over the eyes of the magician and which are held in place by having a handkerchief tied around the head. Having the eyes bandaged in such a manner seems to preclude any possibility of the magician's being able to see. However, thanks to the way our heads are constructed, this is not true. The magician shows the powder puffs and holds them over his eyes and instructs the spectator to tie the handkerchief so it will hold the puffs in place. As soon as the spectator has the handkerchief over the puffs, the magician closes his eyes as tightly as he can. This action will lower the eyebrows. The magician holds the puffs so that the handkerchief will tie them against the lowered eyebrows. As soon as the handkerchief is drawn tight enough to hold the puffs in place, the magician takes away his fingers. The magician insists that the handkerchief be tied tightly around his head. To the audience, having the handkerchief so tight is assurance that the magician will be unable to see. Actually having the handkerchief tight is an aid for the puffs are held over the eyebrows. After being tied in this manner, the magician will find that by opening his eyes, the puffs, because of the movement of the eyebrows, will be taken away from the eyes enough so that he can see downward.

The magician takes the envelopes one at a time from the table on which they had been placed. He puts his hand on the table and feels around until he has found an envelope. He feels around because he is not supposed to be able to see. It is very important that in his actions, he impress on the audience that he cannot see. He can even fumble and have difficulty finding the table and ask a spectator to guide him. Picking up the envelope will give the opportunity to observe the mark. The instant the mark is noted, the magician holds the envelope up in the air—waits a moment as if concentrating—and announces the design on the card inside.

The magician asks to be blindfolded, he says, because he has found darkness makes it easier to concentrate. He never mentions not being able to see for the audience are assured of that because they have witnessed an opaque blindfold being tightly tied around his head, and over the puffs.

A memory aid for the magician, to recall which marked envelope contains which design, is to have the cards in order at the beginning of the trick. This is the order easy to remember: 1) a circle—a circle is drawn with a single line; 2) a cross—drawn with two lines; 3) waves—three lines; 4) a square—four lines and four sides; 5) a star—five lines and five points. The marked envelopes should be given out so that reading the marks clockwise will indicate 1-2-3-4. The fifth envelope is recognized because it has no mark.

At the end of the trick, the magician should have a spectator remove the blindfold, and as the puffs are removed, he should blink several times and shake his head, as if the bright lights now are blinding him.

Eleven. MAGICAL THOUGHT TRANSFERENCE

ONE of the most difficult feats of magic to learn to do, and to perfect in performance, is that of apparent thought transference. That is true of all of the various methods used by professional magicians, which require many years of daily study and practice. Magical thought transference, and I gravely doubt the existence of any other kind, requires two people. One to send the thoughts and one to receive them. It is customary for the magician to enact the role of sender and his assistant to be receiver or "medium." Thought transference is always a sensational act and, therefore, to those who earn their living by magic, is well worth the time and effort necessary to acquire proficiency. Few amateurs, because of the long study necessary, have bothered to attempt the feat. This chapter is devoted to a quickly and easily learned method, which brings this astounding branch of magic into the list of mysteries an amateur can do. This method is not like any the professionals use, and is more limited as to the thoughts which may be transferred, but it requires only a few hours of study instead of years.

MIND SIGNALS

PERHAPS the best way to describe what can be done with this method is to give the introductory talk of the magician. Parenthetically, I wish to note that while in this introduction the magician refers to his assistant as his wife, it is not necessary for one to marry to perform the trick. The assistant may be a brother, sister, son, daughter, cousin or merely a friend. However when a friend is used, the audience should be given the idea that it is a close friendship, for it makes the feat sound more probable.

"Whether our minds have the mechanism to communicate with other minds without resorting to speech, writing, telegraphy, or any other signaling device is a question which has plagued scholars for centuries. These scholars have given a name to the idea and call it telepathy, though other terms, such as thought transference, or mind reading, sometimes are used. There is great disagreement in the scientific world; the majority seem to disbelieve in the possibility of telepathy, a number believe that the subject merits further study, and some few are convinced that telepathy is a fact. *Webster's New International Dictionary* defines telepathy as 'apparent communication from one mind to another otherwise than through the channels of sense.' In short, ideas are transmitted without using sight, touch, or hearing.

"My wife and I became interested in the subject and have been experimenting for some time. We are convinced that our study very likely would not interest the scientists, but we hope that a few experiments will amuse, and may even interest, you. We experimented first with playing cards and later with other objects. Some she seemed to sense quickly and with others she had great trouble, if she was able to receive at all. For instance, she cannot seem to get a mental picture of cloth. Cloth, whether it be a silk handkerchief, or a woolen coat, is apt to make no impression on her mind. We also discovered that it is merely necessary for me to see an object for some picture to come into her mind. I do not need even to bother, consciously, to concentrate on what I want her to know.

"My wife tells me that the ideas come to her mind in picture form and that the pictures develop slowly—that is, only one part of the picture comes at a time. Frequently, too, she seems to sense some totally irrelevant thought before she can see the object I have in mind.

"We will begin our demonstration with a few playing cards and then attempt other small objects such as you may have in your pockets or handbags. Please don't suggest articles of furniture, or things about the room, for large objects do not make clear pictures. Something of your own is most interesting.

"One further request: As this requires deep concentration on the part of my wife, please do not talk, or, in case she cannot see an object, insist upon her trying again. I know you do not wish to tire her.

MAGICAL THOUGHT TRANSFERENCE

"In order that my wife can use only her mind to see, she will stand across the room and turn her back to you."

The magician then permits the free selection of several cards from a deck and the medium describes them, one after another. She also describes various objects shown to the magician such as: a watch, a card with printing on it, a necklace, a five dollar bill, a cigar, a knife, and a twenty-five cent piece. The magician never says anything to the medium except to acknowledge when she is correct.

So much for the effect upon the audience. As you have discovered, many pages back, the effect upon the audience and the method of performance are two entirely different stories. In this trick that still is true. The method depends upon how very few categories everyday objects fall into and how easily each can be identified. The pictures which the medium "sees" are conveyed to her by what the magician says, and as what he says is limited to only five words, the system must be simple. The system is simple and is easy to learn, when taken a little at a time. Even taking the entire system at one dose should not be alarming, for nearly everything a person is apt to carry with him from a penny to a flashlight, and from a lipstick to eyeglasses, will have one of fifty-two names. As you already know the names of all the objects, the memorization is not difficult. The identification of objects is the same as the identification of playing cards and there are just fifty-two playing cards, too.

The tricky, and mystifying, part of the system is based on the fact that there is so much which may be said about any object that is generally true about the object and does not need to be "coded." As example, a Queen of Clubs is a black card, a Club, a picture card, a Queen, a Queen of Clubs. When described in that manner, it seems as if the medium gradually were getting a detailed "picture" and yet all she need know is the name of the card. Let me give you what both the medium and the magician say when the selected card is a Queen of Clubs.

Medium: You are thinking of a card.

Magician is silent.

Medium: The card is a black card.

Magician: That's right.

Medium: It is a Club.

Magician: Yes.

Medium: It is a picture card—a Queen—The card is the Queen of Clubs.

It will be noticed the medium always makes her statement before the magician says anything and that his words are merely acquiescence. To be exact, that is the effect, while actually she depends upon what he says. The magician never says anything except: "Yes," "Right," "That's right," and "Fine." He has one further signal and that is maintaining silence.

Remaining silent is his first cue. The word "Yes" is his second. "Right" is the third signal and "That's right" is the fourth. The fifth and last code cue is "Fine."

Thinking of the suits in the order of the word CHaSeD (see Chapter 5). Clubs would be the first suit, and the code for that is silence. The word "yes" would indicate Hearts; the word "right" would signal Spades; the words "that's right" would be the cue for Diamonds.

In the example previously given, the medium states: "You are thinking of a card." Of course, that is most definitely known to the medium and the magician even had said in his opening remarks, "We will begin our demonstration with a few playing cards," but the audience will not notice a detail seemingly so unimportant. After the medium has made the statement that a card was being thought of, again referring to the example, the magician remains silent. Silence stands for Clubs, but the medium announces first the color, and then the suit itself. Not only is this more impressive to the audience, but it gives the magician the chance to make two further answers. These answers indicate to the medium the value of the card.

The manner in which the value of a card is signaled will be made clear in the following diagram:

	SILENT	YES	RIGHT	THAT'S RIGHT	FINE
SILENT	ACE	FOUR	SEVEN	JACK	TEN
YES	TWO	FIVE	EIGHT	QUEEN	
RIGHT	THREE	SIX	NINE	KING	

The diagram shows four vertical columns and three horizontal ones. The ten is by itself. Silence, or one of the code words indicates one, or other, of the vertical columns. Then the horizontal row likewise is indicated by silence or one of the code words. These cues are given when the magician seemingly is agreeing that the medium correctly has named the color, and the suit, of the card. Once again referring to the example, you will see that when the medium said: "The card is a black card," the magician answered: "That's right." The diagram shows "that's right" indicates the vertical row with "Jack, Queen, King." When the medium said: "It is a Club," the magician agreed with the word "yes." Following the diagram, "yes" indicates the second horizontal row. Going across the horizontal row until the proper vertical row is reached gives the value of the card. In the example it was a Queen.

Studying the diagram a moment will show you that silence followed by silence would indicate an Ace. As silence followed by "right" would mean a three and "right" followed by silence would call for a seven, it will be seen that it is very important to remember that the vertical row always is given first. In the case of cuing a ten, only the one word "fine" is needed.

When the medium finally states both the value and suit of the card, the magician in acknowledging her to be correct gives the cue for the suit of the next card. In short, the magician always is one ahead in his signaling, and yet seemingly the medium is the only one to talk. The magician must be very casual in his answers. He should say his words as though to himself, though taking care that they be said loud enough for the medium to hear. He must know the system so thoroughly that his answers are immediate. The medium may take all the time she needs to figure out her answers. There is nothing to be gained by stalling, but the answers should not be given too quickly, for remember "her mental pictures have to develop."

There is the entire system for "telepathically" sending the name of any card in the deck and as many cards as one may wish. That is, all the fifty-two cards are included in the code system. In the event that sometime a Joker comes to light, "that's fine" will take care of him, and the cue is given at the time when the medium expects the signal for the suit.

If the medium names six cards, it is quite enough of a demonstration. More might become boring. Whatever the number used, it must be decided upon before the show by both the magician and the medium. The reason for this is that the medium must know which card is the last to be named, for then is when the magician gives the signal for whatever object is next to be described. As these objects have the same signals used for the four suits in cards, it is essential to know when the change is made.

Before going on to the remainder of the trick, I want to note that the way the cards are first selected by the audience is very important. It is important because everyone must be certain that the cards were chosen freely and without influence on the part of the magician. The best way, perhaps, is after having had the deck shuffled by a spectator to ask that same person to spread the cards out on a tray held by the magician. The magician goes from one person to another with the tray until the right number of cards have been selected. But a single card is to be taken by each person. In the event that some person unexpectedly grabs a card, so that more cards are selected than the number agreed upon secretly by the magician and the medium, it is quite permissable for the magician to ask someone to count the number of cards held by spectators. The medium naturally listens to whatever is said and thereby gets the change in instructions. This is not an occurrence which is apt to happen but it serves as a fair example of the fact that both the magician and the medium have to be prepared for emergencies.

Exactly as silence, yes, right, that's right indicate Clubs, Hearts, Spades, and Diamonds, those same cues indicate four lists of articles. The first list is money and the cue therefore is silence. The various denominations of money are put in boxes in vertical and horizontal rows exactly as were the denominations of the cards.

1	SILENT	YES	RIGHT	THAT'S RIGHT	FINE
	It's a coin		*It's a bill*		
SILENT	PENNY	QUARTER	ONE DOLLAR	TEN DOLLAR BILL	POCKET PIECE
YES	NICKEL	HALF-DOLLAR	TWO DOLLAR BILL	TWENTY DOLLAR BILL	
RIGHT	DIME	SILVER DOLLAR	FIVE DOLLAR BILL	FIFTY DOLLAR BILL	

This is an example of using the code with money:

Medium: It is a piece of money. (Of course she had been cued previously by silence.)

Magician: Yes.

Medium: It is a coin.

Magician: Yes.

Medium: It is a half dollar.

Saying, "it is a piece of money" gives the magician opportunity to cue the vertical row. When either of the first two vertical rows is indicated the medium says: "It's a coin." When either the third or fourth is signaled, the medium says: "It is paper money." Either of those statements permits an opportunity for the magician to give the cue for the horizontal row.

"Fine" indicates any coin not on the list (and there are thousands of examples) and the completely satisfactory answer of the medium is: "It is a coin, quite odd, it is carried as a pocket piece." This answer also will be accepted for any metal token even though it is not money.

The second, or "yes," list is for jewelry. As with cards and coins there are but thirteen items in the list. It is true that the medium does not give a detailed description of any piece of jewelry but the terms given on the jewelry list are quite satisfactory to audiences. The trick is aided if the medium, by her tone of voice, acts as if she knew more than she says.

This is the jewelry diagram:

2	SILENT	YES	RIGHT	THAT'S RIGHT	FINE
	It is something to be worn		*It is more than ornamental*		
SILENT	RING	PIN	NECKLACE	WATCH	EYEGLASSES *(magnifying glass)*
YES	EAR-RING	BROOCH	CHAIN	CUFF-LINKS	
RIGHT	BRACELET	CLIP	CHARM or PENDANT	BUTTON *(lodge emblem)*	

Upon being cued with the word "yes," the medium says: "It's a piece of jewelry." In acknowledging the accuracy of that statement the magician gives the code sign for the vertical column. For any one of the first three vertical columns the medium then says: "It is something to be worn" and the magician's reply, as with both cards and coins, indicates the horizontal row. When the fourth, or "that's right" vertical row is indicated, the medium says: "It is more than ornamental," to permit the magician's next cue.

In the box labeled "button," of the diagram, will be seen in parentheses the words "lodge emblem." Those words are not to be spoken by the medium but merely suggest that a lapel emblem of any sort can be described by the word "button." The box labeled "pendant or charm" covers everything from a "jeweled drop" or a "bangle," to a "key" of an honorary society. It is perfectly natural for the medium to use both words and while it sounds as if she were giving a fuller description, she actually covers a wider variety of objects by saying a pendant or charm.

Unless you are one of those rare men who are familiar with the names of women's jewelry you should talk over the subject thoroughly with your medium during rehearsals to be certain you know into which box a piece of jewelry would be properly classified.

In the same column as eyeglasses appears "magnifying glass." If the object is a magnifying glass, the medium is cued to say "eyeglass" and the magician says, "no." "That is odd," replies the medium, "I get the impression of a glass to see through—would it be a magnifying glass?" Rather than spoiling the trick, this mild error of the medium enhances the effect.

The "right" and "that's right" lists are quite varied as to articles and both are called the "personal property" objects. When either is cued to the medium she says: "It is a piece of personal property."

In the diagram are given the medium's statements after the cue is given for the particular vertical column. For instance, in column one (silent cue) appears the word "sharp," which is descriptive of a knife, a pair of scissors, or any kind of cutter. The one word "sharp" is all the medium need memorize but what she actually says is: "It is something sharp." The magician's agreement to that statement indicates precisely what the sharp object is.

The difference between "book" (second box of the second column) and "pad" (third box of the third column) is that anything bound is a "book" and any memorandum block is a "pad."

"Pocket-book" is found to be an acceptable term for wallet or handbag.

This is the diagram for the "right" list:

3	SILENT	YES	RIGHT	THAT'S RIGHT	FINE
	Sharp	Paper	For writing	For money	
SILENT	KNIFE	LETTER	PEN	POCKET-BOOK	PICTURE
YES	SCISSORS	BOOK	PENCIL	BOOK FOR MONEY (bank book, check book, etc.)	
RIGHT	CUTTER (cigar, nail. paper)	CARD	PAD	MONEY HOLDER (coin case, bill clip, etc.)	

As in the previous diagram, the words in parentheses suggest the various items which will fall under the heading of the box and are not mentioned by the medium.

The fourth, or "that's right," list has the following diagram:

4	SILENT	YES	RIGHT	THAT'S RIGHT	FINE
	For smoking	It is something useful		A beautifier	
SILENT	CIGARETTE	CASE (pouch)	KEY	COSMETICS (compact, lipstick, nail polish, eyebrow pencil)	MIRROR
YES	CIGAR	FOR A LIGHT (matches, lighter)	NAIL FILE	PERFUME	
RIGHT	PIPE	SMOKING AID (holder, cleaner, etc.)	FLASH LIGHT	FOR THE HAIR (comb, barette, hair pins, bobby pins)	

As in the previous list, the medium first says: "It is a piece of personal property." The magician's reply gives the vertical column of the list. In the diagram are given the medium's next statements: That is, for the first vertical column, "It is something to smoke"; for the second and third columns, "It is something useful"; for the fourth column, "It is a beautifier." The word "beautifier" is an amusing word and is used for that reason, as it keeps the audience from noticing how incomplete is the final answer. Again the words in parentheses in the diagram indicate the variety of objects which come under one heading.

That is the complete system. At first glance it seems complicated but when studied column by column and list by list, it is amazing how simple the whole matter becomes, for one already knows, for instance, that the smallest coins are a penny, a nickel, and a dime. One also thinks of a pen, pencil and pad together and cigarette, cigar and pipe are naturally connected in our minds. The best way to learn the system is to take but one diagram list at a time and study it one vertical column after another. After a very short period of analysis and study it will be found that all the items fall naturally into their positions on the lists.

It is amusing how odd objects unexpectedly fall into one or other classification on the lists. As example, a pill box would be covered by the word "case." Of course, any calling card, driving license, membership card, etc. is a "card with printing on it," just as a woman's elaborately jeweled clip is no more a clip than a man's tie clip. While most common objects are covered by these lists, the pleasant part of the entire matter is that an occasional slip does not ruin this branch of magic but, oddly enough, makes the rest more impressive.

Once the system is mastered and practiced it will not need rehearsal, although it is advisable for both the magician and the medium to run through the lists in their own minds before attempting public performance, if there has been a long interval since last sending "mind signals."

When a telepathic performance begins to drag the audience loses interest, but dragging may be avoided for the effect of speed almost entirely is regulated by the magician's instructions to his audience. While the cards are being selected, he should give instructions to the spectators to have ready the objects they wish described. He patters along, "Please have the money, the jewelry, or whatever it is you wish described, in your hand and ready for your test. It makes no difference what the object is but please have it ready."

Another thing which gives the effect of speed in performance is for the magician to take first one type of object and then another. This requires that he look about him, as he gives one set of signals, so that he can turn instantly to the next object to be used. Whenever possible do not follow a coin with a coin, or even a ring with a bracelet, but select items completely unrelated.

When a magician and his medium have memorized the system thoroughly and have practiced the performance of "mind signals," they may want to go one step further in the work. This next step transmits the signals more rapidly and it becomes possible for the medium to omit one of her statements in describing each article.

This speed up of signaling is brought about by giving at one time the two signals necessary to indicate a particular box in a list. One signal—that to indicate the vertical row in which a box lies—is given by silence, or one of the code words, as previously described. The other signal is given by the position in which an arm is held. To indicate a particular horizontal row, but three signals are necessary and instead of silence, "yes," and "right," one arm is held in one of the three different positions.

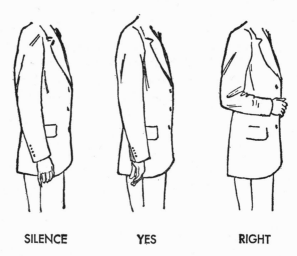

SILENCE   YES   RIGHT

Of course, using signals which must be seen cannot be done when the medium has her back to the audience and therefore she faces the audience. In order that no one suspects that she can see what she describes, or that she is signaled, a blindfold is tied about her eyes. The blindfold is so made that it does not impair the medium's vision. The magician does not suggest that the medium is blindfolded to keep her from using her eyes. He tells the audience, "I shall tie this black cloth over my wife's eyes for darkness helps her to concentrate."

The blindfold is made quite like a mask except that no notch is cut for the nose. As with a mask there are two ribbons which tie at the back of the head and like a mask there are two eye-sized holes to see through. Where the mask and blindfold differ is that the eye holes are not visible when the blindfold is worn. This is due to the thin transparent silk which covers the entire pad of the blindfold. Care must be taken by the magician when he first displays the blindfold that he does not permit any light behind him to betray the holes. When performing intimately it is an excellent idea to have a duplicate and really opaque blindfold which may be exhibited to the in-

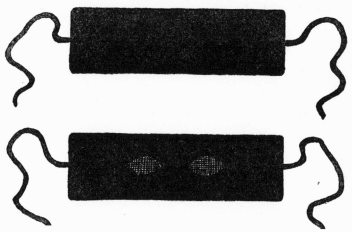

quisitive. One is exchanged for the other—as you already know—by putting the prepared one in a pocket and taking out the fair one. The magician should have ample time to do this as his wife takes the applause. The medium, by the way, is the only one to acknowledge applause, for the magician's role is that of only a very passive assistant.

The signals are given by one arm and which arm is used depends upon which way the magician is facing. He always stands sidewise towards the medium and he uses the arm nearest her, but as he has to turn from one spectator to another to look at the different articles, he has to be able to use either arm.

The signal for the top (or silent) horizontal row is for the arm to hang at the side with the palm of the hand towards the leg. For the second (or yes) row the arm moves back so that the hand is at the thigh and the wrist is turned so that the back of the hand is toward the body. The third (or right) signal is given by bending the elbow and bringing the hand up to the waist in front of the body.

These three positions of the arm are natural to make and easy to assume and will attract no attention if the magician will make them slowly and hold them as long as possible.

Due to the fact that the magician must give two signals simultaneously, he has to know his lists so well that he does not have to think them over. He must know the instant that he sees a King that his signals are "That's right" and his hand at his waist. He must know without consideration that a quarter dollar is cued by "yes" and his arm at his side. And he must be quite as certain of every other signal.

Mind signals will be found to be an interesting mystery and quite good enough to show by itself, although it may be used as a finale of a program of magic.

Twelve. TRICKS UNLIMITED

MAGIC is a most flexible art and this Chapter explains how a magician can take advantage of that helpful quality to add to his repertoire and the delight of his audiences. The reader will find, through the suggested combinations and changes of what apparatus and knowledge he has, that he is possessed of new magic as appealing to the audience as it is varied. In addition are given new feats to show how changes in patter and presentation will make different magic. The reader also will discover that if he is flexible in his thinking and performance, there will be no end to his magic powers.

Tricks generally are quite flexible and it usually will be found that a trick which may be done with a penny also may be done with a silver dollar and when appearing before many people the dollar would be seen more readily. For instance, the trick of the "Rings and Strings" in the second chapter becomes an excellent stage trick when the magician uses a cane, two ropes, and several bracelets instead of a pencil, twine, and finger rings. On the stage, however, it is advisable to use his own glass, or plastic, bracelets or even wooden curtain rings, rather than slowing the speed of performance by stopping to borrow bracelets. The reason for using glass, plastic, or wooden rings is that the material itself convinces the audience that there is no trickery about the rings. The magician also should use soft and pliable ropes. As far as method of performance is concerned the size of the objects used makes absolutely no difference to the magician.

It is not always necessary to use large objects in order to have them visible. Of course, the man in the back row cannot see the date on a penny, but he can see the penny if his attention is called to the coin. Robert-Houdin, the great French magician, said that it made no difference how cleverly a magician caused an orange to disappear, there would be no trick unless the audience were aware that the magician had an orange in the first place. The spectators should be given ample opportunity to see the objects used by the magician and before a larger audience the objects should be exhibited for a longer length of time, because distance increases the difficulty in seeing things.

Another example of a small trick which is very effective when made larger is the platform version of The Jumping Arrows described in Chapter 3. The square upon which the arrows are marked can be made of heavy white cardboard one foot square. However, it will be worth the extra trouble, because of the way the audience receive the trick, to make the "sign" of thin plywood, which, after sanding, is painted white. Black arrows are carefully painted on the white board.

In this bigger version the square is held between the two hands when it is turned diagonally. The palms of the hands press against the opposite diagonal corners and the board is turned by the fingers of both hands.

Even as a small trick The Jumping Arrows has other versions. Two of them, both amusing, are handled as is done with the small card but different stories are told. One trick is done with a small square soda cracker such as is served with cheese. The magician picks up one cracker and asks if everybody has heard about the manufacturer's problem in boxing his crackers. He goes on to say they wanted the crackers all to go into the box in one direction but were not certain the machine was packing them in that way. Therefore the factory owner drew a line on each side of the cracker to mark the way he wanted the cracker to go into the box. At this point the magician with pen, or soft pencil, draws a line on one side as the shaft of the arrow is marked on the card. He turns the cracker diagonally and draws a second line. Doing the trick the magician explains that the cracker manufacturer was frantic because sometimes the cracker was packed this way, sometimes that. The same routine is followed as is done with the card and arrow. At the conclusion of the trick the magician says, "I don't see why the man was so bothered for no matter how the crackers are packed they still are tasty." With that remark the cracker is eaten. Incidentally, the amount of ink, or graphite, needed to make the lines will not be found to be at all indigestible.

The other version of The Jumping Arrows can be done with some of the folders of paper matches having advertising printed on them. The way the advertising design is printed on some packets, it can seem to be made to jump so it is upside down part of the time. If the reader will keep his eyes open he is bound to find a paper match folder so designed that he can use it magically.

Tricks can be varied by combining the story of one with the method of another. An excellent trick depending on the use of the marked envelopes used in Arches, Loops and Whorls in Chapter 4, is done in connection with Kikeri Kikeri Ki described in the same chapter. A number of envelopes are given to the spectators. One half the number of envelopes is given to men and the other half to women. Each man is told to put in his envelope some completely masculine possession. Each lady is asked to put some completely feminine object in her envelope. After the items have been put in, the envelopes are to be sealed. The envelopes are collected by a spectator and mixed before they are given to the magician. He with his Kikeri Kikeri Ki sorts the masculine objects from those which are feminine. Only the envelopes given to the men have to be marked and each is marked in the same manner.

Not only can individual tricks be varied by substituting one article for another but parts of one trick can be used to make a complete new trick or combined with parts of another trick to make tricks that follow in natural sequence. Flowers—with Thanks (Chapter 9) becomes an excellent effect to present to an audience of men by changing only a few details. Inside the metal box are put several wrapped cigars and a folder of paper matches. The matches are put on top of the cigars and at the end of the box which does not open. The metal box is wrapped with brown wrapping paper and tied with string. The wrapping and tying is done in the same tricky way as when the trick is performed for ladies but this time a less fancy package is made. The paper bag in which the package is put should be utilitarian rather than decorative. Instead of borrowing a ring as was done in the feminine version of this trick, the magician asks for money. He insists that he requires a bill of large denomination and considerable amusement can be derived merely from the chore of getting a big bill. The bill is folded four times and put in the handkerchief. The pocket in the handkerchief contains a piece of paper of the same weight as that used in paper money and folded in the same manner the borrowed bill is folded.

A bill folded that number of times will be stiff enough so there will be no difficulty pushing it into the box.

In presenting to men this version of the trick the magician does not suggest that he bought a present as is done when showing the trick to ladies. Rather he says he won a prize in a raffle and he wonders if the gentleman would find acceptable whatever it contains now that his money is lost. If raffles are illegal in your locality offer some other, and law abiding, way in which the box with its unknown contents came into your possession.

One part of the routine of the Boy and Box of Candy (Chapter 7) is the disappearance of a box of candy. This means of causing a box to disappear is very effective when done before an audience of men provided the box is the size of a cigar box and wrapped in the manner and with the type of paper usual with such boxes. The man who is asked to aid in the trick is not requested to recite the alphabet but is asked a few trick questions. Such questions as, "Is the capital of Kentucky pronounced Louie-ville or Lewis-ville?" Even the reader, were he asked the question in public, might momentarily forget that Frankfort still is the state capitol regardless of how Louisville is pronounced. When the spectator fails on a question the box of cigars disappears.

Following the disappearance of the box, the magician may show the Bottomless Boxes (Chapter 7) to advantage by producing cigars for everybody. Frequently at a club the entertainment committee will be glad to have the cigars made part of the show—cigars which they had intended should be given out during the evening.

The easel described in ESP (Chapter 10) can be used to perform a really marvelous card trick. The effect is that a spectator shuffles a deck of cards very thoroughly. He then deals, as he decides, four, five, or six poker hands. He deals one hand to the magician, one to himself and the others to spectators he selects. When the magician gets his hand he puts the cards face down in the five spaces of the easel so they are in full sight of all the spectators. He announces that he will stand pat, sight unseen, for he has great faith in the dealer. He suggests that the others holding hands draw as many cards as they wish. At times when this trick is shown one, or more, of the spectators will have excellent hands but they will not beat the Royal Flush the magician shows as his hand. This trick needs a little more practice than does the ESP version where only one card has to be turned over in the easel, but the trick is well worth the effort. It, undoubtedly is needless to explain that when the deck was given to the spectator to shuffle and deal that it was minus the five cards which the magician had concealed on his easel prior to the performance.

Another trick, which children find fascinating, is done with the easel designed for the ESP trick and a deck of alphabet cards. Such cards are the size of playing cards and are very generally sold at the toy counter. In addition the magician has some 40 small white cards on which words are written. On each card a pair of words appears. The words may be names of objects in a like category such as: piano-banjo, peach-lemon, table-chair, bread-beans, knife-ladle. These words are, respectively, in the categories of musical instruments, fruit, furniture, food and kitchen utensils. In none of the words is a letter repeated and each word is made up of five letters. Other pairs of words which are antonyms also may be used such as: above-below, adult-child, beast-human, white-black, demon-angel. These words also have five letters all different. Heart and brain are another pair of words possible to use and it is immaterial whether one considers them related in terms either physiological or poetical. What is required are some forty pairs of words, each pair associated in some manner, and every word must have exactly five letters and all five letters have to be different. Unusual words should not be selected for, it will be remembered, the words are for magic for children and must be familiar to them. A suitable list of pairs of words will not take long to write out and it is more satisfaction to make up such a list than it is to solve the crossword puzzle another person made up.

This is the effect of the trick. The pack of cards upon which are written the pairs of words is shown to the audience. The magician then shows a pack of alphabet cards (one letter on each of 26 cards). These cards are mixed and five cards selected and put face down in the five spaces of the ESP easel. Then the pairs of words cards are mixed and a spectator freely selects one card. He also chooses one word of the pair written on his card. When the alphabet cards are turned over on the easel, they spell out the selected word.

Understanding the way the ESP easel works makes it quite clear how it happens that the letters placed on the easel by chance will spell out the selected word. Forcing the word is very easy as they are two packs of cards having pairs of words written on them. One pact having 40 different pairs of words is exchanged by the magician for a second pack having the same pair of words written on each card. The magician puts the cards he has shown into his pocket at the time the alphabet cards are introduced. Later he merely takes out the cards which are all alike.

While the spectator really has no choice of the pair of words, as is apparent, he does select one of the pair. If he names the one set up on the easel the trick is over. If the other word is announced, the magician says: "That is your word, fine, now what is the word left for me?" The magician then has "his word" appear on the easel.

The alphabet cards to use in this trick should be of regular playing card stock. Flimsy cards cannot be handled in connection with the easel.

The cigarette case described in Card and Cigarettes (Chapter 9) can be used to great advantage in other ways. In one way the magician starts his trick by offering a package of small white cards to a spectator. These are blank cards about the size of a business card and are sold by stationers in packets of 25. They are held together by a band of paper. The spectator is asked to break the paper band and to select one card. He is told that his task should be easy for all the cards are blank and all the same size. As the card is being chosen, the magician takes the cigarette case from his pocket and opens it. He asks that the card be put in the case for its protection. The case is closed and the magician takes it towards his pocket. Before the case is near the pocket he says, "Did I ask you to write your initials on your card? I didn't. Well then will you please do so." As the final word is said the magician has the case open so that the spectator can put his initials on the card. Again the case is closed but it is placed on the table rather than put back in the pocket. Another spectator is requested to choose a card from a deck of playing cards. The magician then tells the audience, "You all know that every medium has a spirit guide. I am going to ask mine to write on that blank card in the cigarette case the name of the card just chosen." The case is opened, the initials on the card verified, and the card taken out. On the other side of the card is written in large letters, "The card just chosen is the seven of hearts," and signed "Spirit of Turpentine." The magician holds the card where the writing can be seen and reads it aloud. He stops before the last three words and says, "Oh, I see my guide signed his message. Spirit of Turpentine."

The card with the message was in the case before the show began. The playing card referred to in the message, of course, was forced. The subtle part of the trick comes from the magician's "forgetfulness" in asking the spectator to write his initials on the card. When the case is reopened it is done so that the back of the duplicate card with the message is exposed. The magician keeps his finger on the card while the initials are written supposedly to hold the card so the spectator can write more easily. Actually it is to keep the card in the case so that it cannot inadvertently be turned over so the message would be seen.

Another way the cigarette case can be used is to cause a card to disappear and, naturally, is done exactly in reverse of the method used to make a card appear in the case. If a card is forced, and by means of the case made to vanish, a duplicate card can be used for a reappearance. The duplicate card can be pushed into the earth in a flower pot. It can be folded and wrapped in foil and put in a candy box after taking out one piece of candy. Or the card can be mailed a couple of days before the show and be found in a tightly sealed envelope. There are 1001 ways of bringing the card back which will interest and amuse audiences. If sometime you have the opportunity to slip the duplicate card in a pocket of some guest's suit, this makes a most surprising finale for the trick. It is so obvious that you have been no where near that person during the performance of the trick.

One most effective way of causing a card to reappear is inside the nest of envelopes described in Traveling on a Wish (Chapter 8). The duplicate card is in the envelope which the mechanism of the special tray delivers behind the nest of envelopes the audience know about and can see. A very strong addition can be made in this trick. Prior to putting the duplicate card in the envelope, a corner is torn off the card. This corner the magician keeps in a pocket where, when he needs it, it will be easy to get.

After the card is forced the magician takes it and tears off a corner. The corner removed must be at the same location as the corner torn off the duplicate card. Care should be taken to tear off approximately the same size piece. The magician offers the corner to a spectator to hold. Actually the corner received by the spectator is the one from the duplicate card. This is the way the exchange is made. The magician takes from his pocket the corner of the duplicate card while the spectator is "choosing" his card. The corner is held on the tips of the middle fingers of the right hand by the thumb. When the card is taken from the spectator, the left hand takes it and transfers it to the right hand. In this transfer the right thumb is raised a little so that the card can go on top of the corner. The thumb again presses and thus holds the card and the corner. The left hand tears off a corner of the card and puts it on top of the card. Without releasing the corner just torn off, the left hand takes the card away from the right hand. The corner from the duplicate card left in the right hand is given to a spectator to hold. Seemingly all the magician did was to change card and corner from hand to hand and the exchange of corners is unseen and unsuspected. After the spectator has the corner, the magician takes the card back in the right hand but leaves the extra corner in the left hand. As soon as opportunity permits the corner is pocketed.

The card is caused to disappear by using the cigarette case, described in "A Card and Cigarettes" (Chapter 9).

Nothing was said above about how the card was to be forced on the spectator as previously a number of methods were described and the reader undoubtedly has his favorite.

Not only can the same equipment and methods be utilized to produce tricks which seem to the audience to be completely different, but tricks may be changed merely by the type of presentation and patter.

This amazing feat and the two excellent tricks which follow are described first as demonstrations of magic. At the end of each description is given the change in presentation required to perform the trick as an exhibition of power beyond the five senses. Both types of presentation are given to draw attention to the fact that the manner in which a trick is shown is all important to the audience's acceptance of the type of feat performed. A trick in magic, by altering the presentation, becomes a demonstration of mysterious mental powers.

In this trick one spectator shuffles a deck of cards and another spectator selects one of several pennies. After both have completed their tasks it is shown that the date on the chosen coin is identical with the values of the four top cards of the deck.

The magician requests someone to shuffle the deck thoroughly. He then puts the cards back in the case and gives them to the spectator. The magician next takes all his change from his pocket and picks out the pennies. The pennies are placed, tails up, in a row on the table. The spectator, who holds the deck of cards, is told to choose one penny. The magician instructs the spectator how to make the selection.

"Please choose one penny in any manner you please. You may say eeny, meeny, miny, mo, or use any other counting system, or you can move the coins about to change the order and pick one out by chance. The thing which I want to impress upon you is that I do not influence your choice in any way."

When one penny has been selected, the magician asks the spectator to look at the date on the coin. While this is being done, the magician picks up the other pennies and puts them in a pile on the table. The spectator next is asked to take out of the case the four top cards of the deck. The spots on the four cards are discovered to be the same as the four figures of the date on the chosen penny. The other pennies are found to have various different dates.

There are two parts to the trick; one is forcing the selection of the coin with the correct date, and the other contriving to have the right four cards on top of the shuffled deck.

To arrange to have the right penny selected is simplicity itself, for the coins on the table all bear the same date. To prepare for this trick the magician must watch the pennies which pass through his hands until he has four of the same date and three more of other and different dates. The four pennies alike in date, he puts in his pocket, or his purse, with the rest of his change before he offers to show the trick. Naturally they must be the only pennies among the other coins. The pennies with unlike dates are put in another pocket where they are easy to get with the left hand. All the pennies used should be alike in design and worn to about the same degree.

When the magician brings all his change from his pocket and selects the one cent pieces, it never occurs to the audience that the magician would know the dates on the coins, nor, for that matter, even how many pennies he has in his pocket. Few people know exactly how many pieces of small change they carry, and no one notices the dates of the coins. Therefore at the start everything is quite unsuspicious.

The reason the magician makes a point of the spectator's being certain he makes a free choice is that it makes absolutely no difference which coin is selected, while at the same time the trick becomes more impressive. He puts the pennies on the table tails up because the dates, which should not be visible, are on the heads of the coins.

While the spectator is looking at the date of the one penny the magician picks up the remaining three with his right hand. At the same time the magician gets the differently dated pennies from his pocket with his left hand. The next move the magician makes is very easy to do and is most effective when done easily and naturally. The alike pennies are picked up from the table with the fingers of the right hand while the different pennies are held in the left fist. The moment the last penny is taken from the table, the two hands are brought together in front of the body. The left fist is held with the back of the hand down. As the hands meet, the left hand is opened and held flat. The instant it is opened, the left hand is moved over to the left and the right hand, with its pennies still in the fingers, is dropped to the side. A few seconds later the right hand calmly is stuck in a pocket and the pennies left there. The hand should not be put into the pocket quickly, nor jerked out, but slowly stuck in the pocket as if it were done absent-mindedly. The pennies in the right hand will be masked by the fingers, in the rare event that anyone is looking at the magician at this point. After the right hand has gotten rid of its pennies, the left hand puts its pennies on the table. There is absolutely no manipulative difficulty in this series of moves. It is a matter merely of timing and confidence. By timing is meant that, of course, the left hand should not be opened and its pennies disclosed until the instant the right and left hands are brought together. If you find that you lack confidence in making these moves, there is a more simple way of exchanging the coins which is almost as effective. This substitution is made by picking up the coins, putting the hand in the pocket, leaving those three pennies and taking out the others, which are placed on the table. Again, to be unnoticed, this exchange depends upon slow movement and calm, natural manner. By the way, it is advisable to use older coins for new ones excite suspicion whatever the reason may be.

Before the trick, the magician has extracted four cards from the deck, put them in the case, and closed the case. As example, the magician takes an ace, a nine, a five, and a four to match the date on the coins which in this case would be 1954. These cards are put in the case face up so that when the magician puts the shuffled pack into the case, he can slide it over the four cards. That is, the cards are slid into the case if it is one with an open end. If the case is a box, the cards are dropped in place. The deck, in either instance, is held face up as it is put into the case for then the four cards (in the case) are added to the top of the pack. When the four cards are put into the case before the trick is begun, it must be remembered to have them in the correct order to bring the figures of the date in the right sequence when the spectator later takes these cards from the deck. As no one knows anything about four cards having been hidden in the case, the presence of the cards will not be suspected. The magician only has to remember to hold the case so that the spectators cannot see inside. The magician not only need not, but should not, hurry in putting the deck into the case. When he inserts the cards slowly, he will find the extra cards add no difficulty to the action.

In presenting this trick as a demonstration of some power beyond the five senses, the performer begins with the explanation that he wishes to make a test to find out whether two members of the audience are psychically attuned. The various steps are followed exactly as is done when shown as a trick until the climax is reached. At the point where the shuffled deck still is in the case and one penny still is held by the spectator, the presentation is changed. The performer states, "Two people have been kind enough to perform acts. The acts were done separately and seemed to be totally unrelated. This has been a test of each person's imaginative projection of consciousness into the action of the other." Turning to one spectator, he says, "Will you please read aloud the date of the coin you selected." Turning to the other he continues, "And will you please tell the value of each of the four top cards of your shuffled deck." After date and cards are given the performer concludes, "The numbers agree, the test is positive, and I am delighted to find you are so attuned to each other."

This feat is performed with borrowed dollar bills. The chief distinguishing feature between two or more pieces of paper money of like value is the serial number. Each bill has a different number and the series letters are considered part of the number. The serial number is printed twice on the face of each bill; along the bottom near one end and along the top at the other. When a person secretly memorizes the number of one of five bills of the same value, it would seem impossible, even for a magician, to discover which of the bills carries the number held in the person's mind. It not only would seem, but very probably is, impossible and yet in this trick the magician convinces his audience that he has such powers.

The feat is started by the magician's requesting the momentary loan of five dollars. He states that he wants the money in dollar bills—bills which are neither brand new nor yet old. He explains that the reason he specifies used money is that he wants bills which look alike. Upon the successful negotiation of the loan, the magician displays the bills to show the audience how alike they are. He next folds each bill, vertically and face out, and fastens the ends together with a paper clip. The clip is used, so the audience is told, in order to hold the fold. All five folded and clipped dollars are handed to one spectator. This spectator should be selected by the audience as the one having the best memory for numbers. He is instructed to look at the money and secretly to memorize the serial number of one bill. As there are eight figures and two letters in each serial number, there are few people who can learn the number without study. The audience usually derives amusement from the length of time needed for the memorization.

The magician takes back all the bills and, as if in worry that someone might suspect him of trickery, says: "I want everyone to be certain that I hold five one dollar bills." As this statement is made, the magician, seemingly quite absent-mindedly, mixes the order of the dollars. Then he slowly holds up one dollar after another so that the spectators may count the five bills.

"In order that neither you, nor I, can see the money," the magician tells his audience, "I shall put it all in this empty pocket." The bills are pushed into the right trousers' pocket. The magician continues, "It is quite obviously impossible for anyone to know which of the five dollars has been selected, for nothing has been done to that bill to distinguish it from the others. Only one person knows the dollar that has been chosen and he has the serial number locked in his mind. Although it is impossible to discover which bill has been selected, it is possible to know the bills which have not been chosen. Watch, I take from my pocket one of the wrong bills." The magician looks intently at the bill. "Yes, I am certain this is not the selected bill. Now another wrong one." The same action is gone through for the third and fourth bills.

Holding four bills in his hands, the magician tells the audience that if he has been successful in choosing the wrong bills, the selected bill must still be in his pocket. He asks to have announced the number of the selected dollar, draws the fifth bill from his pocket, and gives it out so that the number may be verified.

All that remains is for the magician to return the borrowed money and to thank the lenders for their kindness and confidence.

What the audience does not know is that the magician has a secret working capital of four dollars. These four bills are folded as the magician folds the borrowed money and likewise have paper clips attached. The magician's bills are in his right trousers' pocket before the show begins, though otherwise the pocket is as empty as the magician claims it to be. The unstated reason for borrowing bills which are neither very old nor very new is that they must be the same in appearance as the bills the magician has in his pocket. That is the prior preparation.

The magician does nothing except what the audience sees him do, until he has the money returned to him after the one serial number has been memorized. It is at that time when he takes such great care to have the audience know that he has five dollars, and holds them up one at a time for the audience to count, that he does something the audience does not know about. As he slowly holds up one bill after another, the magician looks at the first figure of the serial number on his side of each bill, and memorizes these figures in order. For example, the figures might be 7-4-8-2-5. By the way, most people find it much easier to remember a series of figures if they combine them in pairs; that is, "seventy-four, eight, twenty-five" stick in the mind more readily than "seven, four, eight, two, five." Whatever his mnemonic method, the magician memorizes the first digit of the number on each bill and in the order in which he has the bills.

Note. It is amazing, in performing this trick, how infrequently a duplicate figure occurs, but, when one does, the magician notes two figures of each bill having numbers with alike first digits. When he folds the bills at the beginning of the trick, the magician has opportunity to discover whether any numbers are in duplicate.

Knowing the five digits, the magician puts the bills, being careful to keep them in order, in his pocket with the paper clips uppermost. The five bills are put behind (i.e., next his body) the four bills of his own already there. These four bills are the ones the magician takes from his pocket one at a time as he states his certainty that "this is not the selected bill." Having

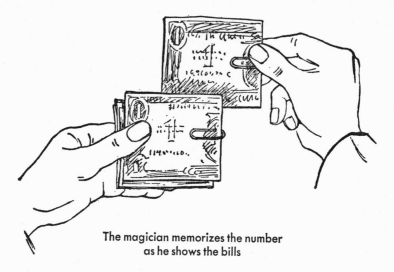

The magician memorizes the number
as he shows the bills

four bills in his hand, the magician asks to have the number of the selected bill announced and puts his hand in the pocket as he asks the question. As soon as the spectator names the first digit, the magician is aware which of the bills in his pocket is the selected one, for they are in the same order as the memorized digits. While the spectator announces the other figures in the number, the magician has ample time to locate the right bill in his pocket. No difficulty should be had in picking out the correct bill from among the five. In the first place, the paper clips are very easy to count by touch, and in the second place, he need never count above three to find it. The right bill is either one or other of the outside bills, second from one side or other, or the middle bill.

Naturally four spectators do not get back the same bills which they gave, but as they neither know nor care, it makes no difference.

It should be impressed on the spectator memorizing the serial number that it is important that he remember the number. Having the audience select the person with the best memory is fair assurance that the number will be remembered and it is also a convincing way for showing that no confederate was used. The trick is much more effective when the number is held only in a person's mind and it will be found inadvisable even to permit having the number written down.

When the trick is all over and the money returned the magician says, "I do hope that everyone realizes how much easier it is to get the right answer the wrong way."

That is the ending when the trick is presented as magic. When presenting the feat as a demonstration of mental phenomenum the routine is practically the same. However, at the point in the demonstration where the performer takes out of his pocket the four dollar bills of his own, the patter is changed. The new version would be to this effect.

"When one person thinks strongly of a way he has of identifying one of several like objects it often is possible for another person to see what he has in mind. However, if it is not possible for the second person to use his eyes such mental communication has little value. Experiments are being made to discover whether a person's thoughts can bring any identifiable changes in the object thought about. This is the basis of what I shall now attempt. I feel no change in this bill and I believe it cannot be the one about which the gentleman is thinking. Again no change—so it is not this bill. Nor this bill—for I sense nothing. Not this one either. The remaining bill should be the one. To find out if I could feel the way your mind affected the bill, please tell me the number of the bill still in my pocket. Here it is. Please check the identifying numbers."

By adding a single sentence in concluding this feat the audience is lead to look upon it as being due to mind power rather than to trickery.

"Luck is a strange thing," the magician tells his audience, "and for most of my life I have had but little faith in it, although as a boy I was told that the man who didn't believe in luck was a fool. Recently I have had the strangest experiences with a children's word game and I can account for it in no other way than by luck."

With some such introduction, the magician takes from his pocket a stack of cardboard discs. He shows these discs to have words printed on one side and to be blank on the other. He suggests to the audience that undoubtedly everyone has seen children play the game in which they use these word-cards. (Possibly there are such discs used in a game that children play, and while I never have heard of such a game, its existence has been unquestioned by every person to whom I have shown the discs.)

All of the discs are given to one spectator, who is told to look over the words and, in his mind, to select one word and remember it. The spectator drops all of the discs into a hat, a small empty box, a bowl, or any other innocent receptacle. The container is shaken to mix the words and the magician puts it on a table and steps in front of the table.

The magician explains to his audience what he is about to do.

"Some eight, or ten, word-cards are all mixed up in the receptacle on the table behind me. One of the words has been selected, but which word is known only to one person. Were I to look over the cards, it might be thought I have the power to receive some mental radio message telling me the chosen word, but I shall not look at the cards. Blindly I reach behind me and take one card out of the container entirely by chance. If my luck continues, I hold in my hand the disc bearing the chosen word. Which word was selected? Thank you. Let me see. Yes, that is the word I took. Isn't my luck amazing?"

The trick depends upon the particular eight words used on the cardboard discs. These words are in two sets and each group of words needs a total of only five different letters to spell the four four-letter words. This is due to the fact that the letters used in spelling the words always run in the same sequence and when all five letters are printed around the edge of a disc, it can be shown as having any one of four words merely by hiding the extra letter. The magician has such a disc which the audience knows nothing about. The extra disc has the five letters of one set of words on one side and the five letters of the second set of words on the other side. By showing the correct side and holding a finger over one letter, this disc can be exhibited as any one of the original eight discs shown to the audience.

The illustration shows the eight discs of which the audience are aware and also both sides of the extra secret disc.

At the beginning of the trick, the magician has the extra disc in one of the pockets on his left side. When the point in the trick is reached where the container is placed on the table, the magician takes that disc from his pocket. If the disc is placed so that the magician need do no fumbling in getting hold of it, the audience will not notice even that he has put his hand in his pocket. Of course, the magician gets the extra disc before he stands in front of the table. At that time the disc is in his left hand, which hand is held, loosely closed, at his side. There need be no fear either that the disc will be seen or that it will fall out of the hand, if it is held at the base of the

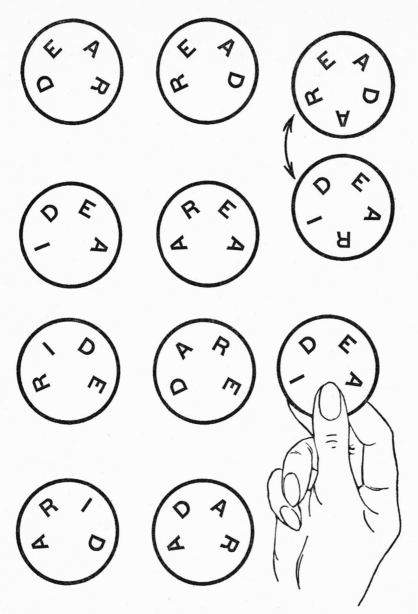

All the discs can be reproduced inexpensively by having a photostat made of the page, cutting out the discs and pasting them on round cards.

fingers. Neither is it odd appearing for the hand to be closed, for one's hands naturally are closed when they hang at the side.

When the magician says, "I will reach behind me," his words are very slightly preceded by the gesture. Having gone through the motion of taking out one word-card, the magician brings his hand in front of his body and holds it up. At this point he holds his fist tightly closed.

The trick is better when the magician knows which side of the disc is next the palm of his hand. It is easy to know this if the magician puts the disc in his pocket, before the show, knowing which side is up. Knowing which side of the disc is next his palm, the magician can open his hand so that the correct group of letters face him. In order to have the side next his palm face up, he holds his hand back up and opens his fingers as he bends the wrist down. The disc will lie on the fingers. To get the other side up, he holds his hand back down, before opening the fingers, and the disc will be on the palm. The magician looks at the disc, puts his thumb over the letter to be hidden and slides his first finger under the card. Between forefinger and thumb, the magician holds the disc in the air face towards the audience. Care must be taken in lifting the disc from the hand that the other side (supposedly blank) is not seen by the audience. This is easy but must be kept in mind.

The reason for "taking the disc from the container" with the left hand is that, for a right-handed person, it is easier when using the right hand to exhibit the disc at the end of the trick.

When in his patter the magician says, "eight or ten word-cards" he is well aware there are but eight but he thereby gives the idea to the audience that the number of words is immaterial.

All the words used in the trick are in everyday use with the one exception. Adar is the name of the twelfth month of the Hebrew calendar and is mentioned frequently in the Bible. All cross-word puzzle addicts will know it.

Putting the trick on a basis of luck rather than skill, besides being an amusing idea, makes the trick easier to perform.

All the performer has to do to change the presentation of this effect is to add one sentence at the very end. "Those who are students of the subject have been making a deep study and believe that luck frequently has psychic causations."

It is unbelievable how many times a magician can perform miracles by being prepared to take advantage of what chance will bring. I shall never forget the occasion in Wichita when the officers of a men's club were kind enough to entertain me at the home of one until time for my very late night train. In the attractive room where we sat were two mirrors. Through the aid of those mirrors and a deck of cards I never touched, I performed what the gentlemen assured me were the most astounding card tricks they ever had seen. Come to think of it, they were about the most fantastic I ever saw. They derived a lot of fun and I was given a great deal of credit merely because I noticed those mirrors and took advantage of them. In the second chapter the suggestion was made for the magician to take advantage of those occasions when he happens to get a glimpse of a card. That suggestion is endorsed here with the additional suggestion that the magician will be wise who takes advantage of every chance occurrence he can turn to his advantage for the mystification of his audience.

Here, as example, is an excellent way to make use of the information luck can bring. If chance has permitted the magician to notice the bottom card of the deck while the cards are held by a spectator, the spectator is instructed to place the deck on the table if he has not already done so. He is told to take a substantial number of cards from the deck and to put the heap on the table. He then is asked to take more cards from the deck and to make a second heap. The remainder of the deck he is to deal alternately on to the two piles. Except for using only one card and two heaps, this is the same force as was made in By the Sense of Touch (Chapter 6). The performer merely has to notice upon which pile the last card was dealt. As that card had been on the bottom of the deck when the magician saw it, he now knows the name of the top card of one of the piles. The assistant is asked to choose one of the two piles by placing his hand on top of it. If it is the pile having the known top card, he is told to look secretly at the top card, to remember what it is, and to put the card somewhere in the middle of the deck. If it happens that he put his hand on the other pile, he is told to hold it there and secretly to look at the top card of the other pile. He then is told to put that card somewhere among the cards under his hand in the pile he has chosen. In either case, the spectator, then is told to put the two piles together and to shuffle the entire deck for exactly ten seconds. The magician agrees to tell him when he is to stop shuffling and that he is to stop instantly. This emphasis on time is to put the idea of mathematics into the spectator's mind. The spectator then is asked to deal face up in a row the top six cards of the deck. The magician studies the cards, names two or three of them aloud, and announces the name of the card selected. Among the six cards there almost inevitably are some which by addition, or subtraction, the value of the known card can be "deduced." Often I have one of the same value appear and a few times the actual card. The proper suit is, or isn't among the six cards, or there are more, or less cards of that suit. In short, the magician derives (in effect) the name of the selected card from some formula connected with those six cards. Actually once having caught a glimpse of the card, the magician has nothing to do but to talk and think.

While an effect may seem similar to a magician, by changing the articles used and the method of performance, a new trick will result. For example, the "Rings and Strings" trick involved the release of objects from a string. Here is an identical effect which is well to know and which will be a new trick to the audience. The magician in this trick uses only one string and a personal card. First he folds the card in half and then into quarters and tears off a corner of the folded card. The corner torn is the one at the double fold and which is the center of the card when opened. Tearing off this corner makes a hole in the center of the card. The magician publicly prepares his card, opens it, and threads it on the string. The ends of the string are given to two spectators to hold and the magician covers the card and all but the ends of the string with an opened handkerchief. Reaching under the handkerchief, he magically releases the card from the string and gives it for examination. After pocketing the handkerchief, the magician also submits the string for inspection.

Unknown to the audience the magician has a duplicate card in his pocket. That card also has the folds and the hole in the center and it is left folded. When the magician has reached the point in showing the trick where he has spread the handkerchief over card and string, he gives those holding the string instructions to hold each end tightly. This interlude gives him a chance to get the card from his pocket which, because it is folded, will be hidden in the closed hand. Reaching under the handkerchief the magician tears off the card on the string and folds it. He unfolds the duplicate card and with one hand gives it to a spectator as with the other hand he pockets the handkerchief and with it the original card.

It may well be asked which form of the trick is better. The method just described needs a little more practice and assurance than the other, but they are equally effective and impressive. Circumstances of performance vary and a trick which merely is astounding on one occasion may be a complete miracle on another. For instance, one group may be partial to tricks with cards and another may find tricks with coins more interesting. In each instance, therefore, the better trick from the spectators' point of view is the one using the objects in which they have most interest. Seldom can a magician know the bias of an audience before a show but when he does he will be wise to arrange his program accordingly.

There is no best trick in magic, except that each person will think that feat best which is shown to him personally. When he chooses the card, or when his coin is used, or when he takes part in any other way, the trick has an added glamour and, in his opinion, becomes the best trick he has ever seen. We professional magicians constantly are told of super-marvels people have seen performed by other magicians. Invariably these super-excellent demonstrations are ones in which those recounting them have taken part.

Magic has flexibility in another way that has not been mentioned. It is not only possible but often desirable to group tricks in such a way that the show has a theme rather than being an exhibition of disassociated mysteries. There are three basic types of magic-show themes and the variety in each is limited only by the ingenuity of the magician.

The first type is limiting the magic to a series of feats with objects of like character. Gus Fowler successfully toured the world with his magic done solely with watches and clocks. Ade Duval had equal international acclaim when all his magic was done with pieces of silk. T. Nelson Downs was the first to confine his magic to feats with coins. A long list could be given of the wide variety of objects different magicians have built magic acts around.

The second type of theme is nationality and the magic is presented as being from one country. Theodore Bamberg and his son David, and William E. Robinson each built his wonderful show on the Chinese theme, and even adopted Oriental names, Okito, Fu Manchu and Chung Ling Soo, respectively. They were so successful that they became known by their Oriental rather than Occidental names. Still other Occidental magicians have had East Indian, Japanese and Egyptian mystery acts. This is a partial list but it makes obvious that the magicians in each instance could make their performances more realistic by wearing the individualistic attire of the country. However, there is much more to making this kind of act acceptable than merely changing clothes. The magic, too, must be changed in presentation and often in form. Merely painting a few Chinese characters on some obviously Occidental object will not make it acceptably Oriental to any audience. For an extreme example, it is not likely that an audience will visualize an Indian turban because a magician put a sign on a high silk hat. Audiences are very knowing and object strongly to any performer who, by what he does or says, seems to assume that they are ignorant.

The third type of theme is where all the magic is based on the particular interest of the audience. An act in which all the tricks are done with postage stamps would be bound to be fascinating to a group of philatelists and might even have general appeal. But most such highly specialized acts will be found interesting to one group only. However, a number of professional magicians have devised acts for the butcher, the baker, or the candlestick maker because single firms, or organizations, have wanted such shows for promotional reasons. I have performed acts of magic with everything from automobile parts to silk stockings. Truly magic is very flexible and anything can happen when the magician is willing to work hard and to think in a pliable manner.

Magic depends upon leading the minds of the audience away from the true basis for the tricks. In earlier chapters, tricks devoid of science are offered as scientific marvels. The following three tricks, actually based on scientific principles, are disguised as feats of magic.

For instance, a lump of sugar will ignite and burn with a blue flame when a magician holds a match to the sugar. A spectator will find it impossible to get another lump to burn even though his sugar is taken from the same bowl that the magician used. This trick is entirely a chemical phenomenon though the magician is careful not to let that fact be discovered. The magician dips a corner of his sugar into cigar or cigarette ashes before he holds a match to the lump. Of course, getting the ashes on the sugar is done before the magician calls attention to his feat but it will be found he can do that quite openly.

Another bit of scientific magic is called the "Jumping Flame." Two candles are used and both are burning. The flame of one candle is blown out and the flame of the second candle is held an inch or two above the wick of the one just extinguished. Part of the flame of the lighted candle may be seen to jump to the wick of the other candle which then also begins to burn. This is due to the fact that the smoke which rises from a candle just blown out has a high carbon content and is highly flammable. The effect of the

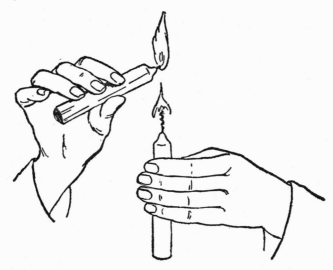

jumping flame is caused by the ignition of the smoke. The wax of the candle accounts for the large amount of carbon in the smoke. The trick also may be done with most paper matches as their smoke too will burn. The magician will find by experiment that he can see the rising smoke and he holds the flame in that smoke and as high above the other candle, or match, as possible for the greater the distance jumped by the flame the more impressive the trick.

One last trick of science is well worth the bother of experiment necessary for its performance. A small object is dropped into a glass of ginger ale, or other carbonated drink, and it immediately sinks to the bottom. The magician commands it to come to the surface and slowly the object rises to the top of the glass. The magician causes it to sink which it does and then once again rises on command. The trick is caused by the bubbles of gas adhering to the object and carrying it to the surface. There the bubbles burst and it sinks again. The rise and fall will continue while the gas is freed from the liquid. The experimenting necessary is caused by discovering the object to be used. It should be heavy enough to sink but only that heavy. All sorts of things have been used for the trick from a seed of a fruit, such as a grape or apple seed, to a carved piece of coral. The more odd the object the more fanciful a story can be told by the magician and a good story will keep the minds of the spectators from thinking of the bubbles of gas. Another reason for trying out one's own object is that the amount of carbonation used in drinks varies in different localities.

Such phenomena when presented in the guise of magic can be very striking and good entertainment and a magician will do well to keep on the lookout for all natural marvels. Almost anything unusual can be made into a piece of magic. I saw a Chinese magician in Peiping wave an ordinary wooden parlor match in the air and cry, "Fire." All who witnessed the match bursting into flame on command were startled. I was amazed as well as startled and didn't know until he told me that he struck the match by running his thumb nail along the tip. I not only was well aware that a match could be lighted in that manner, but, as a boy, had developed the knack. What drew me entirely away from that idea was the waving of his arm about in the air and calling on the match to light. The big motion completely hid the action of the thumb and because the command instantly was obeyed it seemed magical.

The more magical he can make everything he does the more genuinely will the magician be a person who can do the impossible. However this one word of caution—never make a magical move which will confuse the audience. As example, don't startle the spectators by lighting a match magically in the middle of another trick upon which they are supposed to concentrate.

Nate Leipzig who could perform brilliant magic with any object—literally anything he could handle—said, "The first rule for a magician is that he must keep the effect of the trick simple." He felt that the best way to follow that rule was to do only one trick at a time and to remember not to talk too much.

Returning to the subject of flexibility of magic, in the previous pages, suggestions are given for varying the presentation of some of the magic described earlier in the book. A few of those tricks, incidentally, are my variations of magic other magicians have originated. Exactly in the same way that my changes made new effects from old ideas you will find you will devise changes that will bring new magic into the world. You will derive both pleasure and satisfaction from devising new feats of magic. But don't limit yourself only to the tricks in this book or those of your own invention. You will find a number of books on magic available to get more tricks. However, do not attempt to do too many different tricks. A magician is judged by how entertaining and interesting is the magic he does and not by how many feats he can do. It obviously must be better to learn to do a few tricks well than merely to know how many are done, for audiences are interested only in magic which is done well.

Thirteen. CONCLUDING SECRETS

IN the previous pages, the how and why of a number of feats of magic have been set down, but the vital part of a trick cannot be written—that part is the interest in the trick the magician is able to engender in the audience. What makes a trick effective, as was said previously, is the agreeable personality of the performer and the timing, naturalness, and smoothness of the presentation. It seems almost unnecessary again to mention practice, for practice is needed in everything one does well, and who wants to do a thing poorly? But perhaps it might be well to jot down the reminder that to be effective practice must be done thoughtfully and with understanding of the results wanted. It will be found necessary only to practice hours on the magic in this book rather than having to spend the months and years needed to learn so many other subjects.

Always keep in mind the three steps to be taken in learning a trick. First, it should be studied so that every detail is thoroughly understood. Second, everything to be done must be memorized. Third, it must be repeated in private until everything done and said runs along evenly, effortlessly, and interestingly. When a magician has practiced to the point that he automatically knows and can do each step in a trick, he will find he can concentrate on making the trick interesting to an audience and that will make him, and his magic, more pleasant.

The manner in which a trick is presented is of much more importance than the trick itself. Every trick in which the secret is based on sound psychological principles is a good trick and when the basis for the mystery is not sound, it simply is not a trick. Therefore it may be said that there is no good or bad magic but only good or bad magicians. All the tricks in this book have been proven by the test of public performance to be completely sound mysteries and there is no reason why you should not be a good magician provided you will take the pains to learn the tricks.

Because the secret of a trick is simple, beginners in magic are apt wrongly to scorn the trick. The secrets of many of the most incredible magic feats are utterly simple. When I was about eighteen years old, I witnessed Houdini perform a trick to the delight and amazement of an audience of several thousand people. I was as mystified as anyone and yet the trick looked quite like one I had discarded when I was about twelve because it was too simple for a magician of my skill. (That opinion of my prowess at twelve, by the way, was quite exclusively my own.) After the performance I asked Houdini if he had performed the trick I knew. He handed me the equipment and I could see that it was the same. "Always remember, Johnny," he told me, "it is not the trick which impresses the audience but the magician."

The means employed by the magician to make his mysteries are of no interest to an audience provided they do not discover them. When the magician is caught in a trick, it is immaterial whether the secret be simple or involved, the audience immediately loses interest in the magician, in that trick, or in any future magic he may show. People will forgive a flat note of a singer, or a pianist's discord, but never, so help them, forgive a magician his failures. All audiences insist on the magic shown them being inexplicable. There is an old saying in magic that the test of a good magician is how well he gets out of his errors. Magicians fortunately are not prone to slips and usually can cover over their difficulties without the audience's being aware they occurred. In the first place, an audience does not know what the magician intends to do until he tells them and he very carefully should refrain from announcing his intentions until he can do so safely. Not knowing what is to happen, the audience does not know whether or not the magician intends to do whatever it is he is doing. When the magician finds something amiss in the early stages of a trick, he frequently can change to another trick with the audience being no wit the wiser. For instance, were a spectator to drop the cards when the magician was using a stacked deck, he could change to one of the tricks which do not require the cards to be in a special order. There are occasions when a magician needs to exercise ingenuity to extricate himself from difficulties but he will find almost every situation may be overcome. This has not been written to be frightening, but rather as advice to look for a way out of a difficulty when, rare instance, one occurs.

Even if an escape cannot be found, do not admit error, but merely stop the trick and say, "I just happened to remember I was told never to do this piece of magic on Wednesday."

Most difficulties are caused by spectators' forgetting which cards they had selected or not following instructions. Both of these troubles may be avoided. When a person chooses a card, he must be told to remember what it is and it is an excellent plan to have him show it to those near him. Someone is bound to remember the card. Instructions should be given twice. First the magician describes what is to be done and then he tells a person to do it. Care should be taken not only to be explicit but to be certain that the instructions are worded correctly. Because I had discovered that when I asked a spectator to choose either an American half-dollar or a British penny, he would pick up one coin rather than stating his choice, I fell into the error of saying, "Please name one coin." Alexander Woollcott greatly added to the amusement of the audience at one of my performances by following my instructions precisely. He pointed at one coin and said, "I name this one Elmer."

Almost all other troubles a magician is heir to, come about through faulty preparation. He fails to make certain, prior to his performance, that he has an extra coin, or that the cards are in sequence, or the matches are in the right pocket. One of the greatest aids to insure proper preparation is for the magician to make a list of everything needed for each trick and refer to those lists before his performance.

As the mystery in magic depends upon details to a very large extent, the successful magician is the one who considers all details as being important. That is the correct attitude for in magic nothing is so minor as to be unimportant. In making a reference list of everything needed for a trick no detail can be excluded. These lists are valuable for several reasons. First, when a magician understands a feat of magic well enough to be able to write a full list of requirements for its performance, he is well on his way towards its mastery. In this way, the list serves as a test of knowledge. Second, by scanning the list prior to performance, the magician can assure himself that he is possessed of everything he will need for the trick, and that each item is ready to work, and is properly placed. Thus the list aids to insure a good performance. Third, reading the list will review in the performer's mind what he has to do in performance. Used in this way the list gives a quick mental rehearsal. Professional magicians have such lists, even those who do the same show day after day. For the amateur, who performs only occasionally, these lists are imperative. For the magician who plans to change his show in any way, such as substituting one feat for another, or adding a trick or two, again these lists are of great help. For instance in the routine the magician has outlined, he finds that the third trick he had planned to do requires that a certain pocket be empty while for his fourth trick that same pocket had to hold a needed object. The middle of the show is no time to discover there is something in the pocket which should be empty. Perhaps all that needs to be done is to reverse the order in which the tricks are performed. Or at times it will be found it is necessary to choose which feat to show, as both cannot be done in the same performance. By the lists the performer will become aware of his problems and at a time he can do something to avoid having difficulty during his show.

Magicians identify their tricks by name and frequently the names seem bizarre. Originally outlandish names were given for two reasons: 1) they were impressive on the printed programs; 2) they gave no clue to the spectators as to what the feats would be. Some of the names I recall are: Chronometrical Bullets, Homological Evaporation, The Thalmo-Thaumatic Problem, and the Aqua-Avial Paradox. While none of those names would give a spectator the vaguest idea what he would witness during the performance, they are not too easy for the performer to recall. Today magicians name their tricks for their own benefit and an attempt always is made to have the name serve as a mnemonic device which will remind the performer of a trick, or sequence of related tricks. As example, "The Hungry Jackass" will remind the magician of the doggerel by the use of which a deck of cards may be arranged so as to perform a series of tricks. Some names will recall method, others effect, and still others the basis for the patter but all should, one way or another, recall the trick to the performer's mind.

When giving a formal performance, the magician will find it very helpful to have a program list on his table, or someplace where he can refer to it during his show. This list is merely of the names of the magic he is to do and in the sequence he plans to do them. Having such a list handy relieves the magician of ever having to wonder about what comes next. Something may occur during the show to make the performer momentarily forget the order in which he had intended doing his feats. While such occurrences are apt to be very rare it is a great comfort to know the list is there. There was an incident in a theater during one of my shows when a child toppled over the railing along the front of the balcony. Something caught in his clothing and kept him from falling to certain injury. So as not to panic the audience, I kept on with the trick I was performing until the boy was jerked back to safety. It is true I did the trick automatically and probably I finished what I was doing but I don't remember. I do recall I was glad to have the list to remind me what came next. The program list has another most important use. It can be saved and annotated by the magician telling which tricks the audience liked most and for what group the tricks were done. The next time the magician appears before the same group, he can repeat one or two of the tricks that received the most favorable reception and make up the rest of the repertoire with tricks he has not previously shown this particular group.

The trick and program lists mentioned are of the utmost importance and that is why they are used in all shows from a Shakespearean performance down. In a show there are quite enough things to think about and whatever can be done to relieve the mind should be done. It is part of a magician's job to confuse the minds of his spectators but he never should be befuddled himself. The less he has to remember prior to a show the clearer his mind will be and the better the performance. So let me redundantly state that it is better to depend upon lists than memory.

While there are tricks suitable only for presentation to adults because they require the audience to have knowledge, or skills, children do not have, magic for adults as compared with magic for children is usually merely a matter of presentation. Magic for children has to be kept simple but it is a great mistake to make it childish. It never can be assumed that children enjoy being made aware that the performer feels a superiority because of his adult status. I was deeply impressed by a remark a youngster made after listening to a man tell stories to a group of children. "I know I am a kid so what did the guy have to rub it in for? Doesn't he know I'll outgrow it?"

The details of good magic must be within the knowledge of the spectators. By details, in this instance, is meant the plot of the feat, the various ideas mentioned, the properties used and the vocabulary employed. These facts must be kept in mind when showing tricks to children and, even, in presenting magic to different groups of adults. There are certain subjects about which women have more knowledge than do men, and the reverse equally is true. A city man will know things a country man will not know and vice versa. Both the Eskimo and the Hottentot have knowledge the other lacks. Possibly the reader never will perform his magic both in the Arctic and in Southern Africa, but he must realize that audiences differ and that it is his task to cater to each in order properly to please and entertain.

The words the magician uses in his patter not only have to be understood by his audience but should be ones to which they are accustomed. I had an interesting experience with one word of patter. The trick in which the word was used was similar to the Boy and Box of Candy in that it required having an ordinary and unprepared paper bag. In New York where I first performed the trick, I introduced the bag by saying, "Here is an empty paper bag." As I traveled around the United States, I found suspicion of the bag was apt to be created unless the local term for paper bag was used. In the southwest "paper sack" was more generally used. In parts of the deep south, "paper poke" was the common name. In a district of Pennsylvania I found it better to use the word "toot." It was not that the word bag was not understood in any locality but the word was unusual locally and people are naturally suspicious of the unusual word, the unusual action, or the unusual object. The magician does well to avoid the uncommon word, or act, as far as it is possible to do so.

I like to perform all the tricks mentioned in this book, but as Elmer P. Ransom used to say, "That is a detail—what matters is that audiences like them." Audiences do like them, as I know because they tell me after the show and ask me to repeat them at future shows. Audiences like these tricks because of their simplicity and apparent fairness. The magic, without any fuss, or bother, or cumbersome paraphernalia just goes ahead and occurs. Such magic always is more mysterious as well as more impressive.

Throughout the book many tricks are described which can be performed almost anytime and anywhere—at a dinner table, a card table, at a tea party or a cocktail party—anywhere where it would be suitable to tell a humorous story, anywhere a moment's entertainment is indicated. While thought and practice have to be given even to these tricks, the reader will find them easy to do.

All of these tricks can be presented extemporaneously. That is, the reader will recall, some of them actually may be given without any prior preparation and the others seemingly so. These tricks, besides entertaining those to whom they are shown, train a person to think, act and talk in the ways a performer of magic should do. Mastery in presentation of such feats makes learning more elaborate magic far, far easier, because the magician learns to keep his audience always in mind. Performing magic is very much like driving an automobile. Being a skillful operator is not enough and the safe driver is the one who pays constant attention to what is being done by drivers of other cars on the road. In magic the audience is a component part of the show. The magician works with his audience and not merely in front of them, as is done with all other branches of the theater. To repeat, learning to perform extemporaneous magic in a way to make it interesting and entertaining is the best training for becoming a really good magician.

Giving a more formal performance, one consisting of a sequence of several feats and done before more people, requires that the magician have additional knowledge. Each trick, by itself, becomes no more difficult but the magician must not only think of his various tricks but also about the show in its entirety. A show has to have variety. In a show one feat has to follow another smoothly. A show should be designed so that the interest of the audience not only is maintained but increased trick by trick. These things are not difficult to accomplish once they are realized and consideration is given to them.

No general rule can be set down which will indicate how long a time any trick needs for proper performance. Horace Goldin was able to delight his audience for a half hour when performing at the rate of one trick a minute. Houdini was able to thrill his audiences by performing but two feats in a half hour. Neither speed has ever been successfully duplicated by other magicians. Goldin alone could work at that accelerated speed and Houdini was unique in holding an audience in suspense for a length of time. Through experience a magician learns to vary his speed of performance by altering details of presentation. At New York's Radio City Music Hall, I did in eight minutes exactly the same tricks of a program of Chinese magic which, in most theaters, I take four times as long to do. It will be obvious that the time required to perform a trick varies according to the magician, the place of performance, the audience, and the trick itself.

While it is impossible to specify the time needed to do one trick, it is quite practicable to put a time limit on a performance. Twenty minutes for the entire program is all that any magician should attempt until he has had considerable experience. That is ample time to do an impressive show and is longer than the majority of the acts of professional magicians. In twenty minutes a magician should be able easily to do five tricks and until considerable experience is gained five tricks are ample.

While on the subject of time, and the fact that all magicians do not and should not work at the same rate of speed, here is a helpful suggestion. After a trick has been privately rehearsed until it is ready for public performance, it should be timed to give the approximate length of performance. Again it should be timed when done in front of an audience, and this time recorded on the reference list for that trick. Knowing how long is required to do a particular trick is helpful in making up a program.

Two final points on time. The first is always have the show short enough so that the audience feels it would like to see more magic. The second is when working on a program having other acts, a performer must be certain to take only the time alloted him. A magician may be forgiven for having his performance shorter than the time he was given. He never will be forgiven for filching more time than was specified.

Following are the tricks suggested for various programs. In brackets following the name of each trick listed is given the number of the chapter in which the trick is described.

First will be given several programs for the "Parlor Magician." That is the old term for the magician who gives his show in a home. Probably the performance will be given in a room designated by some name other than parlor, but the conditions are quite the same. Because of space, the number of spectators at such a show will number less than thirty. All the feats listed can be seen by that number without difficulty.

For a mixed group of adults at a parlor show, the following program is suggested: Rings and Strings (2), Scientists' Dollar Dinner (6), The Prophetic Pennies (10), Card Automation (2), The Sheikh's Ring (9).

For a parlor show for men these tricks are suggested: Money No Object (4), Return Fire (6), Arches, Loops and Whorls (4), The Pirate and the Strongbox (4), Beelzebub's Letter (6).

For a parlor show which will appeal to the majority of adults and consisting only of card tricks: Shuffling the Deck and a Trick in Connection Therewith (5), To Know How Many Cards Are Missing from the Deck (5), By Number (5), By the Sense of Touch (6), A Card and Cigarettes (6).

For a children's parlor show it is suggested using the challenges and odd tricks from Chapter 3. These tricks bring in more audience participation, use no appreciable amount of apparatus and a greater number of feats may be shown.

One word of caution in regard to a parlor show in another person's home. The magician should always bear in mind that he must do no trick which will harm or disarrange his host's house.

There is not a great deal of difference between a parlor show and one done on a platform in a hall. Each has certain advantages and disadvantages. As the spectators in a hall are apt to be considerably greater in number the performer must take pains to be heard and understood. On the other hand the spectators in a hall are not under the toes of the magician as they are very likely to be in a parlor. For that reason when working on a platform the magician can with ease perform tricks which might be hazardous in a parlor.

For a platform show before a mixed audience of adults and children, these tricks are excellent: String for a Parcel (6), Magic Dye (7), Boy and Box of Candy (7), Ho Chang (9), Astronaut Cards (9).

For a mixed adult audience, or one limited either to men or to women, Mind Signals (11) will be found to be most effective.

For a platform show for ladies: Another Century (7), Chromatic Vibrations (10), Clever Poltergeist (10), Flowers—With Thanks (9), Bottomless Boxes (7).

For a platform show for men: To Know by Sound Which Card Is Missing from the Deck (5), Wrong Way for the Answer (10), The Flight of a Coin (6), 10,000 to 1 (10), ESP (10).

For a platform show for children the following tricks, all taken from Chapter 8: Flying Silk, Obedient Colors, Ball, Paper and Nothing, Coin and Cord, The Elusive Block.

In giving a platform show consideration has to be given and plans made in advance about getting tables and paraphernalia on and off the platform quickly and without a lot of fuss and bother. No matter how brilliant the actual performance might have been the spectators are bound to wonder what kind of a magician he is if he has trouble before or after the show. Another point to know in advance is where secretly can the apparatus be set up and where can it be kept before the show.

Mentioning tables reminds me that a promise was made earlier in the book to go into some detail about tables for magic shows. As we mentioned these are of two types: performance tables and prop table. The prop table (usually one is enough) should be large enough to hold everything the magician plans to use during the performance, except whatever he has on his person. The better the appearance of all of the tables used during the performance, the more attractively "dressed" will be the show. Some magicians use a card table as a prop table. There are card tables and card tables. A flimsy legged one, which gives the effect of having had rickets in its youth, is apt to cause the audience to pay more attention to its imminent collapse than they are to the magician. On the other hand there are very good looking and substantially made card tables which can be used to advantage. The use of a card table as a prop table is not required but such a table has ample surface space. There are also good portable tables available that are made for camping. They are sturdy, of light construction and fold into easily carried cases. Personally I prefer to use an oblong table for my props as, for me, it makes each item more readily available. However, the prop table is largely a matter of individual preference.

While the prop table is where the equipment is placed until the performance of each trick, it also is where most of the articles are returned after the tricks are completed. In his rehearsals the magician should take into consideration that he has to clear his performance tables after one trick and prior to starting the next. In many instances he will find that as he does a trick he can so arrange his props and apparatus that the objects can be removed quickly and without any effect of fumbling. Often it is just as easy to replace articles on a tray as it is to scatter them about the table.

The performance tables, on the other hand, should meet definite specifications. These tables are used constantly through the show and should be of such a size as to make it easy for the performer to work from them and yet stand erect. The usual height of such tables is thirty inches. The way to discover the correct height for you is to measure the distance from the floor to the knuckles when your hand is hanging at your side. Not only do magicians come in a variety of sizes from short to very tall, but their arms, too, vary in length. A short man, therefore, with very short arms may require a table of the height needed by a tall man with very long arms. So much for the table height, except to note that the first magicians to use performance tables used candle stands, common at the period. Such stands were greater than table height in order to raise the candle so it would throw its light on a book held by a seated reader. Candle stands usually

CONCLUDING SECRETS

had round tops (12″ to 14″ in diameter), attached to an upright having three feet. Traveling magicians copied the candle stands but had them made so that they could be taken apart in order to be more easily packed for transportation. Later magicians made tables having feet and uprights of metal tubing. These had the disadvantage of appearing to be just what they were —tables made for magicians.

The tables I made are of mahogany with a 15″ square top, four legs and a shelf. Two tables when taken apart pack into a case 16½″ x 16½″ x 6″. Because of the way they are made they are extremely light.

It is quite possible, for those who give magic shows infrequently, to attach detachable lifts to the legs of lower stands and make most usable performance tables.

The reason the old term for these tables is side tables is that the magician customarily had one on each side of his stage.

And speaking of each side of the stage, it must be remembered that the magician's right as he faces the audience is the spectator's left. Throughout this book whenever giving instructions for the magician, the words left and right always refer to his left and his right and not to the right and left of the audience. If the magician in speaking to the audience ever has occasion to mention "on the left," or "on the right," he must remember to use the words that the audience will understand. The audience's right is the magician's left. Because there can be real misunderstanding in the theater in regard to these words, stage directions are written "stage right" or "stage left" and refer to the right or left of the actor.

"Upstage" and "downstage" also are helpful stage terms. The terms are very old and originated when the stage floor actually was built on an incline with its lowest edge that nearest the audience. Actors actually walked down a slope when they went toward the audience, or downstage, and when they went away from the audience they walked upstage. It is helpful for all performers to think in stage terms for it tends to make everything less confusing and is helpful even in thinking about the space a magician reserves for his performance in a parlor.

For instance, in placing his tables he will find the best location for his prop table to be upstage center. The performance tables are fairly far down stage—one stage left and one stage right. It will be found helpful always to have the performance tables the same distance apart in rehearsal and in performance because conditions then will be alike in the show and in practice.

With the exception of Mind Signals (Chapter 11) all the magic described in this book may be performed with only the aid of volunteer assistants. While those from the audience who help the magician are called volunteer assistants, it always is wiser, as has been noted, to draft such service. However, these people always must be treated in a kind and courteous manner by the magician and never be permitted to realize that actually they are impressed labor. They should be treated respectfully and never, never to the nth degre, be ridiculed, made to think that they are stupid, awkward, or have any other failings. As soon as a volunteer assistant has completed doing whatever was required, he should be thanked and told that his help was appreciated. Stating his gratitude, the performer will find also is a polite way of indicating that the assistant is to return to his seat. An assistant should never be left in the embarrassing position of not knowing when to leave the platform and go back to his chair.

Many magicians like to have trained assistants to aid them in their acts. One of their reasons is that they believe the performances run more smoothly when assistants hand to the magicians whatever they require and remove those items no longer needed. Another reason offered is that every person added to a show is supposed to make it more impressive. An assistant to be really helpful has to rehearse his part almost as much as the magician does his. And the assistant has to rehearse with the performer and can do nothing alone. The magician who uses an assistant for an occasional show must know when he, or she, is without a conflicting engagement. There are advantages and disadvantages to having assistants. Whether or not an assistant, or assistants, is used in a magic act is optional. However, an untrained assistant never should be used.

In this book the reader has been exposed to several words from the technical vocabulary of magic. These words were mentioned because they are useful and helpful. There are two other words of magic which the reader should know. The first word is "gimmick." Originally the word was found only in the vocabulary of the magician. In its magic meaning it refers to something required for the successful working of a trick and of which the audience is unaware and never sees. As, in the English language, there was no single word for "the hidden factor necessary for success," the word was appropriated by those magicians of words—the advertising copywriters. The word was found to be so useful that it was adopted by those in television production and in much of the business world. After newspaper and magazine writers began using the magician's word, gimmick came into fairly general use. The spring clip which holds open the secret door in the Chinese box, used in "Flowers—With Thanks," is a gimmick. The loop of thread for the ribbon in the Elusive Block trick is a gimmick. And in the Clever Poltergeist, the knocker is a gimmick.

The other word of magicians the reader should know is "misdirection." Misdirection often is rather loosely used to encompass the entire field of the psychology of deception. More specifically the word may be defined as leading the minds of the spectators away from the secret part of a trick. Misdirection is simply making use of the knowledge of the way normal people react to certain situations. By trial and error, magicians have, through the centuries, learned many reactions that are completely dependable. A few examples of the ways misdirection works will be more clear than any definition could be. At the end of the series of card tricks at the very beginning of the book, an explanation is given of how to separate the red cards in the deck from the black without the spectators' knowledge, although the separation is done in their sight. The misdirection consists of dealing the cards in six piles in order to separate the red cards from the black. Because it is totally unnecessary to make six piles in order to divide the deck in half, no one ever suspects that is what is being done. In addition the magician seems to be playing a game of solitaire. This is an example of misdirection by doing an act in an unusual and complicated manner. Another example, that of misdirection by simulation, is found in Coins, Paper Napkins and Olives and also found in Ho Chang. In both tricks the audience is convinced that the magician has an object in his hand because he acts as if he did, at the instant the object is removed from the sight of the audience. As the audience is unaware that the action they see is fake, it accepts the feigned action as genuine. In the trick 10,000 to 1, the spectator is convinced the four numbered tags hung on the rack are those of his own free choice because he was permitted to handle and examine forty tags and select four. This is misdirection by examination coupled with slackening of attention which is natural after completing a task. The rest of the audience always accepts the judgment of one of their own number. A final example is the audience's conviction in the trick, Boy and Box of Candy, that there is a real box of candy in the paper bag. The thud heard when the weighted skeleton box is dropped into the bag is convincing proof that a filled box of candy went into the paper bag. This is misdirection by sound. In each of these few examples the mind has been led astray by the unsuspected and unexpected as always is the case with misdirection.

It will be obvious that misdirection depends upon the knowledge magicians have of the way people think and react. It does not have anything to do with the personal magnetism or any other innate quality of the magician. It is not a form of brain washing, nor does it rely in any way upon hypnotism. Above all there is nothing obscure nor esoteric about misdirection. In this book the misdirection has been included in the description of how each trick is done. While the misdirection was not pointed out as such nor stressed particularly, it has been noted many times that every detail mentioned has importance. Particularly the detail having to do with misdirection never should be omitted from a trick.

Another way in which the minds of the spectators function is of great help to the magician. People convinced of the normality of one of several like common objects will accept, without further demonstration or proof, every other object in the series to be likewise unaltered. As example, in his show all the trays the magician uses to hold his props should be alike in appearance. The audience is given the opportunity to notice that the first tray is only a tray. It should not be obvious that is what is being done, nor should anything be said on the subject. However, when the spectators are made to realize that the first tray is an ordinary tray and is used only for its usual purpose, the magician can make use of a prepared tray with complete confidence for every person is certain that what looks alike is alike. In the Magic Dye trick, for another example, six silk handkerchiefs are used. As everyone can see the first five are simple silk handkerchiefs, to the audience the sixth must be like the others. People are very consistent in thinking in this way and the magician need have no qualms in his performance that they will change. However, he too has to act as if each article is identical and must handle the prepared exactly as he does the unprepared object.

If prior to a performance before a sizable audience the reader develops a case of stage fright he should not be perturbed. It is apt to happen to anyone and at anytime in his career. While there is no known cure for the ailment, there is a practically infallible palliative which is so simple. Lick the lips. That is all that is necessary. When a person becomes afflicted with stage fright, or even frightened by meeting a lion, his mouth becomes dry. That condition not only makes talking difficult but is quite uncomfortable. The action of licking the lips automatically causes the glands in the mouth to function. When the mouth again is moist, the stage fright will disappear in almost every instance. Taking a sip of water does not have the same effect. As a young magician, having chronic stage fright, I appeared on the same program with a veteran of great experience and he gave me the lip moistening secret. I used the method then with success and still use it on those occasions when I get an attack of stage fright.

After a performance a magician does well immediately to pack whatever equipment he has used. In a show in someone's home this should be done if only as a matter of politeness. A very important reason to start packing the moment the show is over is that what is put away cannot be handled or examined. Even adults, who daily tell each of their children to "look with your eyes, dear, not with your hands," have no compunction themselves when it comes to examining equipment for magic. It is well to remember that only those secrets are safe which are not available.

There also are a few things which are well to know about meeting members of the audience after having given a show. One thing is always to accept the proffered compliment. Never give your opinion of the show for the spectator likes his opinion better. Probably it is best merely to say, "Thank you. I am glad you enjoyed the magic." Above all never mention any trials you had getting to the show, nor any problems which occurred before, during or after the show. Naturally such items will be uppermost in your own mind, but no one else will find your troubles interesting and, of course, they are not entertaining. It is necessary to maintain your role for to the spectators you still are the magician even though, to you, the show is over.

Frequently people tell a magician of tricks they have seen in the hope that he will explain how the tricks were done. When those who have been mystified by a feat of magic attempt to describe what occurred the story very likely will be most inaccurate and the magician may not have the faintest idea what had been seen. Even though he is able to guess what the trick had been and how it might have been accomplished, he should no more explain the other fellow's magic than to explain his own and for the same reasons. If he is asked a direct question he will find, "Oh, I haven't any idea," an excellent answer. Invariably that answer is understood as being a nice way of saying, "I know but I won't tell."

When, after one of his shows, John William Sargent would be told, "I know how one of your tricks was done," he would reply, "I am certain you must be right." That usually closed the subject but in the instance when the individual would insist on giving his idea, Mr. Sargent would interrupt to say, "Pardon me, but I feel I must warn you, I always tell everyone he is right." People do occasionally analyze correctly how a magician has performed his trick, but the person, who comes bouncing back to tell you what unquestionably you already know, is wrong almost always. Mr. Sargent's method will be found a pleasant and effective way of quieting him.

The public or, to be more accurate, a certain proportion of the public, holds fixedly to a number of weird opinions about magic and magicians. These people not only will give you their opinions as facts, but will relish the opportunity to argue about the validity of their ideas. Two or three samples of these erroneous ideas will show what magicians are up against.

"Of course, I know that everything depends upon the hand being quicker than the eye."

"I suppose that any person who is double-jointed can learn to be a magician."

"It must be very expensive to have your clothes especially made for magic."

"I realize we were hypnotized and only thought we saw all those wonderful things."

It is a complete waste of time to attempt to explain that rapidity of movement plays no part in magic; that a magician is not a person of unusual construction; or that neither the magician's suit nor hypnotism are magical requisites. Not only is it useless, for these people are certain of their ideas, but it is never entertaining to anyone to be told he is wrong and a magician should never forget that he is an entertainer. A magician may be sorely tempted to forget his position, but let him steel himself when someone, who has read a book, insists the vanished article went up the sleeve. These individuals are fond of their little errors, so let them keep their notions for, bless them, they are nice persons in every other way.

One pitfall which all magicians have to learn when to avoid is accepting the challenge of a spectator. It is dangerous ever to let anyone suggest the way a trick is to be done or even which trick to do. Now and again a magician will come across the person who will state that he is thinking of a card and wants the magician to tell him which card is in his mind. Or someone will be met who will challenge, "Let me see you make this sugar bowl disappear." At times the idea suggested is one the magician is prepared to do and he may do it only if he will remember that the audience knows what to expect and that he must take more care with the trick to avoid detection. Very likely he can distract the spectators by what he says but he will know that he cannot be caught if he doesn't do the trick at all. Usually these challengers get their ideas only at the end of a performance and, if such is the case the magician can say, "Sorry, but I have finished with magic for tonight." He should make his statement nicely but with a tone of finality. He must take care not to sound as if he wishes to be coaxed. If a spectator interrupts the magician's performance with a suggestion for a trick, it is perfectly proper for him to refuse the challenge. An excellent way to refuse is to look surprised at the suggestion and say very pleasantly, "Oh, no—why that was one of last year's tricks." While it is a direct refusal, it always is taken by everyone to mean that for him the magician intends showing only his newest magical powers.

It may well be wondered if the various rules set down in this book apply to all magic shows and to all magicians. They do. Magic is a universal art and a very old one. For hundreds of years magic has been practiced and magicians have learned that the basic principles are applicable whether the audience is one person or thousands of spectators in a huge theater. Furthermore the same rules hold true whether the audience is from Broadway, Main Street or Calcutta's Howrah Bridge Road. The principles of magic are as sound as they are universal and one need have no fear in relying upon them.

My final suggestion is to attend the performances of as many professional magicians as appear in your locality. Not only will you find magic even more interesting than the shows you saw before you became a magician, but you will notice ways to improve your own performances. Naturally I do not suggest that you copy either their style of work or their tricks, but notice the little things they do which make their magic more interesting and better entertainment. Notice what most impresses each audience. Compare the work of one magician with that of another. You will learn a great deal and have an excellent time in the process.

As I travel about giving my shows, it is a rare city, or town, where I fail to hear about the triumphs of the local magician. Hearing of another magician's achievements always is pleasant and the fact that the shows are remembered and talked about is evidence of the public's great interest in magic. I shall be made particularly happy when they tell me of your successes.

17 TENSILE RINGS

10

MATCHES
94